BARRIERS TO SMES INTERNATIONALISATION: EVIDENCE FROM INDONESIA

RITA R. PIDANI
FRANK W. AGBOLA
AMIR MAHMOOD
PEIK FOONG YEAP

Title : Barrier to SMEs Internationalisation: Evidence from Indonesia

Authors: Rita R. Pidani, Frank W. Agbola, Amir Mahmood, Peik Foong Yeap

Cover Design: Ali Khiabanina

Publisher: Supreme Century, USA

ISBN: 978-1939123992

SYNOPSIS

This book investigates some of the major barriers that may affect export development of manufacturing small and medium-sized enterprises (SMEs) in Indonesia. Although SMEs are a major source of growth and job creation, little is known of how SMEs in developing countries represented in international economy relative to their contribution in national and local economies. This lack of evidence in the literature provides a strong rationale for this study. A review of the literature suggests that many of the problems facing SMEs' efforts to internationalise are known, regarding internal and external factors. An investigation of export development in developing countries therefore should include the broad range of internal and external constraints as the key forces influencing the process. This line of reasoning highlights the role played by managerial perceptions of export barriers in shaping the export development process.

The findings suggest that export development of manufacturing SMEs in Indonesia is constrained by a lack of knowledge to identify foreign business opportunities, lack of resources to develop new products, difficulty in maintaining control over foreign middlemen, and verbal and non-verbal language differences. These are areas where export strategies could be addressed and improved. This study provides strong empirical evidence to suggest that to improve export performance there is the need to enhance economic and social development in Indonesia. This could be achieved through a more transparent government policy, promoting coherence among agencies supporting SMEs export development and adopting structured and relevant export development strategies in Indonesia.

CONTENTS

CHAPTER ONE
INTRODUCTION

1.1 Background of the Study

In this dynamic era of globalisation, Small and Medium Enterprises (SMEs) play a pivotal role in the development of a country. SMEs are considered the backbone of an economy, whether we are referring to a random state, or if we are talking globally. SMEs respresent a critical source of economic growth, dynamic and flexibility in industrialized countries as much as they do in emerging and developing economies. The central argument for conducting this study is that SMEs are the dominant form of business organisation, representing roughly 90 to 99 percent of all companies. An economy that can create conducive environments for its entrepreneurs in SMEs increases its chances to upturn overall productivity, industrial revenue, employment creation which then translates into a vibrant entrepreneurship ecosystem. It is therefore pertinent to understand the operation of SMEs and establish effective support systems to help boost growth within these enterprises. In this study, SMEs are defined as firms having less than 300 workers.

It is widely acknowledged in the international trade literature that continuing advances in production, transportation, information technologies, financial systems, and regulatory environments, and business networks, have impelled firms of any sizes to increasingly extended their operations to international markets in order to survive in today's global environment (Bartlett and Ghoshal, 2000; Katsikeas, 2003; Leonidou et al., 2002). Internationalisation in general and exporting in particular is still considered an attractive and less risky method particularly for SMEs as it does not require as much resource commitment as other modes of international entry such *as* licensing, strategic alliances, joint ventures, or international subsidiaries (Hutchinson et al., 2006, Rasheed, 2005). Through this mode of entry, firms in developing countries, such as Indonesia, are exposed to the international ecosystem of trade and payments. Accordingly, trade becomes the engine of economic growth among countries as well as for firms operating within them (Wignaraja et al., 1991). The various benefits of international trade has also prompted the Indonesian government to reverse much of the imbalance created by past inward-oriented development policies. In recent years, this outward oriented strategy has emerged as the dominant strategy outperforming import substitution industrialisation which was once the orthodox thrust of development economics in the country (Soesastro and Basri, 2005).

Public policy makers in both developed and developing countries are increasingly aware that the benefits of this export outward-oriented strategy are not restricted to the individual firm itself. Countries can also benefit from foreign operations of domestic firms because from a long run perspective these activities foster socio-economic development, increase employment opportunities, generate spillover effects such as ecosystem prosperity and support to boost productivity, as well as solve the trade deficit problems faced by many countries (see for example Dollar, 1992; Edwards, 1998; Katsikeas and Skarmeas 2003; Leonidou et a. 1998; Sachs and Warner, 1995). This has generated a plenitude of studies that examine firm-level organisational and managerial characteristics and how these impact on exports. In the international trade literature, a number of studies have particularly examined problems perceived by firms at various stages of export development. For a review, see for example, Bilkey, 1978; Ahmed et al., 2004; Katsikeas and Piercy, 1991, Suarez-ortega, 2003. These studies conclude that by identifying problems faced by exporting firms, corporate and public policy makers who deal with export promotion programmemes will have a better perspective in formulating and implementing more effective trade policies and national export promotion programmemes (Gray, 1997; Suarez-ortega, 2003; Wilkinson and Brouthers, 2006).

Indonesia is heavily dependent upon commodities from the rest of the world as many other developing countries. The Indonesian economy has recorded longstanding practices in international trade. Its severe economic downturn in the last three decades, however, has led to major macroeconomic and trade policy reforms and impacted on the way SMEs conduct their activities in Indonesia. Most of the SMEs have for a long-time been recognised as a large provider of employment and a potential source of export revenue. They constitute more than 90 per cent of all firms outside the agricultural sector (Indonesian Ministry of Cooperatives and SMEs abbreviated herein, henceforth MOCSME's website, 2009).

The SMEs in Indonesia contribute immensely to growth in the production, distribution, and service sectors of the economy. According to BPS, in 2007, of all formal and informal enterprises, there was an estimated 189.000 SMEs operating in the manufacturing sector and employing 3.6 million of the 14.7 million people employed by SMEs (*BPS*, 2008). The contribution of SME's to the country's GDP increased from 712 million in 2000 to 2.1 billion rupiah in 2007. This represented 53.6 per cent of total GDP in 2007, suggesting that SMEs in the manufacturing sector are contributing a larger share of GDP than that of the large enterprises (abbreviated herein, henceforth LEs) in the same sector (*BPS*, 2008). Despite this, the value-added by small enterprises in the manufacturing industry declined from 39.7 per cent in 2000 to 37.81 per cent in 2007, while those of medium and large enterprises rose only marginally from 15 to 15.88 per cent and from 45.5 per cent to 48.40 per cent, respectively (BPS, 2008). The Indonesian Statistics database also indicates that, in 2005, the rate of economic growth of small-scale enterprises stood at 5.82 per cent, of medium- scale at 6.25 per cent, and of large-scale at about 5.37 per cent. In 2007, the figures for the small-scale enterprises grew by 6.18 per cent, medium scale by 6.84 per cent and large-scale by 6.24 per cent. These facts, as well as SMEs related role as downstream assembling industry, have forced the Indonesian government to change their policy strategies by focusing on promoting SMEs as a vehicle for achieving economic growth and development within the country.

The Indonesian government has introduced successive trade policy reforms to minimize the strong anti-export bias of the past protectionist policies. The primary goal of these trade policy reforms has been to convert the import-substituting pattern of industrialisation during the oil boom era of the late 1970s and early 1980's to an export-promoting one (Wie, 2006). It is expected that this shift, from reliance on the oil and gas sectors to other sectors of the economy, particularly the manufacturing sector, would create confidence among entrepreneurs and investors thereby stimulating non-oil exports to offset the decline in tax revenue derived from oil exports.

Indonesian government's policies were initially and mainly targeting large enterprises within the manufacturing sector. SMEs was early regarded as trivial in the Indonesian government's agenda due to the inherent limitations of size and resources of SMEs. In the wake of the Asian financial crisis which saw LEs hit hard and SMEs rebounding from the shocks (Berry et al., 2002; Asia Foundation's website 2009; Wengel and Rodriguez, 2006), awareness raising among policy makers in Indonesia that SMEs are capable of ensuring continued growth of the economy. With the SMEs turning out to be more resilient than the highly indebted conglomerates, and exhibiting their flexibility and agility to the ever-changing market conditions, SMEs through their exports, are seen as capable of playing a key role in improving the balance of payments of the Indonesian economy (Urata, 2000). In a study conducted by the Asian Development Bank (ADB), the contribution of SMEs to total non-oil and gas exports after the Asian economic crisis of 1997 increased by 11 per cent (ADB, 2004). The recent data from the

Indonesian Central Board of Statistics showed that the figure stood at 27.68 per cent in 2009 (*BPS*, 2010). Thus, although the SMEs' share of total exports has more than doubled in six years, they still represent less than one third of the total export value of Indonesian goods and this indicates that there are opportunities for further enhancements. This study, therefore, aims to enhance an understanding of the export behaviour of SMEs by investigating export barriers facing SMEs and to explore the efficacy of the Indonesian government's SMEs export promotion strategies.

1.2 Problem Statement

Since export outward-oriented approach is an economic reality that can generate multiple benefits and spillover effects to boost economic growth and development in Indonesia, the efforts to stimulate economic development through import substitution of locally produced goods needs to be combined with an export expansion approach to optimize gains obtained from trade has grown dramatically over the years. To achieve this objective, we need to have a greater understanding and a further identification of the barriers hindering their export development.

One motivation behind this study is the responsiveness of SMEs to the changing global environment. In periods of declining exports, SMEs may respond in a variety of ways. For instance, they may engage in intensification in the production of products for export or expand the production base through diversification. Given the changing global economy in recent times, and the limited research on the operations of SMEs in Indonesia, it is pertinent that we investigate the perceptions of exporting and non-exporting SMEs and the constraints facing them. This would aid in policy formulation and implementation to assist their export drive and thus foster sustained economic growth and development in the Indonesian economy.

1.3 Objectives and Hypotheses of the Study

1.3.1 Objectives

The main objective of this study is to undertake an empirical investigation of the nature and magnitude of export barriers facing SMEs and the interaction between those barriers and the level of export development of manufacturing SMEs in Indonesia. The specific objectives are:

1. To develop a conceptual framework for explaining export behaviour of manufacturing SMEs in Indonesia.
2. To identify the importance of different export barriers faced by manufacturing SMEs in Indonesia.
3. To examine the interrelationships between managerial perceptions of export barriers and export development, export intensity and export propensity
4. To make recommendations to assist in policy formulation and implementation for improving manufacturing SMEs' export performance in Indonesia.

1.3.2 Hypotheses

Based on the extant literature and the objectives of this study, the following hypotheses have been developed:

H1: Non-exporters are perceived to rate export barriers higher than do exporters.

H2: There are significant differences between exporter and non-exporter groups in relation to the factors they perceive as important barriers to exporting.

H3: An export barrier is perceived to have a negative effect on the level of export development, thus having a negative effect on export propensity and intensity.

1.4 Methodology of the Research

Based on research objectives, a survey questionnaire was designed and personally administered to elicit information on managerial perceptions about export barriers. The questionnaire contains a series of questions which were compiled following the review of previous empirical studies on export barriers. The structured questionnaire was pre-tested for clarity, difficulty and ease of response before the execution of the full-scale study. The pilot survey was administered to 24 SMEs from each of the 4 major provinces with manufacturing SMEs. The questionnaire was revised following the pilot survey and subsequently personally administered to achieve higher respondent participation. In the end, 197 surveys of SME operators were usable, which is considered satisfactory for subsequent analyses (Comrey, 1978; Gorsuch, 1983; Guilford, 1954; Hair et al., 1998; Lindeman et al. 1980; Long, 1983).

The study focuses on manufacturing SMEs in Indonesia engaged in the garment, footwear, and furniture and wood products industries. The selection is based on their significant role and contribution to the Indonesian economy (for further discussion, see Section 2.6 of Chapter 2). The analysis is narrowed to only manufactured goods due to their major role in the industrialisation of the Indonesian economy in the last two decades and the increasing share of Indonesia's manufacturing SMEs in recent years.

Following the data collection, the sample was grouped into four levels of export development. This follows the approach used by Leonidou and Katsikeas (1996), Suarez-Ortega (2003), and Jansson and Sandberg (2008), whereby *non-exporters* are defined as firms in the first two levels of export development, distinguished by their intention to engage in export operations, and *exporters* are those in the next two levels of export development, identified by their levels of export intensity.

The empirical investigation in this study consists of two phases. The first step involves performing multivariate analysis of confirmatory factor analysis to group constructs into factors influencing export development, intensity and propensity. The second step involves running a structural equation model to determine which export barriers have significant effects on export development, intensity and propensity of manufacturing SMEs in Indonesia.

1.5 Organisation of the Study

The study consists of seven chapters. Chapter 2 reviews the major transformation that has taken place in the Indonesian political and economic landscape since 1945. This chapter also reviews the recent development of Indonesian SMEs, focusing on the contemporary shift in sub-sectors of the manufacturing SMEs. Chapter 3 provides a critical review of theoretical and empirical studies that examined export barriers and export performance of SMEs. This chapter also discusses the export behavioural model of the firm and the internationalisation stages of export development of SMEs. Chapter 4 discusses the methodological framework adopted in the analysis of internal determinants of export development of Indonesian manufacturing SMEs. This chapter formalises the model empirically and discusses the sources of and methods used to compile the data for the analysis. Chapter 5 discusses the results of construct validation of managerial perceptions of export barriers. The confirmatory factor analysis (CFA) is chosen to predict factor structure of a number of observed variables and assess how well the predicted factor structure is corroborated by the sample data. Chapter 6 reports and discusses the causal relationships between managerial perceptions of export barriers and export development. Chapter 7 summarises the empirical results, concludes, and draws several implications of the empirical results for policy formulation and implementation in the manufacturing SME sector in Indonesia.

CHAPTER TWO
THE POLITICAL ECONOMY OF INDONESIA AND SMEs

2.1 Introduction

Chapter 2 provides an overview of Indonesia from a political-economy perspective. The main purpose of the chapter is to introduce and explore how the political institutions, the environment, and the economy of Indonesia influence each other. It will also explicitly discuss government efforts to promote development of SMEs in Indonesia. This information is central to this research as the explanation acts as background material and performs as the data reference point for the analysis in subsequent chapters.

To advance the above purpose, the chapter starts by describing the Indonesian geographic location in Section 2.2. It then discusses the Indonesian political landscape from 1945 to 2009 in Section 2.3. Next, it examines key features of the Indonesian economic landscape in Section 2.4. It then provides an analysis of government efforts to develop SMEs in Indonesia in Section 2.5. A discussion of the recent development in the three selected sub-sectors is presented in Section 2.6. Finally, Section 2.7 summarizes the key points of the chapter.

2.2 Geographical Location and Indonesian State Institutions

Indonesia is an archipelagic country located in South-East Asia, between the Indian and the Pacific Oceans. Its archipelago consists of five main islands and islets of which about 6,000 are inhabited. The territory consists of 84 per cent sea and 16 per cent land. The Indonesian land area is about 1.9 million square kilometres. The five biggest islands are Kalimantan or two thirds of the island of Borneo (539,450 sq.km.); Sumatra (473,606 sq.km.); Papua which forms part of the island of New Guinea (421,952 sq.km.); Sulawesi (189,035 sq.km.); and Java including Madura (132,035 sq.km.). The climate is generally tropical, hot, and humid but cooler in the highlands. The geographical features of the country consist of coastal plains with mountainous interiors. In 2008, Indonesia's population stood at 227,345,082 people with a growth rate of around 1 per cent per year (World Bank's website, 2010). The official language is Bahasa Indonesia, while English is commonly used as a foreign language. The national capital is situated in Jakarta in the island of Java.

The birth of modern Indonesia is dated from the declaration of independence on 17 August 1945. Executive power is exercised by the President who also acts as the head of government, the chief of state, and the commander of the armed forces. The legislative power of the country is exercised by the People's Consultative Assembly (*Majelis Permusyawaratan Rakyat* in Indonesia, henceforth MPR) which consists of House of Representative (*Dewan Perwakilan Rakyat* in Indonesia, henceforth DPR) members, and the regional representative's council members. The House of Representative and the regional representative's council members are elected by direct popular vote for five-year terms. The judicial system of Indonesia comprises several types of courts such as the justice court and the constitution court that are under the oversight of the Supreme Court (*Mahkamah Agung* in Indonesia, henceforth MA). Following the civil law tradition of The Netherlands, Indonesian courts do not apply the principle of precedent which is familiar among common law jurisdictions.

2.3 Political Landscape

2.3.1 Soekarno Administration (1945-1966)

The Indonesian political environment from the time of independence till 1966 was highly unstable in nature. The first decade of the Soekarno administration was marked by a revolutionary spirit and filled with political turmoil and uncertainty. After adopting a presidential system which lasted for only one year, Soekarno embarked on an unpopular approach of a semi parliamentary system. In this half presidential and half parliamentary system, parliamentary government was led by the prime minister who also acted as the vice-president of the presidential system. Soekarno's administration was under constant pressure from the Dutch military who wanted to restore their colonial interests by supporting armed rebels and aggravating conflicts among political parties. To deal with this issue, Soekarno decided to move the administration centre to Yogyakarta and led the struggle from there. The administration centre returned to Jakarta after the Dutch completely acknowledged Indonesian sovereignty at the round table conference in 1949 in The Hague, Netherlands.

Soekarno's semi parliamentary system was heavily criticised as an illegitimate way to run the nation as the parliament was not appointed through a formal general election. All members of the DPR or House of Representative and MPR or People's Consultative Assembly were appointed by the president and came from political parties established under vice-presidential decree in 1945.

In order to formulate a new constitution that could accommodate a semi parliamentary system, Soekarno needed to replace the 1945 constitution via the formation of a constituent body determined by a general election held in 1955. This was the first and the only general election within the 20 years of Soekarno's administration. The majority of votes were won by four major parties: Partai

Nasional Indonesia (henceforth *PNI*); Masjumi; Nahdatul Ulama (henceforth *NU*); and Partai Komunis Indonesia (henceforth *PKI*).

Following this general election, the newly appointed National Constituent Assembly started their sessions to develop a new constitution. But despite multiple sessions over five years in a row, the assembly failed to reach an agreement to establish a new constitution. Political conflicts among major political and religious groups were also escalating due to this failure. Seeing the risk of national disintegration, Seokarno, with the support of the armed forces, announced, by decree on July 5, 1959, the dissolution of the constituent body and reversion to the 1945 constitution. From 1959 onward, Soekarno conducted the administration by decree and without general elections. He also appointed himself as president for life.

In the second phase of Soekarno's administration, he implemented the so called "guided-democracy" whereby all members of DPR and MPR were appointed directly, without any election process, with the expectation of gaining support for government political programmemes and the embrace of the new political-ideology which identified nationalists, religionists, and communists (henceforth *Nasakom*). Despite criticism of Soekarno's authoritarian style in this 'guided democracy", the Nasakom concept was actually helpful in overcoming the huge differences of political orientation from the various political and religious groups of that era.

Amid the political crisis of the early 1960's, Soekarno became embroiled in liberating West Papua from the Dutch protectorate in 1963. The domestic unstable situation was aggravated when the Indonesian communist party launched its insurrection on 30 September 1965. This tragedy claimed the lives of six leading Indonesian army generals and caused chaos across the country. The communist party was later dissolved by the Presidential letter of 11 March 1966. Soekarno, particularly in the last years of his administration, had to balance the tension between his increasing reliance on his communist party support base and the army's internal security role (Kingsbury, 2005). Nevertheless, he was held accountable for the events of 30 September 1965 and was forced to leave power on 15 March 1966. In a special hearing of MPRS in 1967, Soekarno's speech and plea were rejected. General Soeharto was then elected by DPR and MPR to become Indonesia's second president in March 1968.

2.3.2 Soeharto Administration (1966-1998)

Under Soeharto's administration, the Indonesian political environment could be regarded as stable, but it was highly controlled by the government. The people's freedom to express their opinions and to pass judgments on government policies was suppressed to the highest level. The style of Soeharto's government was also largely influenced by his method of achieving power. In the most recent review of Indonesian politics, it is revealed that the PKI movement was known to Soeharto and he used the incident in order to gain power over Soekarno and to bring back "the West" influence in the country. Soeharto's propaganda and manoeuvres over the event, however, were concealed until well within 32 years of his office. Once the true plot was eventually disclosed, it bred doubt and strong resistance to his policies, and there were increasing clashes between the civilian and the military groups and increasing corruption issues involving Soeharto's immediate family members, particularly after his third term in office.

In the early years, Soeharto gained strong support from the Indonesian people to restore order and law by reforming the legal system in the country. This social contract, however, was never honoured as, in the main, he was simply replicating and implanting Soekarno's (Javanese) centralized control approach with its emphasis on respect for individuals who hold power (as kings, sultans, or aristocrats during the Dutch colonial era). Due to the suppression of open politics and the high risk associated with change, people became petrified of being on the "wrong" or contradicting side of the government. Anyone who was on the opposing side was treated as fundamentally opposed to the state and was thus classified as an enemy.

Under Soeharto, the armed forces acquired extraordinary privilege in the Indonesian political structure. The armed forces were initially maintained as the only institution qualified to produce the leaders to run the country. This forced convention was reflected in the dual-purpose of armed forces both in military and in government administration from the provincial level down to the village level (Kingsbury, 2005).

Soeharto, in addition, banned the idea of a plurality in political views. This political style was manifested in unpopular measures during his administration. First, the PKI and its affiliates were entirely dissolved and banned from the Indonesian political landscape. Second, Soeharto strongly disallowed the liberalist view to grow in the country by blocking people's freedom to participate in the democratic process. The number of parties where people could channel their aspirations was limited and severely controlled. In 1973, several small parties, which were established in the late 1950s, were either dissolved or merged with bigger ones. Three parties, which were established under Soeharto's order (and continued to exist till the regime fell in 1998), were PPP, PDI and Golkar. Former Islamic parties were united in PPP, ex-nationalist and Christians were merged in PDI, and Golkar became the party of government. It can be claimed that all election processes held between 1971 and 1993 were fabricated shams (Kingsbury, 2005) and not genuine, as Golkar, through government and military ploys and interventions, always gained the majority of the total vote. Third, the role of media in Indonesian politics was tightly controlled, censored, and suppressed. The media could only report items which promoted national development and harmony. Criticism against the state leaders and their policies, the role of the armed forces, and the national ideology (Pancasila) was strictly forbidden. Although this media control was justified as maintaining national stability, it also served the Soeharto government's vested interests.

As Soeharto's wiliness and increasing corruption were slowly unveiled, a number of events occurred which could be considered as the root of his downfall. One of them was the Sumitro and the Malari riots in 1973 which reflected a growing public concern about the government failure to eradicate issues of corruption and patronage among a number of leading generals and a small group of ethnic Chinese businesspeople. The Tanjung Priok (port district in the northern part of Jakarta) clash in 1984 was probably the next controversial event during Soeharto's administration. The protest, which caused a death toll in the hundreds of victims, was initiated when officials attempted to stop Moslems gathering who wanted to talk about the declining economic condition of the time. The case was the subject of an investigation by Indonesia's National Human Rights Commission till mid June 2000. However, it did not settle due to the interference of the government and the involvement of high ranked generals in the event. The Dili incident in 1991 was another prominent case in Seoharto's regime. The incident, which took 200 lives in East Timor, was actually a result of significant division within the armed forces, where vying factions were trying to assume power over Soeharto's government by sacrificing civilians in the conflict area. This case was not resolved and is still under investigation of the domestic and international judiciaries.

The international supports for the new order of government were disappearing as Soeharto entered the fifth term of his office and the Indonesian economy was near collapse in mid 1997. Soeharto, as a result, had to face increasing opposition over his continuing tenure, accusations levelled against his corrupted cronies, and the frequent demonstrations of the pro-democracy movement. The strong calls to completely replace Soeharto's long regime, and his followers, were rising and reaching a dangerous level in the beginning of 1998. Protests and riots were increasingly taking place in and outside Java and taking many lives. A rumour of a coup was also spreading, not only in the armed forces but also amongst Golkar members. As these events were unfurling, Soeharto's wealthy elite families and cronies continued to live lavishly with drugs, expensive cars and properties as amusements (Kingsbury, 2005). In May 1998, the new order government entered its final phase when the angry mobs, comprised mainly of university students, occupied the MPR building and called on the president to step down. Large-scale riots, which were sparked by the security force's shooting on university's students, took place in Jakarta on 13-15 May 1998. Following the death toll of more than 1000 and the public protest calling for his resignation, Soeharto finally resigned on 20 May 1998. The next day Habibie was sworn in to become Indonesia's third president.

2.3.3. Post Seoharto's Administrations

2.3.3.1 Bacharuddin Joesoef Habiebie (1998-1999)

The appointment of Habibie, who was a trusted ally of Soeharto, had been carefully planned to cover Seoharto's quiet exit from Indonesian politics. The plan worked as Soeharto managed to expatriate most of his wealth out of the country when the transition took place. Although strongly affiliated with Soeharto's regime, Habibie, with his civilian background, was still considered a better option than continuing with Soeharto. The real power at this transition time, however, remained in the hands of the armed forces which were in every way opposing the growing democratic aspirations of the people.

Despite people's anxiety over his weak administration, Habibie took a number of initiatives in responding to the people's calls for reform. Several moves that were evident in the Habibie era were the legalisation of labour unions which were banned under Soeharto; the further liberalisation of the news media; the prohibition of an association between government and business; the prohibition of monopolies; and the approval for all qualified political parties to take part in the elections. To deal with public complaints of the excessive centralisation of political economic power in Jakarta, Habibie also signed the two laws on regional economy. The law number 22/1999 and number 25/1999 provided greater autonomy to district governments and allowed the regions to retain a larger proportion of incomes, except for those derived from oil and gas. In November 1998, his administration passed a law that specified Indonesian commitment to promoting and protecting human rights as stipulated in the United Nations charter. Habibie, in addition, began the separation of the police and the military in order to dismantle the military role in the enforcement of law and order.

Habibie's administration brought optimism to the majority of Indonesians for better representation and participation in the political process and implementation of institutional reform. This hope, however, was far less than expected as the reform was still only partially achieved. The power of the elites, conflicts between groups, and the power struggle within institutions meant that efforts to clean up corruption, for instance, could not be delivered in one fell swoop. The government provision on human rights was also partially achieved as the abuses continued and even increased in some places like East Timor, Aceh, and West Papua.

The East Timor crisis in mid 1999 and the increasing pressure from international society over the widespread death and destruction in the area, pushed Habibie's government to allow the people of East Timor to vote in a referendum on autonomy within the Indonesian state. Through United Nations intervention, East Timor, however voted for its independence and separated from Indonesian territory in

2000. The electoral reforms which were demanded soon after Soeharto resigned from his office progressed as people expected. There was an expansion to 149 parties before the electoral culling process, which then brought them down to a generous, but more manageable, 48. The first open national election since 1955 was conducted in June 1999 and attracted 130,000,000 electors at polling stations across the archipelago. Through a coalition, Abdurrahman Wahid was elected as the fourth Indonesian president on 20 October 1999.

2.3.3.2 Abdurrahman Wahid (1999-2001)

The appointment of Abdurrahman Wahid in Indonesia's first democratic election came as a shock to most people. Although he was generally well respected and well known for his honesty, he was a less than ideal option not only due to his physical shortcomings but also his organisational inexperience. With his strong traditional Javanese religious leader background, Abdurrahman Wahid led Indonesia in a very traditionalist Islamist style.

The ministerial cabinet under Abdurrahman Wahid reflected Indonesia's new democratic landscape as it mainly consisted of representatives from the five major parties that won the majority of votes in the election. The armed forces also managed to gain a small presence for its personnel in the cabinet with the inclusion of six generals in the structure. This, again, indicated that the military's influence, albeit less intense, still permeated the Indonesian political landscape.

Wahid's poor management skill was immediately noticed in his first cabinet that was not only large but also segregated. The first cabinet functioned poorly as there was often overlap between ministries which created conflicts within the cabinet and generated public doubts about his ability to lead the country. Within ten months of his administration, Indonesia had made very slow progress in areas which needed to be addressed.

In response to public criticism of his lack of competency to perform presidential tasks adequately, Wahid appointed Megawati (Soekarno's daughter) as executive of cabinet affairs and formed his second cabinet structure. In this new structure, Wahid appointed Bambang Yudhoyono as Coordinating Minister for Political and Security Affairs. Wahid also appointed a number of new ministers that he felt would be more accountable to him, but these too did not function as expected due mainly to the absence of mutual support within the cabinet, with ministries dominated by the political parties to which they were attached.

During his tenure, Wahid made some controversial moves such as funding the West Papuan congress and allowing Papua to fly the Morning Star flag over Indonesian territory. The decision was seen to undermine the integrity of Indonesia, as the flag symbolised Papuan independence and the move was strongly opposed by the armed forces. Wahid also lifted the ban on the use of Chinese characters, symbols, and practices in order to show sympathy for Indonesia's ethnic Chinese minority and increased his political influence within this group. But the increasing public sense that the President was not in any way in control of the country, led the DPR to pass a censure motion on 1 February 2001 over Wahid's Brunei and Bulog corruption allegations. This was then followed by his impeachment in July 2001.

2.3.3.3 Megawati Soekarnoputri (2001-2004)

On 24th July 2001, the MPR reaffirmed its lack of faith in the President and passed a decree to revoke Abdurrahman Wahid's mandate as president. On the same day, the MPR also appointed and swore in Megawati Soekarnoputri as Indonesia's fifth president. After a runoff between Akbar Tanjung from Golkar and Hamzah Haz from the PPP party, Hamzah won the ballot, with the support from PDI-P party votes, to become the new vice president.

Megawati's appointment, which was mainly based on the legacy of her father's founding presidency, brought Indonesia into a slightly better shape than Wahid's administration. Due to strong support from her constituency and despite her ineffectual approach in addressing the multitude of problems facing Indonesia, the economy was stabilized under her administration. One of the first public responses to her election was an improvement in the speculative value of rupiah which had become exceedingly volatile and undervalued since Soeharto's resignation. By fulfilling most of the International Monetary Fund's requirements of establishing a cut-off limit to government spending and reducing official debt, Megawati managed to meet the minimum economic growth. The inflation rate, which had stood at 58 per cent in 1998, was reduced to 5.3 per cent in 2004.

A significant change in the Indonesian political landscape during Megawati's period was the passing of Law number 23/2003 in July 2003. In this law, the presidential electoral process was separated from the legislative electoral process. This also led to the removal of the MPR involvement in the voting process of the election as the decision was directly placed into the hands of the people. Although the law was not fully supported by the DPR, it was eventually passed and marked a most important step in Indonesian democracy.

Foreign investments which were expected to accelerate growth in the country, however, remained very low in this period. After the Asian financial crisis in 1997 and the subsequent economic restructuring, the standard of living of Indonesians was even lower than that in the mid 1990's due to the increasing cost of imported goods and the increasing rate of unemployment. Disputes between her two economic advisers Kwik Kian Gee and Laksamana Sukardi over conglomerates issues also typified Indonesia's continuing economic problems in this period. Megawati with her indecisive leadership style was far from capable of solving these matters. Her initial move to deal with Indonesia's problems of corruption was also bound to fail due to the conflict of interests within the political and institutional system in the country. With increasing public dissatisfaction in her way of handling issues in the country, Megawati lost in the second round of votes of 20 September 2004 presidential election. The presidential polls showed a strong support for the Yudhoyono and Kalla duo.

2.3.3.4 Soesilo Bambang Yudhoyono (2004-2009)

The first direct presidential election in Indonesia ran well and peacefully at polling booths throughout the country on 20 September 2004. Yudhoyono and Kalla won 60.8 per cent of the vote and were sworn in as the sixth Indonesian president and vice-president, respectively, on 20 October 2004. In his first days in the office, Yudhoyono brought back the reform manifesto to gain the people's support and restore confidence in his upcoming programmemes to address Indonesia's problem of corruption and to rebuild the Indonesian economy.

Although not fully supported by the segregated DPR's members and coalitions, Yudhoyono, with his government experience since Wahid's administration, started to remove obstacles that hindered investment, growth, and employment in the country. In his five-year development agenda, Yudhoyono formulated immediate steps to improve the investment climate, to maintain macroeconomic stability, and to raise public welfare and eradicate poverty (Soesatro and Atje, 2005). To address the magnitude of infrastructure problems that were inhibiting improvement in the investment climate in the country, the Yudhoyono government opened up the infrastructure sector to private investments, rather than maintain the monopoly of state enterprises. Yudhoyono, in addition, took steps to counter terrorism groups which were an issue for foreign investment and were the source of political instability in the country. His concrete action in addressing corruption was initiated by the arrests of several high-profile officials in 2005. With the destruction on the northern part of the Sumatran island caused by the earthquake and tsunami of 26 December 2004, Yudhoyono faced multiple challenges in developing the country's political economy including the reconstruction of Aceh which had been ruined by the natural disaster and the long term confrontation between the armed forces and the free Aceh movement.

2.4 Indonesian Economic Landscape

2.4.1 Soekarno Administration

The performance of Indonesia's economy under the Soekarno administration was very poor. Spiralling inflation due to the economic crisis compounded conditions exacerbated by wartime and post-war destruction of industries, uncontrolled population growth, and the ensuing food shortages. The illiteracy rate, infant mortality, and other social indicators were lower than those of comparable neighbouring ASEAN countries (Aswicahyono & Feridhanusetyawan, 2004). Higgins (cited in Hill, 1996b) referred to Indonesia in this period as a "basket case" due to the sluggish and even falling growth of production and investment and falling real per capita income which was lower than that of 1938 (McCawley, 1981). Data in Table 2.1 highlights the worsening inflation rate between 1940 and 1961. Prices as recorded by the Jakarta cost of living index doubled each year and increased by 800 times during the period 1962 to 1968.

Table 2.1: Inflation and Money Supply Growth in Indonesia, 1940 to 1961

Period	Inflation	Money Supply
1940-51	32	28
1951-56	12	22
1956-61	28	39

Source: Indonesian statistics in Papanek, 1980.

Due to the limited documentation of Indonesia's economic performance under Soekarno's administration, this review will mainly focus on important changes in the economy since the 1930s or mid-1960s whichever data is available. As can be seen in the following Table 2.2, Indonesia's population was 97 million in 1961 and increased to 119.2 million by 1971, representing an average annual growth rate of 2.1 per cent over the decade 1961-1971. The most densely populated among the five large islands in Indonesia were Java and Madura islands (Papanek, 1980). This unequal distribution of population resulted in pressure on land and resources on Java island, particularly as the agricultural sector was regarded as the main source of income.

Table 2.2: Population of Indonesia, 1930-1971

	People (in millions)			Annual Growth Rate (in per cent)	
Year	1930	1961	1971	1930-61	1961-71
Total	60.6	97.0	119.2	1.5	2.1

Source: Indonesian statistics in Papanek, 1980.

Nevertheless, in a newly established nation where political stabilisation was more of a concern than economic growth, Soekarno's administration undertook some important measures to provide a foundation for the economic system in the country. Among these measures were: (1) nationalising "Bank Java" which later became the Indonesian central Bank or "Bank of Indonesia" and establishing two financial banks that were "Bank Industri Negara" (henceforth BIN) to help finance industrial projects and "Bank Negara Indonesia" (henceforth BNI) to help provide foreign-exchange and finance export-import activities; (2) Introducing Oeang Repoeblik Indonesia (henceforth *Booth*) as the first currency of the Republic of Indonesia which was later changed into Rupiah. This was also carried out to address the massive inflation rate which was mainly caused by the unmanageable circulation of more than one currency as an exchange tool (ORI, the Dutch currency, and the Japanese currency); (3) Securing enterprises that engaged in provision of public utilities and establishing state enterprises to manage them; (4) gradually diminishing the Netherlands' involvement in Indonesian export and import activities.

The results of the Round Table Conference in 1949 very much benefited the Dutch economy. In order to support the Dutch economy after the second world war, it was considered essential to retain the Dutch owned companies in Indonesia. The importance of Indonesia to the Dutch economy was reflected in the official data from the Dutch statistics which revealed the total export revenue derived from the Indonesian colony represented 7.8 per cent of the Dutch national income (Booth, 1998). This proportion gradually diminished in subsequent years until 1957 when all Dutch companies were taken over by the Indonesian government.

The struggle to remove the Netherlands' control in the export-import activities was also carried out by establishing a central trading company in 1948. This company was appointed by Soekarno to export agricultural products from Indonesia. He, in addition, established another institution, named USINDO, in 1956 to export products from manufacturing industries and to import raw material needed by these industries. Most of the manufacturing industries operated under BIN's assistance.

Soekarno's government took various economic interventions to build infrastructure for the development of indigenous entrepreneurs in the country. In 1953, for instance, BIN disbursed 160 million rupiah to finance various industrial projects in the country which were mainly owned and by managed by the government. Indigenous entrepreneurs who owned business licenses, however, were not able to make the most out of these opportunities to become partners of these industries or establish profitable businesses. Due to their inadequate business capabilities and lack of entrepreneurship, the indigenous entrepreneurs consisted of noblemen who would rather just rent their business licenses to non-indigenous Chinese businessmen who were able to run the business efficiently or used the licence to obtain credit assistance from the government.

The trend in the work force distribution partly confirms the lack of business acumen of indigenous entrepreneurs and their failure to take up opportunities. According to Table 2.3, there was an increasing share of employment in the agricultural sector, a minor increase of share in trade, and a decrease of share in manufacturing and services. Thus, given the pressure on land on Java island, the work force was increasingly concentrated in agriculture and exposed to falling real wages (Papanek, 1980).

Table 2.3: Distribution and Size of Work Force in Indonesia, 1930-1961
(in % unless otherwise stated)

Sector/Year	1930	1961
Agriculture	68.8	73.6
Manufacturing	10.6	7.8
Trade	7.7	8.9
Services	12.9	9.7
Total	100.0	100.0
Total number (in millions)	20.9	34.8
Annual Growth (in per cent)		1.7

Source: Indonesian Statistics in Papanek, (1980).

As a result of the "guided democracy' implementation over the 1959 to 1965 period, the Indonesian economic structure followed the "socialism market" model where everything was set and controlled by the government. The provisional economic system which was expected to provide equal prosperity to the people, however, was not able to improve the economic situation in Indonesia due mainly to government failure in monetary and fiscal policies and the unfavourable confrontation with Malaysia in the 1960s.

2.4.2 Soeharto and Post-Soeharto's administrations

2.4.2.1 1966-1995 Period

The change of regime in 1966 marked a transformation from the old order into the new order of government. Despite some shortcomings such as authoritarian leadership, disproportionate military role in politics, corruption, collusion and a nepotism (KKN) based bureaucracy, Soeharto's administration led the country to better economic achievements. Under the new order from 1967-1998, Soeharto and his ministry achieved results well beyond people's expectations. Through a series of five-year development plans known as Repelita which were designed to establish development priorities and set specific growth targets, hyperinflation, which was at about 1,136 per cent in 1966, was successfully reduced to around 15 per cent by the 1970s and further reduced to 8 per cent in the 1990s (World Bank's website, 2010). This single digit inflation rate was carefully monitored by the government until the unexpected economic crisis of 1997. Macroeconomic stabilisation, favourable investment laws, liberalisation of the capital account, and an oil boom in this era contributed to Indonesia's increasing capability to finance economic development.

A comparison of economic conditions and indicators at the beginning of the new order era and some 30 years later shows a progress in almost all posts. Real per capita GDP increased almost fourfold in just a decade (see Table 2.4). The crumbling economy in the first half of the 1960's triggered a positive growth for almost the entire period of 1966 to 1995. The growth rate of GDP has been relatively stable since the second half of the 1960s and has kept around 7 per cent per annum (World Bank's website, 2010). Population growth reduced from an average 2.0% in the period of 1960-1990 to an average of 1.6% in 1991-1995 (World Bank's website, 2010) due to an intensive family planning programmeme. The transport infrastructure has experienced a revolution in terms of road and air capacity and the passenger fleet. The expansion of the economy in this period, however, was underpinned by the increase in the world demand for commodities and the oil shock. The abundant mineral resources, which have been exploited extensively during the past three decades, have allowed the mining sector to play a significant role in the balance of payments.

Despite the dominance of foreign aid as a major source of funds for economic development, the circumstances prior to the 1997 crisis demonstrated that the country had exports and investments capacities to restore the debt. The economy which was once dominated by public investment has gradually been taken over by private and foreign investment. The reliance on oil revenue was slowly replaced by non-oil exports which continued to increase to around 70 per cent of total exports in the 1990s (World Bank's website, 2010). This was a significant increase which improved the country's buoyancy in relation to external shocks during this period.

Table 2.4: Indicators of Indonesian Economic Development, 1965-1995

Indicators	1960-1965	1966-1970	1971-1975	1976-1980	1981-1985	1986-1990	1991-1995
Real GDP per capita:							
Growth	2	6.2	7.8	8	5.4	7	7.8
2000 $US	200	213	277	358	448	546	740
Gross capital formation as % of GDP	10	11	21	24	28	31	31
Inflation (% increase)	141	280	20	15	10	7	9
Debt:							
Total ($US billion)	2.4	4.7	8.0	18.7	32.5	64.8	110
Transport/infrastructure :							
Domestic air travel							
(Millions departures)	0.4	0.8	1.8	4.2	6.1	8.3	12.7
Roads, total network (km)	N.A.	N.A.	N.A.	N.A.	N.A.	288,727	332,530
Current account balance ($US billion)	N.A.	N.A.	N.A.	N.A.	-3.2	-2.3	-3.7
Population growth (%)	2	2	2	2	2	2	1.6

Notes: N.A. = Not Available
Source: World Development Indicators (World Bank's website, 2010).

Rapid structural change was the common feature of Indonesia's economic development during the new order regime. Figure 2.1 shows that the agricultural sector, which once dominated the economy, declined from 56 per cent of GDP in 1965 to 16 per cent in 1997 (World Bank's website, 2010). The manufacturing sector, in contrast, grew at approximately 13 per cent per annum over 1975-97. The manufacturing share of GDP which was as small as 8 per cent in 1965, exceeded the agricultural sector in 1991, and contributed 24 per cent of GDP in 1995; this was three times more than its 1965 level. Indonesia's well-balanced economy was achieved in the beginning of the 1990s. This momentous transformation was achieved, by all major sectors playing about an equal role in Indonesia's economic development. Agriculture which historically had been the dominant activity in both employment and output was slowly matched by the manufacturing sector (Pangestu in Aswicahyono and Feridhanusetyawan, 2004).

Figure 2.1: Indonesia: Structural Change, 1960-2008 (% of GDP)

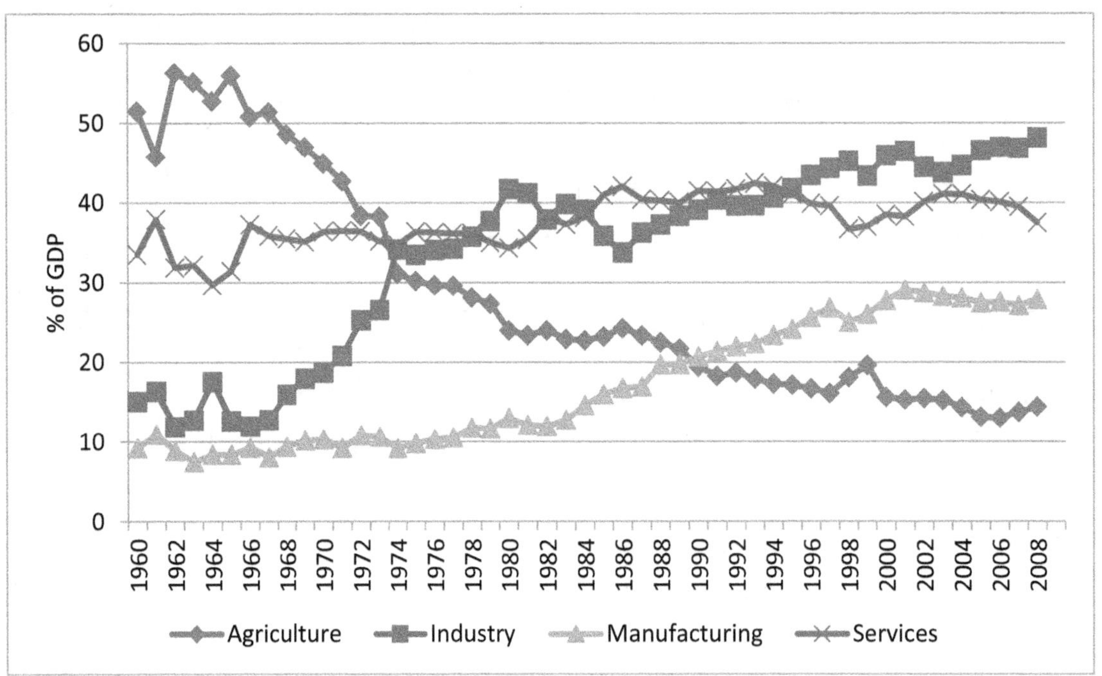

Source: World Development Indicators (World Bank's website, 2010).

Manufacturing output was increasing at an average of 12.4% per year under the import substitution industrialisation policy and open economy strategy. Enduring economic reforms, especially export promotion and sound macroeconomic management have produced significant export growth since the early 1980s. The manufacturing and services sectors, fostered by the tourism industry, have also come into play in a later stage of economic structure (World Bank's website, 2010). Around the mid-1980s, with the implementation of trade and financial liberalisation policy, Indonesia reduced its dependence on primary exports by rapidly increasing its manufactured exports. This development even enabled Indonesia to be included in one of the three 'Newly Industrialising Economies' (World Bank, 1993).

Following the declining share of agriculture in GDP, the share of employment absorbed in agriculture also continued to decline from 65.8 per cent (or about 25 million of the total population) in 1971 to 41.2 per cent (or about 40 million of the total population) in 1997 (Indonesian Statistics in Manning, 2000). Employment growth in the industrial sector, on the other hand, was multiplying through small sub-sectors such as construction, mining, and public utilities (Manning, 2000).

The high growth rate of domestic capital investment was another factor that strengthened economic progress in this period (see Table 2.4 and World Bank, 1993). The introduction of investment laws, favourable tax schemes, and other incentives improved the investment climate for private investors. The substantial amount of rent taxes gained in the 1970s allowed the government to invest in physical infrastructure and social development. During this oil boom decade, a large number of government public investments were undertaken in large scale, capital-intensive, resource processing, and basic industries (Dick et al., 2002).

Private investment started to dominate the economy after the end of the oil boom in the early 1980s within which Foreign Direct Investment (FDI), accounted for 61% of gross domestic fixed capital formation (World Bank, 1998). One of the issues following this capital formation, however, was the efficiency in its utilisation. Many of the investments ended with unproductive outcomes which later resulted in a drain on the budget due to the high cost to the economy.

2.4.2.2 1996-2008 Period

Underneath the strong GDP growth during Soeharto's administration, however, laid a fragile system which required reform. The authoritarian regime that endured for almost thirty years, however, prevented the review of these weaknesses and even allowed the creation and tolerance of a range of distortions which partially explains the collapse of the economy in 1997-1998. Investment became increasingly concentrated in import-dependent manufacturing and property development. Backward linkages in manufacturing and the agricultural sector were neglected. This unbalanced allocation of investment was underpinned by fast but poorly regulated expansion of the banking system after the reform package of October 1988 (Economist Intelligence Unit's website, 2008).

Table 2.5 shows Indonesia's main economic indicators within and after the Asian financial crisis period. GDP growth, in particular, has shown a sharp recovery after being hard hit by the Asian economic crisis of the late 1990s. Some signs of improvements have also taken place in other indicators. The inflation rate fluctuated over the period and settled to a low of 9.7 per cent by 2006-2008. The current account balance indicated a significant increase due to fiscal consolidation and government effort to reduce its outstanding debt stock from over 100 per cent of GDP to 46.2 per cent (ADB, 2006).

Table 2.5: Indicators of Indonesian Economic Development, 1996-2008

Indicators	1996-2000	2001-2005	2006-2008
Real GDP per capita:			
Growth	1.2	4.8	6.0
2000 $US	831	881	1,038
Gross capital formation as % of GDP	22.6	23.8	26
Inflation (% increase)	19.2	9.4	9.7
Debt:			
Total ($US billion)	161	155	151
Transport/infrastructure :			
Domestic air travel (Millions departures)	12.2	18.2	30
Roads, total network (km)	346,371.4	379,684.5	N.A.
Current account balance (US$ billion)	1.1	4.9	38.7
Population growth (%)	1	1	1

Notes: N.A. = Not Available
Source: World Development Indicators (World Bank's website, 2010).

In terms of export performance, the merchandise composition, captured in Figure 2.2, showed that until the late 1970s, manufacturing exports constituted a mere 4 per cent of total exports. But by 1985, the share of manufacturing exports had exceeded the agricultural share of exports. In 1992, the share of oil, mineral, and basic metal exports was superseded by the manufacturing sector's share of exports. Recent developments, however, show that the Indonesian manufacturing exports' share has been experiencing a declining trend.

Figure 2.2: Indonesia: The composition of Exports 1962-2008 (% of Merchandise Exports)

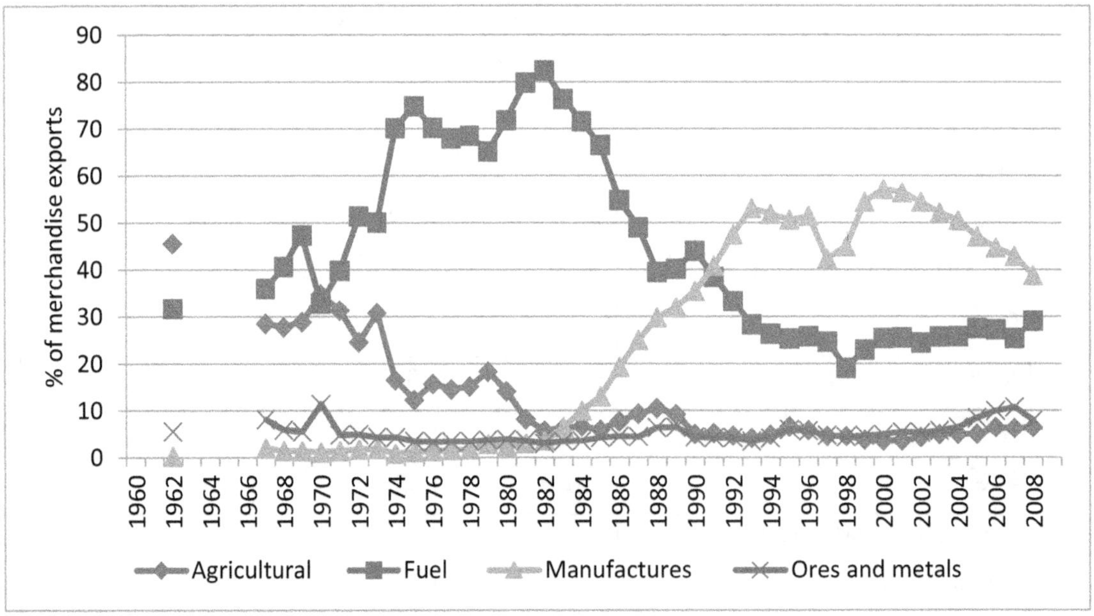

Source: World Development Indicators (World Bank's website, 2010).

Within the manufacturing sector itself, the intensity level of technology of the product exported was also experiencing changes. According to Aswicahyono and Feridhanusetyawan (2004), during the early 1980s, Indonesia's manufacturing export structure was mainly resource based manufacturing products (91 per cent). The value of resource-based manufacturing exports, however, has been declining steadily and was replaced by low and medium-tech manufacturing exports in the early 1990s. The share of low-tech products then diminished from 50 per cent in 1993 to 32% in 2002. Within the same period, the share of medium-tech products levelled-off around 18 to 20 per cent, while high-tech products expanded rapidly at a rate of around 20 per cent during the whole period.

Export promotion programmemes from the early 1980s have achieved most of the expected outcomes. According to Hill (1996a), several factors such as sound macroeconomic management, political inclination toward low inflation, high rates of saving and investment, oil and gas revenues of the 1970s, and the introduction of liberal trade reforms in the mid-1980s have contributed to the effectiveness of export promotion policies.

During the deregulation era of 1986-1996, the government undertook a major about face by rapidly opening-up the economy, reducing its economic intervention and switching support from the capital intensive/import-substitution industry to labour-intensive/export-oriented industry. Although capital growth in this period was lower than that of the earlier period, the economy still grew at more than 7 per cent. Total factor productivity (TFP) growth, during this period was higher than in the earlier period of 1972-1981. The TFP growth was also positive during this deregulation era, compared with four negative TFP growth rates in the 1971-1985 period (Aswicahyono and Feridhanusetyawan, 2004).

Other performance indicators of export growth did not show up as promising as that of TFP. During 1993-1996, for example, export growth slowed to an average rate of 10 per cent, well below the 1990-92 period (around 15 per cent). According to Aswicahyono and Pangestu (2001), the causes of the slowdown were mainly cyclical in nature due to the price decline and market destinations of products rather than structural factors or reduced competitiveness.

From Table 2.6, the dollar value of total non-oil exports grew at an average annual rate of 17.5 per cent during the period 1990-1996. By the mid 1990s, manufactured goods contributed over 50% of total merchandise exports. Indonesia's share in total world non-oil exports increased steadily from 0.47 per cent during the years 1982-86 to 0.77 per cent in 1995. The growth of the share in world manufacturing exports for the same period was even faster, from a meagre 0.21 per cent to 0.64 per cent.

After the crisis in mid-1997, total export earnings in dollar terms contracted by 6 per cent and grew slowly to 12.6 per cent in 1998, with non-oil primary products and manufacturing experiencing significant contraction and oil and gas growing by a mere 2.3 per cent. The decline in export value (in dollar terms) was a general pattern which according to Athukorala (2006), could be found across all countries affected by the crisis, and which was due to sluggish adjustment of both domestic-currency export prices and volumes to massive exchange rate depreciation. As stated by Rosner, massive contraction of domestic demand during the crisis may also have pushed exporters to pass on some of the exchange rate depreciation to foreign buyers in order to boost export demand (cited in Athukorala, 2006).

During 1999-2000 there was an improvement as the export value rose to 15 per cent higher than the pre-crisis average. This was followed by a 9.5 per cent export reduction in 2001, which was explained by the global economic downturn at the time. The following years saw a fluctuating trend and pre-crisis growth showed a sign of recovery in 2003. From 2002 to 2006, the average annual growth of total non-oil exports improved to 14.2 per cent, approaching the annual growth rate for 1990-1996 which was 17.5 per cent.

Table 2.6: Trade Performance: Exports of Indonesia (1967-2008, in USD billion)

Year	Exports in value	Share in Total Exports (%)			Export Growth (% p.a.)			Share in World Exports (%)	
		Oil & Gas	Non-oil	Manufacturing	Oil & Gas	Non-oil	Manufacturing	Non-oil	Manufacturing
1967-72	1	41.4	57.1	1.5	28.7	14.8	18.6	0.36	0.01
1973-81	12.1	68.8	29.4	1.9	49	23.6	45.1	0.54	0.05
1982-86	19.7	70.4	19.1	10.5	13.4	0.8	35.7	0.47	0.21
1987	16.9	49	26	25	2	14.2	47.9	0.52	0.33
1988	18.9	39.5	30.7	29.7	-9.6	32.6	33.3	0.58	0.37
1989	21.8	40.2	27.9	31.9	17.3	4.5	23.4	0.6	0.42
1990	25.6	44	20.6	35.4	28.3	-13.2	30.3	0.59	0.47
1991	29	38.5	20.7	40.7	-0.6	14	30.7	0.61	0.5
1992	33.8	33.3	19.2	47.5	0.9	7.8	35.9	0.79	0.7
1993	36.6	28.4	18.6	53.1	-7.8	5.1	21	0.83	0.75
1994	39.9	26.4	21.8	51.8	1.3	27.8	6.4	0.81	0.69
1995	45.4	25.4	24	50.6	9.4	25.3	11	0.77	0.64
1996	49.7	25.9	22.7	51.4	11.8	3.7	11.3	0.81	0.68
1997	46.7	28.2	23.7	48.1	2.3	-2.1	-12	0.70	0.57
1998	40.8	23.1	24.1	52.8	-28.3	-11.2	-4.2	0.65	0.54
1999	48.7	22.9	26.5	50.5	18.7	-0.3	21.6	0.76	0.66
2000	62.1	25.4	21.5	53.3	40.1	10.1	34.5	0.88	0.80
2001	55.9	25.2	22.1	52.6	-9	-6.6	20.4	0.82	0.74
2002	57.2	24.3	25.1	50.6	-2.5	19	-2.3	0.83	0.74
2003	61.6	25.8	26.0	48.2	12.9	12.3	1.8	1.18	0.48
2004	64.5	17.8	30.1	52.1	-27.0	10.3	14.1	1.09	0.49
2005	85.7	27.7	27.6	44.7	106.9	16.9	13.9	1.19	0.52
2006	100.8	27.4	28.5	42.4	16.5	24.1	11.7	1.27	0.50
2007	114.1	25.6	34.0	40.4	5.8	27.4	7.9	1.15	0.54
2008	137.0	29.0	34.0	37.0	36.2	53.4	9.6	1.20	0.55

Source: UNCTAD's website, 2010.

The Indonesian economic landscape, in conclusion, has gone through a significant change, particularly after the Soekarno administration. Despite chronic problems of corruption and nepotism, several development indicators have by and large been a resounding success. Some indicators like real per capita GDP have tripled in just a decade and, after the economic decline in the first half of the 1960s, nearly all sectors of the economy have performed substantially. The control of inflation and infrastructure development also showed satisfactory progress.

Indonesia, in addition, experienced substantial increases in its terms of trade from the early 1970s. The tremendous progress in trade has continued to be high even after the decline in oil prices in 1985-1986. With improved efficiency, tight economic management, rapid export diversification and the implementation of the trade and financial liberalisation policy in the late 1980s (Hill, 1994), Indonesia reduced its dependence on primary exports by rapidly increasing its manufactured exports. These trends were actually expected by the government to continue to grow because the experience during the second half of the 1990s demonstrated that Indonesia has much to gain from rapid export-oriented growth of industry and services. The gain from outward-looking growth included the ability to address the major problem of employment through a labour-intensive approach.

The major role of this outward-looking policy which was initially given to large enterprises (LEs), however, needs to change and bring in SMEs to sustain the growth in exports. The substantial gap between the actual and the potential export capacity of Indonesian SMEs, as maintained by Wengel and Rodriguez (2006), needs to be reduced by understanding SMEs' dynamics and recognizing the factors that influence their decision to enter the export markets.

2.5 Manufacturing SMEs Development in Indonesia

SMEs play a significant role in Indonesian economic and social development. SMEs in Indonesia account for more than 90 per cents of all firms outside the agricultural sector and micro enterprises. Their larger share in labour earnings, as maintained by Berry and Mazumdar (1991), provide a more equal income distribution to the country's employed, especially women and the young. The most recent statistics from MOCSME showed that small enterprise establishments (excluding micro enterprises) was around 38,669,000 units in 2000 and increased to 49,720,000 units in 2007. In the same period, the total number of medium and large-sized enterprises grew from 56,500 units in 2000 to about 124,700 units in 2007.

Table 2.7: Total Units of Enterprises by Size (Number of Employment Category in Thousand), 2001-2007

Size Category	2000	2001	2003	2004	2005	2006	2007
SEs[a]	38,669	38,854	42,537	43,641	47,007	47,109	49,720
MEs[b]	54,6	51,2	59,6	66,3	95,9	106,7	120,2
LEs[c]	1,9	1,8	2,2	4,1	6,8	7,2	4,5

Notes: a= Small enterprises; b = Medium enterprises; c = Large enterprises.
Source: MOCSME's website, 2009.

SMEs' role as an important source of employment in Indonesia is also reflected in the number of employed absorbed in this category of enterprise. According to MOCSME (2010), the number of people employed in SMEs is larger than that of large enterprises. In 2000, for example, SMEs' contribution was 5,169,329 employed persons. This number increased by nearly 40 per cent or 7,248,559 people in 2008. While the number employed in large enterprises decreased by 0.4 per cent and absorbed 2,776,214 people in 2008.

Despite its role as the locus of employment, Indonesian SMEs are still challenged by lower productivity compared to their larger counterparts. An average GDP per person employed in large firms was consistently five times larger than that possessed by SMEs which clearly shows the considerable gap between the size of the sector and its socio-economic potential (MOCSME, 2010).

Government attention to the development of SMEs was fully initiated in the new order era. Various promotion policies and assistance programmemes were aimed at overcoming the constraints that impede SMEs' growth, such as difficult access to financing, poor managerial and marketing skills, and low level of technology and innovation (Wie, 2006). By undertaking these programmes, it was expected that SMEs would be able to create employment and redistribute income throughout the region and across the nation-states (Hill, 2001).

Appendix 2.1 provides a summary of the programmes for the development of SMEs in Indonesia. It is evident from the table that the new order government made many efforts to support SME development in Indonesia. The most important programme in technology assistance was BIPIK (Small Industry Development) which was then replaced with PIKM (Small-scale Enterprises Development) in 1994 and has been continuing ever since. In terms of financial assistance, the government began with KIK (Credit for Small Investment) and KMKP (Credit for Working Capital) in 1973. These two subsidised programmes, however, were replaced by non-subsidised KUK (Credit for Small Business) in 1990 due to a high default rate (which was more than 27 per cent) and debt collection problem (Wie, 2006).

Another major financial scheme to help farmers, cooperatives, and SMEs is the Liquidity Credit Scheme, which was restarted in 1998 to replace the unsuccessful

KUK (Credit for Small Business) scheme. It is interesting to note that although the government has introduced several financial assistance schemes to promote SMEs, only around 10 per cent of these use credit from formal financial institutions to finance their business operation (Urata, 2000).

Other programmes tend to show the same pattern of ineffective outcomes. According to the World Bank in Wie (2006), these outcomes are due to a lack of coordination between the agencies in charge of SME programmes, poor programme design, and inadequate monitoring and evaluation. Berry, Rodriguez, and Sandee (2001:377) argued that ineffective outcomes of government assistance programmes are mainly due to the philosophy of guiding and helping economically weak groups (golongan ekonomi lemah) most of which are people who work in the SME sector. This credo has caused new order government to pay special attention to SMEs by providing loosely structured and haphazard assistance to numerous micro and small-scale enterprises and then overlook the prospective medium-scale enterprises. Most of the non-formal SME assistance during Soeharto's administration was replaced by efficiency based formal assistance in the Habibie and Wahid administrations (Hill, 2001). A constant confusion regarding the definition used to distinguish SMEs from their micro-enterprise counterparts has further complicated the classification of the characteristics, promotion and assistance needs of the two groups.

Despite the unfavourable results of assistance programmes and the outstanding growth of large-scale manufacturing over exports, the role of SMEs remains unchanged. The ability to exploit market niches that are not in the commercial interest and technological grasp of larger firms (Hill, 1995b) is claimed to be one of the reasons for the latter's resilience. Other reasons are the advantages over low import requirements and less reliance on formal credit (Wengel and Rodriguez, 2006). The clustering feature of SMEs manufacturing, particularly in densely populated Java, also provides opportunity for SMEs to group together based on location and products to exploit economies of agglomeration (Berry, Rodriguez, and Sandee, 2001).

Response to the sudden economic crisis in 1997 was different from one SME to another. The effects were not only varied according to the kind of product, type of input material, and destination of products (Tambunan, 2000) but also to the firm size (even within SMEs), sub-sector, location and market orientation (Sato, 2000). While data from the annual manufacturing survey of 1996 and 2000 (Wengel and Rodriguez, 2006) confirm that SMEs had the most closures, they also proved to be a highly dynamic sector with many entries in the five-year period. The number of jobs in SMEs employing 20 to 49 workers, however, remained about the same; 121,000 jobs were lost due to firm closures, but the expansion of the remaining firms created 28,000 more jobs and newly established firms created 91,000 jobs. This resulted in an employment loss of less than 1%. In other SME categories, firms showed increments of 7% to 11% in total employment during the period. The Les, however, showed retrenchment of 50,000 jobs within the period.

The trend toward demand-driven and more export market-oriented policies from the post-Suharto administrations seem to deliver more benefits to SMEs. Although there are still many internal factors that complicate the economic reforms, the schemes, which are aimed at promoting further entry of participants in the market for exports by lowering the cost of doing business and improving export facilities and infrastructure, will promote exports of Indonesian SMEs.

While the object of the study is exporting and non-exporting small and medium sized firms in Indonesia in general, it is necessary to incorporate as much as possible the specific characteristics of individual sub-sectors where these SMEs are involved. Three sub-sectors namely garments, footwear and furniture and wood products, characterized by having SMEs as main players, are targeted for this study's analysis.

2.6 Review of Characteristics and Performance of Sub-sectors

2.6.1 Garment and Footwear

The first two sub-sectors to analyse are the garment and footwear sub-sectors. These two sub-sectors are commonly grouped together under the apparel classification, hence statistics from these two sub-sectors are analysed concurrently in this section. In this study, the garment sub-sector is defined as those that manufacture ready-made clothes from textiles and from woven and knitted materials which are made by cutting and sewing so that they are ready to be worn. The primary activities of firms in this industry are producing shirts, trousers, blouses, dresses, babies' garments, dancing costumes, jackets, pants, underwear for men and women, sportswear, jeans, overalls, and uniforms. This industry is also identified as downstream of the textile industry which is different from the upstream and the midstream. The upstream sub-sectors are highly capital intensive, large scale, synthetic fibre industries. While the midstream sub-sectors are capital intensive, large spinning industries and the moderately labour-intensive weaving and fabric producing industry.

Another sub-sector is footwear. This sub-sector is defined as those that manufacture leather and leather substitute footwear. The primary activities of firms in this industry are producing ladies' shoes, men's shoes, sandals, thongs, sport shoes, children's shoes, inner soles, baby shoes, chemical resistant shoes, back counters, and parts of sports shoes.

The textile, garment and footwear industries began to grow in the 1970s. Significant amounts of garments and footwear from Indonesia were initially exported in the 1980s as a result of a gradual change in the New Order's policies from import substitution to export oriented policies. As a country with a considerable potential labour force, the export promotion policies concentrated on labour-intensive approaches as a comparative advantage. Trade reforms and the low labour wage increased the output, employment, and exports of the industry for a while. However, rising real labour costs in the domestic market and intense competition from China and other low wage countries in Asia, have respectively reduced the competitiveness and size of Indonesia's market share in international markets.

2.6.1.1 Number of Establishments

The number of garment establishments showed a steady increase during the period of the 1970s and 1990s; whereas, the number of textile establishment has gradually declined since the 1970s. A large number of unprotected small scale hand loom firms closed down and were replaced by larger, power loom weaving firms in the 1970s and early 1980s (Hill, 1995a).

Table 2.8 indicates changes in the numbers of establishment within the garment and footwear sub-sectors over the 1995-2005 period. After the Asian financial crisis, garment and footwear establishments increased by 13 and 6 per cent respectively, while textile establishments declined by 7 per cent (BPS, 2008). The number of garment and footwear firms, however, decreased by 9 and 12 per cent respectively in 2005 which is in contrast to textiles which grew by 2 per cent in 2005.

Table 2.8: Number of establishments in the garment and footwear sub-sectors, 1995-2005

Sector	ISIC	Number of establishments		
		1995	**2001**	**2005**
Textiles	321	2241	2079	2120
Garments	322	2110	2377	2172
Footwear	323/324	606	643	566

Source: *BPS*, 2008.

In terms of ownership, both garment and footwear sub-sectors are dominated by the domestic private sector. The share of domestic private owned firms in the garment and footwear sub-sectors was 89 and 87 per cent respectively in 2001 and has declined slightly to 88 and 86 per cent respectively by 2005 (BPS, 2008). Table 2.9 shows that there is a similarity in the structure of ownership within the three sub-sectors. Despite the slight rise in the percentage of foreign owned garment and footwear firms, the industry is mainly controlled by domestic private firms.

Table 2.9: Percentage of Ownership of Firms in Textiles and Garments, 2001-2005

Sector	ISIC	Ownership			
		Private		**Foreign**	
		2001	2005	2001	2005
Textiles	321	91.14	91.28	8.86	8.72
Clothing	322	89.53	88.55	10.47	11.45
Leather & Footwear	323/324	87.13	86.88	12.87	13.12

Source: Calculations on data obtained from Indonesian Statistics (BPS).

Based on Indonesian Ministry of Industry and NAFED (National Agency for Export Development) current databases, it is evident that most firms in textiles and garments are situated on Java island. Textile firms are mostly located in West Java while garment firms tend to be located around Jakarta. Garment firms in

West Java are more export oriented than in other locations as their total garment exporters are higher than elsewhere. A province outside Java which has shown an exceptional export orientation is Riau (NAFED's website, 2007).

2.6.1.2 Performance

The textile, garment, and footwear industry are one of the major contributors to non-oil manufacturing GDP and export earnings in Indonesia. Although the three sub-sectors were experiencing a decline, they contributed, on average, 12.51 per cent of non-oil manufacturing industry's GDP in the 2001-2007 period (IMI, 2008). These sub-sectors have also accounted for substantial investment formation in non-oil manufacturing industry during the same period, rising from 8.9 per cent in 2000 to around 9.4 per cent in 2006 (MOCSME, 2010).

Table 2.10: Sectoral Share of Non-Oil Manufacturing Industry's GDP

Sector	Sectoral Share of Non-oil Manufacturing Industry's GDP (%)						
	2001	2002	2003	2004	2005	2006	2007
Food, Beverages, and Tobacco	32.6	30.90	29.94	28.28	27.41	27.91	27.89
Textiles, Apparel and Footwear	13.52	13.20	13.23	12.81	12.25	11.78	10.79
Wood and Paper	5.87	5.59	5.33	4.85	4.54	4.30	4.01
Machinery	23.15	25.87	26.57	29.04	30.87	31.54	32.9

Source: Indonesian Ministry of Industry (IMI), 2009.

Based on United Nations data (UNCTAD, 2010), the contribution of textiles and apparel (including footwear) to non-oil exports increased significantly from 4.3 per cent during the 1976- 1980 period to 27.2 per cent during the 1991-1996 period. However, due to the sluggish economy and increasing competition in overseas market after 1997-1998, the share of total non-oil exports of this sector has continued to decline, reaching 11 per cent by 2006-2008.

Table 2.11: Sectoral Share of Indonesian Non-Oil/Gas Manufactured Exports & Imports

Sector	Sectoral Share of Exports and Imports (%)							
	1976-80	1981-85	1986-90	1991-96	1997-99	2000-02	2003-05	2006-08
Exports								
Food	37.2	15.5	9.8	8.2	9.9	5.9	8.2	6.9
Textiles and Apparel	4.3	12.5	22.4	27.2	20.8	15.7	11.3	11.0
Wood and Paper	13.7	31	39	26.4	21.8	10.9	9.0	10.8
Machinery	13.5	8.3	4	13.7	19.9	16.9	16.5	17.4
Imports								
Food	15.2	6.8	4.5	5.1	7.9	8.5	8.2	13.4
Textiles and Apparel	3.5	2	3.2	5.5	6.7	6.9	3.9	2.4
Wood and Paper	3.3	3.3	3.9	3.9	4.8	13	1.3	3.6
Machinery	46.9	53.4	50.9	52.8	48	28.1	27.1	48.1

Source: UNCTAD's website, 2010.

2.6.2 Furniture and Wood Products

The other sub-sector to analyse is furniture and wood products manufacturing. In this study, this sub-sector is defined as those firms that manufacture household furniture and equipment made from wood, bamboo and rattan cane. The main activities of firms in this industry are producing chairs, cupboards, beds, shelves, room partitions, bench seats, boxes, cabinets, other types of furniture, tool handles (plaster trowel, hammers, planes), component furniture, and wood crafts.

The furniture and wood products industry has been growing rapidly since the Indonesian government exercised a ban on log exports in 1985 and placed a restriction on the export of processed wood in 1990. The increasing demand for logs in the early 1990s placed most of the independent producers in a difficult position in procuring raw materials. This also resulted in a sharp decline of the industry's overall performance in 1994 although its export performance was increasing.

The Asian monetary crisis in mid-1997 started to have its impact on the industry's export performance in 1998. To compensate for the drop in domestic demand, the industry increased its revenue through export. The government through its foreign and domestic scheme directed this industry to focus on exports but with high added value products, for example, woodworking and furniture. The revenues in U.S. dollar currency were also considered more profitable and were able to stabilize the plummeting domestic purchasing power.

2.6.2.1 Number of Establishments

The data from the IMI shows that the total number of furniture producers operating in Indonesia in late 1997 exceeded 4,594. These figures include small furniture establishments. In 1998, the population had increased to 4,625 establishments (Indonesian Commercial Newsletter, 1999).

Table 2.12 indicates changes in the number of medium and large establishments within furniture and wood products over 1995-2005. Furniture and wood products establishments declined by 11.4 per cent over 1995-2005 (BPS, 2008).

Table 2.12: Number of Establishments of Furniture and Wood Products Sub-sectors (Large and Medium Manufacturing Statistics, 1995-2005)

Sector	ISIC	Number of establishments		
		1995	**2001**	**2005**
Textiles	321	2241	2079	2120
Garments	322	2110	2377	2172
Leather & Footwear	323/324	606	643	566
Furniture & wood products	331/332	2913	2945	2582
Machinery	382	322	833	626
Other electrical machinery	383	459	312	386

Source: BPS, 2008.

In terms of ownership, both furniture and wood products are dominated by the domestic private sector. The share of domestic private owned firms in furniture and wood products ranged from 93.2 in 2001 to 92.9 in 2005 (BPS, 2008).

The data from the IMI and NAFED current databases shows that most of the furniture and wood producers were also concentrated on Java island. Furniture firms are generally located in Central Java, Yogyakarta, and West Java provinces; while wood products tend to be spread around Java and Bali. The majority of firms in these two sub-sectors are serving overseas markets (Indonesian Commercial Newsletter, 1999).

2.6.2.2 Performance

The furniture and wood products sub-sectors, on average, contributed 10.23 per cent of manufacturing industry's GDP over 2000-2004 (MOCSME's website, 2007). Despite the declining percentage share of investment, the average investment formation of these sub-sectors in the non-oil manufacturing industry in 2000-2004 was around 8 per cent (MOCSME's website, 2007).

In terms of exports, this sub-sector showed a rapid increase in their share of non-oil exports (See Table 2.12). Based on the International Economic Data Bank, the contribution of furniture and wood products to non-oil exports increased significantly from 4.9 per cent during 1971-1975 to 26.4 per cent prior the Asian economic crisis. The share of this sector out of total non-oil exports has since continued to decline to reach 10.8 per cent by 2006-2008.

2.7 Chapter Summary

To conclude, the Indonesian political landscape can be broadly divided into three major eras of the old order, new order, and reform period. Within the 'old order' era, the Indonesian political environment was highly unstable due to political turmoil and post-war uncertainty. As head of a newly established nation, Soekarno searched for the most suitable system to run the country by experimenting with various kinds of legislative system. The presidential system lasted for one year and was immediately replaced by a semi parliamentary system. In this tentative system, Soekarno led the country with a parliament that was appointed not through formal general election but through presidential appointment. Still in his search for the proper approach to manage the country, Soekarno embarked on "guided-democracy" and forced the people to embrace his new political-ideology of nationalists, religionists, and communists (henceforth Nasakom). His leftist political ideology, his hatred of the "West", and unstable domestic situation, brought his administration to a difficult end. His close link with the communist party and the ensuing 30 September 1965 political movement, forced him to stand down from office on 15 March 1966.

Under the 'new order' era of Soeharto's rule, the Indonesian political environment was stable, but it was highly controlled by the government. People's freedom to express their opinion and to pass judgments on government policies was heavily suppressed. Under his administration, the armed forces acquired extraordinary privilege in both military matters and in all levels of government administration. His exclusion of plurality and strong emphasis over stability were reflected in the prohibition against establishment of new political parties other than those he had instituted and the prohibition of the media to criticise the state leaders and their policies, the role of the armed forces, and the national ideology. His fifth term was typified by an increasing opposition to his continuing tenure, accusation of his corrupt cronies, and the frequent demonstrations from the pro-democracy movement. Strong public calls to replace his long regime and his cronies reached an end when Soeharto finally resigned on 20 May 1998. Fuelling calls for his resignation, compelling evidence of his masterminding the coup attempt of the communist movement in 30 September 1965 came to light.

Although the armed forces power remained inevitable in controlling the huge population and multi-ethnic nature of society in Indonesia, the reform era yielded progress for the people in their roles and functions within the political process. Changes such as the legalisation of labour unions, liberalisation of the news media, the people's freedom to participate in the political process, and decentralisation of central government power were apparent in this period. The commitments to eradicate corruption and Islamic extremists were also accepted by the post-Soeharto administrations. Government attempts to overcome economic crisis by creating a favourable environment for investment were overshadowed by the lack of transparency and accountability within the legal infrastructure and power struggle among political parties.

The Indonesian economic landscape has experienced a significant improvement, particularly after Soekarno's administration in 1966. Despite chronic problems of corruption and nepotism, several development indicators have by and large indicated a resounding success. Some indicators, like real per capita GDP, have tripled in just a decade, and after the economic decline in the first half of the 1960s, nearly all sectors of the economy have performed substantially. The control of inflation and infrastructure development are also showing satisfactory progress.

Indonesia, in addition, experienced substantial increase in its terms of trade from the early 1970s. The tremendous progress in trade has continued to be high even after the decline in oil prices in 1985-1986. With improved efficiency, tight economic management, rapid export diversification and the implementation of the trade and financial liberalisation policy in the late 1980s (Hill, 1994), Indonesia reduced its dependence on primary exports by rapidly increasing its manufactured exports. These trends were expected, by the government, to continue to expand because the experience during the second half of the 1990s demonstrated that Indonesia has much to gain from rapid export-oriented growth of industry and services. The gain from outward-looking growth included the ability to address the major problem of employment for the large potential labour force through a labour-intensive approach.

The major role of the outward-looking policy, which was initially given to large enterprises (LEs), however, needs to change and bring in SMEs to sustain the growth from exports. The substantial gap between the actual and the potential export capacity of Indonesian SMEs as documented by Wengel and Rodriguez (2006), needs to be reduced. This will be facilitated by understanding SMEs' dynamics and recognizing the factors that influence their decision to enter export markets.

Most government policies to promote SME development in Indonesia in the past, yielded ineffective results due to the lack of a systematic plan and absence of government capabilities. The Indonesian government, however, can still seize the opportunity and develop output and employment growth by promoting efficient and dynamic SMEs and creating an environment which allows them to grow without long-term dependence on government support. The evidence from SMEs' export response during the crisis corroborates the reality that being less reliant on government support was an additional benefit to growth.

****

CHAPTER THREE
LITERATURE REVIEW

3.1 Introduction

One of the major hallmarks of the twenty-first century business environment is the phenomenal growth of globalisation. Exporting in particular has been one of the fastest growing economic activities, with a growth rate that exceeded the growth of world economic output (WTO's website, 2010a). Exports, in 2008, accounted for about 30 per cent of world gross domestic product (World Bank, 2010). This demonstrates the vital role of exporting in the global economy and its contribution is likely to expand as markets become more integrated (OECD, 2004).

The significant economic improvement that can be achieved through external trade has made export development a very important field for both public and corporate policymakers. Export venture is developed on the premise that it results in benefits to all participants (while acknowledging that it may create competition amongst them), regardless of whether they are nations or individual firms. For the individual firm, this usually means that profits are realized, either directly as in the case of the exporter or indirectly for the buyer who imports inputs into production. Above all, exports allow firms to capitalize on a competitive advantage, increase capacity utilisation, and raise technological standards which lead to better financial positions (Czinkota and Ronkainen, 2001; Julian and O'Cass 2004; Terpstra and Sarathy, 2000). At the national level, the benefits of exporting are determined by the impact on aggregate consumption and production. Since no country is entirely self-sufficient in terms of its ability to satisfy the whole range of the ever-changing desires of its people, international trade allows for the exploitation of competitive advantage in production and maximisation of consumption possibilities in exchange. Beyond that, exporting can improve foreign exchange reserves, provide employment, and create backward and forward linkages which eventually lead to a higher standard of living (Ahmed et al., 2006; Czinkota et al., 1992).

Despite these expected benefits, many exporting firms, particularly those in developing countries, have not optimally utilized their capacity to expand their operation in international markets. This brings up the question as to what role export barriers play in the export decision making process and the export behaviour of the firm (Leonidou, 2004; Morgan, 1997).

The aim of this chapter is to provide a theoretical platform for the analysis of the two important constructs evident in the exporting literature: managerial and organisational characteristics of a firm and export involvement. The chapter reviews key concepts, models, and elements of the macro and micro bases for international trade and exporting. By integrating insights from established theory in economics and export behaviour models, the chapter develops a distinctive model examining the relationship between managerial and organisational characteristics and export involvement of Indonesian manufacturing SMEs. The chapter begins by providing definitions generally used by East Asian countries to classify SMEs. Next, the chapter discusses global trends that are relevant with SMEs development. It then reviews classical and alternative theories of international trade. After describing the theoretical platforms, the chapter provides an overview of export behaviour models; empirical studies in the exporting area; and models that map the relationship between managerial and organisational characteristics and export involvement of Indonesian manufacturing SMEs. Finally, the chapter concludes in Section 3.7.

3.2 Definition of SMEs

There are inconsistent definitions and classifications of SMEs being used amongst the various government agencies globally. Statistics Indonesia, for instance, defines firms with four or fewer workers as belonging to household or cottage industries; those with 5 to 19 workers are small-scale enterprises; and those with 20 to 99 workers are medium-scale enterprises. Another definition is based on the value of firm assets and is generally used by IMI to categorize manufacturing SMEs. Firms with assets of less than 200 million rupiah are small-scale enterprises and those with assets of 200 million to 5 billion rupiah are medium scale enterprises. An additional definition is based on Indonesia's Small Business Law of 1995 which defines firms with assets (excluding land and buildings) of less than 200 million or with sales of less than 1 billion rupiah as belonging to small-scale enterprises. This definition is also used by the Central Bank of Indonesia, and by the Indonesian Ministry of Cooperatives and Small & Medium Enterprises (MOCSME).

Despite these inconsistencies, an alternative view supports flexibility in definition and suggests there is room for evolution. Within this view, SME-related policies are developed and customized in conjunction with the changes that are taking place in domestic and international market operations.

Table 3.1 shows that other countries tend to use employment size, assets value, and invested capital to discriminate between SMEs and LEs (Large Enterprises). The employment size ranges from 100 to 300 workers for SMEs and over 300 workers for LEs. The assets value classification varies from the minimum of US$ 0.6 million to the maximum of US$ 8.6 million. The measure of invested capital has the maximum amount of US$ 0.7 million. Considering this diversity of definitions, the labour-intensive nature of Indonesia's manufacturing, and the orientation of this study, SMEs will be defined as enterprises that employ 300 workers or fewer. To justify this classification, the study will also use the assets criterion from the Bank of Indonesia to validate the size of employment. Note that this definition will permit analysis of Indonesia's "missing middle" (Hayashi, 2002:24), that is the group of firms who receive the least incentives from the Indonesian government but potentially can improve Indonesia's export performance in foreign markets the most.

Table 3.1: Definition of Manufacturing SMEs in some ASEAN Countries

Country/	Organisation	Definition of Manufacturing SMEs	
		Criterion	**Measure[1)]**
Indonesia	BPS[2)]	Employment	SMEs <100
	IMI[2)]	Assets	SMEs < Rp 5 billion (US$ 0.6 million)
	Bank Indonesia/	Assets	SMEs ≤ Rp 10 billion (US$ 1.1 million)
	MOCSME[2)]	Sales	SMEs ≤ Rp 50 billion (US$ 6 million)
Malaysia		Invested Capital	SMEs ≤ MR 2.5 million (US$ 0.7 million)
Philippines		Employment	SMEs < 200
		Assets	SMEs ≤ P 60 million (US$ 1.1 million)
Singapore		Assets	SMEs ≤ S$ 15 million (US$ 8.6 million)
Thailand	Bank of Thailand	Employment	SMEs < 300
	TMI[3)]	Employment	SMEs < 200
	TMI[3)]	Assets	SMEs < 100 million baht (US$ 2.3 million)

Notes: 1. Figures in parentheses in this column indicate the amount in terms of US$ dollars converted by respective exchange rate at the end of 2002 (IMF, International Finance Statistics). Indonesia: US$ = Rp 8,815, Malaysia: US$ = MR3.80, Philippines: US$ = P53.57, Singapore: US$ = S$1.7488, Thailand: US$ = 43.206 Baht
2. BPS = Indonesian Central Board of Statistics, IMI = Indonesian Ministry of Industry, MOCSME = Indonesian Ministry of Cooperatives and Small & Medium Enterprises.
3. TMI = Thailand Ministry of Industry

Source: APEC (2004).

3.3 Global Trends in SMEs Development

The history of industrial economics is filled with descriptions of the growth and strategies of large size corporations that have come to dominate sectors and expand into oligopolies or monopolies. Competition only took place between a few large firms in highly concentrated markets or, in some sectors there were standalone players that controlled the whole supply to consumers within the market. This structure, to a large extent, supports the industrial pyramid which is common in every economy. The head of the pyramid usually consists of a few large enterprises and many SMEs form the base (Scherer and Ross, 1990). This basic industrial structure prevails both for developing and advanced countries. Thus, since SMEs will always continue to be numerically the larger fraction of enterprises within any economy, every government is required to design prudent policies in order to assist and support these small players.

Policy assistance for SMEs, in the past, has been muted due to perceived shortcomings in the capabilities of small firms; however, this reluctance cannot be fully justified. Over time, it is evident that the role of SMEs has remained substantial and in some cases these enterprises have grown and become giant companies. Almost every big company began as an SME. Some reputable big companies, such as Microsoft for instance, started as a couple of guys in a small garage in North America; Vodafone begun as a small subsidiary from Racal; and even Volkswagen was once a small car maker in Germany. Much of this development is recorded to show that SMEs are in fact a 'seedbed' (Berry et al., 2001) for large enterprises.

SMEs substantial role in the process of industrialisation of an economy can be evidenced by their being the largest number of industrial units in both developed and developing countries and their significant contribution to total export and employment. These achievements result from SMEs' active participation in income growth, entrepreneurial training, creation of technological capabilities and job creation. Their activities have also promoted lower wage inequality and dispersion of industry away from urban areas and into regional development. As a group SMEs are also characterised by greater flexibility to changing market circumstances. (Berry, 1992, Humphrey & Schmitz, 1996; Liedholm and Mead, 1999; Little et al., 1987; Strange and Katrak, 2002). Evidence within APEC member countries in 2004, for instance, suggests that despite the whole issue of scale, there were about 6 million SMEs which employed about 25 billion people (APEC, 2004). Most APEC economies have an extremely high percentage share of SMEs, standing at 99 per cent of the total number of enterprises (see Table 3.2). The share was a little bit lower in countries such as Malaysia, Russia, and Singapore, but the contribution was still around 90 per cent. Chile was the only country that had a low share of SMEs at only 15.7 per cent of the total number of firms that contributed only 36.5 per cent of the total employment.

The shares of employment reported in Table 3.2 exhibit substantial difference. Countries such as Brunei and Canada had the highest SMEs' share of employment with 92 per cent and 94 per cent respectively. Other countries such as China, Hong Kong, Indonesia, Japan, Korea, Mexico, and the Philippines had medium to high SMEs' share ranging between 60 per cent and 90 per cent. Malaysia, New Zealand, Russia, Singapore and Thailand's SMEs had a relatively high percentage by total number of firms but a relatively low percentage by total employment. Despite these differences, there is a strong evidence to suggest that capitalizing on national markets and their expansion could lead SMEs to become an engine of export growth and upgrading, particularly in developing countries (Wignaraja, 2003).

Table 3.2: The SMEs' Share of the Total Number of Firms and Employment (%) in APEC nations

Member Economy and Year Joined	SMEs	
	Share of Firms	Share of Employment
Australia (1989)	96.8 (small business only)	50.2 (small business only)
Brunei Darussalam (1989)	98.0	92.0
Canada (1989)	98.0	94.0
Chile (1994)	15.7	36.5
China (1991)	99.0	78.8
Hong Kong, China (1991)	98.2	60.7
Indonesia (1989)	98.0	88.3
Japan (1989)	98.8	77.6
Korea (1989)	99.0	69.0
Malaysia (1989)	84.0	12.3
Mexico (1993)	98.7	77.7
New Zealand (1989)	98.9	52.3
Papua New Guinea (1993)	N.A.	52.9
Peru (1998)	N.A.	N.A.
Philippines (1989)	99.5	66.2
Russia (1998)	85.6	33.5
Singapore (1989)	91.5	51.8
Chinese Taipei (1991)	97.8	78.4
Thailand (1989)	95.8	18.1
United States (1989)	90.0	69.0
Viet Nam (1998)	N.A.	85.0

Notes: N.A. = Not Available
Source: APEC Secretariat, SME Guide, 2004.

Using APEC as a point of reference, the statistics indicate that although SMEs' contribution to exports varies across countries, SMEs from developing countries were active players in the export endeavours (see for example Berry and Nugent, 1999, Tambunan et al., 2007, Wignaraja and O'Neil in Lall, 1999) and they tend to invest in younger industries rather than more mature ones (Acs and Preston, 1997). Yet, since SMEs were using various modes of entry in their export endeavours, including indirect modes of sub-contracting or marketing relationships, their contributions to total exports were often excluded from official statistics. By improving their quality, price, and delivery, a few SMEs made significant progress and were able to survive and even establish their own label in overseas markets. It is estimated that 6 million SMEs in APEC economies shared, on average, 30 per cent of a total export value of US$ 3 trillion in 2004 (PECC: 2004).

The rapid expansion of the global market economy, which is underpinned by technological progress in communication and transportation and systemic synchronisation through economic integration, is likely to open many opportunities for SMEs around the world, including Indonesia. Despite the different viewpoints on the implications of globalisation for SMEs in developing countries, the significant changes in the size and structure of developing country exports is evidence of an increasing integration of the international environment. These current economic realities are likely to improve if a dynamic SME sector increases its participation in international trade and appropriate policies maintain their support for sustainable exports from SMEs.

3.4 A Review of Theoretical Studies and Limitations

The fundamental rationales that move the wheels of trade among countries are not as simple as those that influence trade within the national boundaries. Although it is evident that trade can bring about tremendous benefits to business firms and the nation's economy, a more comprehensive understanding can only be achieved by analysing a selected number of international trade and foreign direct investment theories. These theories offer explanations of trade flows between at least two nations, the nature and extent of gains or losses to an economy, and the effects of trade policies on an economy.

3.4.1 The Classical Theory of International Trade

One of the major concepts of international trade is absolute advantage developed by Adam Smith (1723-1790). This theory is based on the concept of economic advantage and states that countries tend to specialize in those products in which they have an absolute advantage, specifically, in terms of lower cost of production. A condition of absolute advantage exists when one country has a cost advantage (produced with fewer resources) over another country in the production of one product, while the second country has a cost advantage over the first country in producing a second product. With the assumption of a two-country and two-product world, international trade and specialisation will be beneficial to each country when the country is more efficient than its trading partner.

The absolute advantage theory is also aimed at explaining why costs differ among nations. According to the theory, productivities of factor inputs with natural advantage and/or acquired advantage, will determine the cost differences among nations. Natural advantages consist of factors relating to climate, soil, and mineral wealth, whereas acquired advantages consist of special skills, technical, and marketing know-how, and so on. With such advantages, a nation would produce that item at lower cost than a trading partner without the same advantages. The main limitation of the absolute advantage theory is in its assumption which fails to explain the situation of one country having absolute advantage in the production of both products, but still trading with another country in these products.

Another classical concept of international trade is comparative advantage formulated by David Ricardo (1772-1823). This theory argues that for trade to be carried on profitably, it is not necessary for a country to have an absolute advantage over other countries. If one country has an absolute advantage over another country in the production of all products, trade will be gainful if the domestic exchange ratios in each country are not similar. In other words, if the country with the absolute advantage has a greater advantage in producing one product than it has in producing another, the country will benefit by specializing in and exporting the product in which it has the greatest advantage, or superior (comparative) advantage, and importing the product in which it has less advantage. The other country, even though it is at a disadvantage in producing all products, can still benefit by specializing in and exporting the product in which it has least disadvantage. In the real world, however, the power of comparative advantage seems weaker than what its model implies. There is evidence to show that countries tend not to specialize in any product. Despite its significance, comparative advantage theory does little to explain what causes the variation in comparative costs.

3.4.2 The Factor Proportion Theory

The limitation of the comparative advantage theory is solved by the factor proportion theory which explains the differences in comparative costs among trading nations. This theory contends that the differences in supply condition of factor productivities and factor endowments explain much of international trade. If trading nations have the same taste and preference of demands, use factors of production that are of uniform quality, and use the same technology, then productivity of a given resource unit is identical for both trading nations.

The factor proportion theory maintains that relative price levels differ among countries because: firstly, they have different relative endowments of factors of production (capital and labour inputs); and secondly, different commodities require different intensities of factor inputs in their production. In other words, countries will tend to generate and export products that require a large amount of the relatively abundant or cheap input and will import a product which uses the relatively expensive input in their production. This theory, therefore, extends the concept of economic advantage by considering the endowments and costs of factors of production. The fundamental explanation of the pattern of international trade rests on the uneven distribution of world resources among nations, coupled with the reality that products require different proportions of the factors of production. When a country possesses a great amount of resources required to produce a product, its price for that product will be low compared with its price for another product requiring great amounts of scarcer resources.

The empirical test carried out in the United States of America by Leontief (1953), however, showed a contradictory result. As a capital abundant country, the United Stated would be expected to export capital-intensive goods, but the facts revealed that the USA exported labour intensive goods and imported capital-intensive products. This inconsistency can be explained by the human skill in labour-intensive production which was not considered. Corden (1994) argues that the factor proportion theory only mentions the proportions between labour and capital and does not take into consideration skilled labour intensity, technology intensity, and human capital intensity. The same input requirement, therefore, does not simply imply the same factor intensities because the composition of value added might be different from each of the factor inputs.

3.4.3 The Product Life-cycle Theory

Rapid technological progress and the development of multinational enterprises since the 1960s have caused the earlier trade theories, which were based on the economic advantage of factor endowments, to become obsolete. There was then a need to search for an alternative international trade theory that suited the changing realities of the evolving commercial realm. The product lifecycle (PLC) theory developed by Vernon (1966) explained not only the trade patterns of manufacturers but also multinational expansion of sales and production subsidiaries. Figure 3.1 shows the classic rationale of extending the product's lifecycle through international expansion strategy.

Figure 3.1: Extension of product life cycle through international expansion strategy

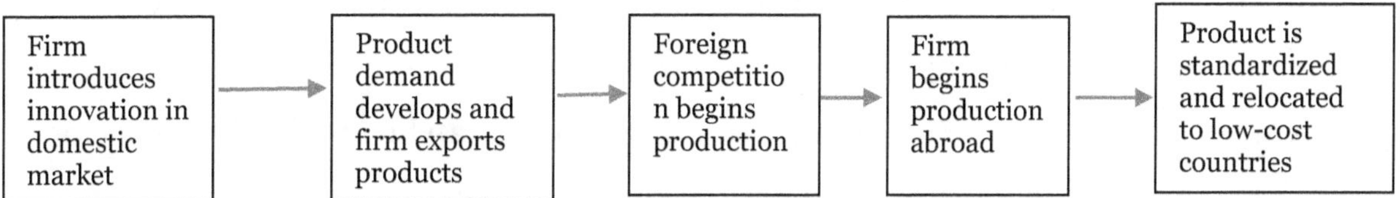

Source: Hanson et al., 2017

According to this theory, many manufactured goods particularly technologically advanced products, experience a trade cycle. The process, which consists of various stages, starts with the introduction stage when the innovator company establishes a technological innovation in the production of manufactured goods. Initially, the relatively small home market and not fully developed technological efficiency may hinder the company in achieving mass economies of scale in production.

In the next stage of growth and expansion, the innovator begins to export its product to foreign markets with relatively similar tastes, income levels, and demand structures. The larger the market becomes and the more efficient the technology, the greater the capacity of the company to switch to mass-production operation and increase the amount of goods to be supplied in the world market.

As time passes and the technology becomes more common place in the foreign market, the domestic company finds it necessary to move its production operation closer to the foreign market in order to protect its foreign sales and export profits. This stage is recognized as mature when the conditions change because the cost advantage enjoyed by the innovator from the outset is not likely to last forever.

Although the innovating country's monopoly position may be lengthened by legal rights such as patents and other intellectual property rights, this often decreases over time. Foreign producers may begin to imitate the production process and the innovating country may start to lose its comparative advantage and its export cycle then enters the declining stage. The cycle is complete when the technology becomes very common and homogeneous such that it can be applied by all nations anywhere in the world. Thus, due to increasing foreign competition, the innovating country may end up becoming a net importer of the product from a place where the costs of production are the lowest (Vernon, 1966, 1979).

The main factors in explaining patterns of international trade, according to this theory, are technological innovation and market expansion (Morgan and Katsikeas, 1997). The main limitation of this theory is in its insufficient explanation of the competitive processes that accompany the market expansion. Lambkin and Day (1989) set out some of the specific limitations. Firstly, the theory overlooks the presence and behaviour of substitutes. The declining stage of a life cycle is often hastened by an emerging substitute with a new basis of comparative advantage. Secondly, the theory also ignores differences between large and small firms, between established and new firms, between firms that develop their own entry and those that enter the market by merger and acquisition, licensing, or joint venture, or between firms that choose to follow different strategies. Thirdly, the simple one-way establishment of the birth-life-death analogy can be misleading due to some evidence of successful strategies to rejuvenate and extend life cycles by sustaining marketing, R & D investments and diversification which in turn will protect the innovator's market share position. Firms usually ready to implement changes when the product is at the growing stage in the PLC, not at the declining stage. Fourthly, it fails to recognize the important role of government and a favourable regulatory environment to legitimize the new industry.

3.4.4 New Trade Theories and its Principles

The conceptual limitations of the standard trade theories which were built on the assumption of perfect competition, free trade, and unregulated trade, suggest that it is imperative to consider trade theories that are not constrained by these assumptions.

The new trade theories began to emerge in the 1970s when several economists were questioning the assumption of diminishing returns to specialisation used in international trade theory. They argued that increasing returns to specialisation might exist in some industries. This section explains some of the important sources of increasing returns by largely focusing on the rise of intra-industry trade, economies of scale and market imperfection (Krugman and Obstfeld, 2003).

3.4.4.1 Intra-industry Trade

Comparative advantage theory suggests that nations with similar production-side capabilities (and relatively similar general demand patterns) should trade little with each other. Industrialized countries with relatively similar factor of endowments (physical capital, skilled labour, unskilled labour, technology, and technological capabilities), therefore, should trade rather little with each other, except in the case of primary products where differences in endowments of productive land and natural resources are significant.

Industrialized countries trade extensively with each other in what is called intra-industry trade. Over 70 per cent of the exports of industrialized countries go to other industrialized countries (NAPES, 2004). Intra-industry trade is the international trade of products made within the same industry such as steel-for-steel, or bread-for-bread (Gerber, 2005). This increasing phenomenon, as argued by Grimwade (2000), cannot be explained within the framework of classical trade theory and has encouraged researchers to look at other explanations. Several attempts to explain and measure this trade were carried out by Grubel and Lloyd (1975), Tharakan (1983), Greenaway and Tharakan (1986), Greenaway and Milner (1986), and Vona (1991).

Much of intra-industry trade involves trade in differentiated products, or exports and imports of different varieties of the same basic product or the same industry. Part of the reasons for the rise of intra-industry trade, according to Pugel and Lindert (2000) is that product variety is considered a luxury in advanced countries. The demand for luxuries is rising even faster due to the increasing per capita incomes occurring in these economies. The higher the incomes of consumers, the more consumers can seek variety in the products that they buy. Thus, prosperous people vary their choices of wines, automobiles, clothing and so on. But, the increasing demand by itself cannot explain the intra industry trade trend. In order to put intra-industry trade in a clear perspective, it is necessary to consider the characteristics on the producer's side of the same expanding markets. At this point moderate internal economies of scale and monopolistic competition come into play in explaining this phenomenon.

3.4.4.2 Economies of Scale

Economies of scale or increasing returns to scale exist if increasing expenditures on all inputs (with input prices constant) increase the output quantity by a larger percentage so that the average cost of producing each unit of output declines (Pugel and Lindert, 2000). Intra-industry trade is driven by the desire for differentiated products and the production of any one variety of product requires some fixed costs. Thus, the more the Mercedes-Benz convertibles are produced, for instance, the lower the unit cost. The role of scale economies allows each country to specialize in producing a restricted range of goods which leads to more efficient production as an alternative to producing everything for itself. This advantage and trade with each other enable each country to consume the full range of goods (Krugman and Obstfeld, 2003).

The model of trade based on economies of scale, however, promotes market structures other than perfect competition. The concept of economies of scale may be either externally or internally propelled. When the cost per unit depends on the size of the industry and not on the size of any one firm, then the economies of scale are said to be externally driven. When the cost per unit depends on the size of an individual firm and not necessarily on that of the industry, then economies of scale are said to be internally driven.

3.4.4.3 Imperfect Competition

Another point of departure from comparative advantage trade theory is caused by the absence of highly competitive international markets. Some important industries in the world are controlled by a few large firms. Commercial aircraft, for instance, is dominated by Boeing and Airbus. Microprocessor production is controlled by Intel and Motorola. The standard model, therefore, may not be appropriate to analyse such industries as the assumption of perfect competition has been violated as these industries move toward global oligopolies. One key explanation of such occurrences is that the exploitation of scale economies, according to Pugel and Lindert (2000), determine why a few firms reach the most efficient level of production and dominate some industries.

Imperfect competition prevails in any market where the producers or consumers have market power to influence prices. Several forms of imperfect competition are found in the literature, including: 1) Monopolistic competition - where there is a relatively large number of small producers or suppliers offering similar, but not identical products. If perfect competition requires the presence of hundreds or thousands of firms, monopolistic competition only needs a fairly large number, such as 25, 35 or 60. Firms have a limited amount of control over market price. Unlike perfect competition that is characterised by a standardized product, monopolistic competition has the fundamental feature of product differentiation. Therefore, despite the presence of a relatively large number of firms, monopolistically competitive producers do have some control over the prices of their products; 2) Oligopoly – where there are a small number of firms that are attracted into markets by high profits but where entry is restricted by barriers. Firms in this structure are characterized by internal economies of scale and the industry is comprised of a few large firms that have the ability to affect prices, but none have the market power of uncontested monopoly.

The opportunity for many firms to participate in an industry will increase if the scale economies are modest and moderate. If, in addition, products are differentiated in quality, sales, installation services, location and so on, then there will be opportunities for imperfect competition of the monopolistic competition kind. If scale economies are substantial over a large range of outputs, then a few firms are likely to grow to be large in order to reap the scale economies. If a few large firms control the global industry, then the industry can be said to be oligopolistic.

Thus, new trade theories suggest that even in the absence of factor advantages, firms can gain cost advantages that will allow them to export. The focus on differences in tastes and preferences and product differentiation in new trade theories can also explain trade in similar goods.

3.4.5 The Competitive Advantage of Nations

One of many explanations for differences in intra-industry performance is the competitive advantage theory. Michael Porter (1990) in this theory maintains that the success of a nation in a particular industry, and thus in an international arena, is invented and is not inherited from its traditional factor endowments, its labour pool, its interest rate, its land, its natural resources, its capital and infrastructure or its currency's value as maintained by classical or factor proportions theories of trade. Porter noted that a nation's competitiveness depends on the ability of its industry to innovate and upgrade. Through the pressure and the challenge of competition in the market, for example, companies can learn and invent a way to cope with strong domestic rivals, aggressive home-based suppliers, and demanding local customers.

The role of a nation, according to this theory, is to encourage the creation of an environment that fosters innovation and the absorption of knowledge into the goods and services being traded. The inimitable characteristics owned by a nation, such as culture, national values, economic structures, and histories, play a crucial role in determining its competitive position. Porter's theory further maintained that these differences lead to a distinctive direction of competitiveness in every country. This distinctiveness, which represents the restrictedness of every home environment, however, also produces an inability of every nation to become competitive in every industry.

In describing the approach that gains success in international markets, Porter concludes that companies with international leadership typically employ distinctive strategies relative to their competitors but fundamentally move in the same path of operation. Through experiences, companies usually identify a new basis for competing or find better methods for competing in old ways. These improvements can be manifested in a new product design, a new production process, a new marketing approach, or a new way of conducting training. Many of these ideas, however, are not original ideas. They are usually pre-existing ideas that have never been followed up intensively.

In discussing the pattern of national competitive success, Porter uses the study carried out in the ten trading nations to distinguish national competitive advantage from idiosyncratic advantage. Some measures of competitive advantage used in the study are the existence of extensive and continuous exports to other nations and/or substantial foreign investment based on skills and assets created in the home country. Based on the findings, it is concluded that successful companies tend to develop a predisposition for certainty and stability. They are inclined to pursue improvements by seeking an increasingly complex source of competitive advantage. They also have the capabilities to solve problems associated with change and innovation.

Porter noted that the above tendencies are strongly influenced by the four determinants that shape the diamond of national advantage (Porter, 1990), which are:

1. Factor conditions. In examining the factor conditions, Porter's theory goes beyond the traditional factors of land, labour and capital by including the quality of the work force (skilled labour) and the quality of individual infrastructure necessary to compete in a given industry. If a country possesses advanced factors such as digital communication system and

knowledge workers and specialised production factors such as specialists in a specific industry, it is likely that the country will serve the industry well and nurture strong home-country competitive firms to compete successfully in the global markets (Hanson et al., 2017).

2. Demand conditions. In reviewing the demand conditions, Porter notes that the existence of large and sophisticated home-market demand helps, in that firms that can survive and flourish in the highly competitive home markets by developing scale-efficient facilities and refined capabilities and core competencies tend to gain a competitive edge as they have a clearer and earlier picture of emerging buyer needs and faster response to innovation requirements. Firms with those facilities, capabilities and core competencies are capable to become global players to sell their products successfully in multiple global markets.
3. Related and supporting industries. The presence or absence of the nation's supplier industries and other related industries are critical for the production, marketing and distribution needs of a firm. A firm that is operating within a pool of related firms and industries gains advantages of close working relationships, proximity to suppliers, and timeliness of product and information flows (Czinkota et al., 2003).
4. Firm strategy, structure, and rivalry. This pertains to the conditions in the home market governing how companies are created, organized, and managed, as well as the nature of domestic rivalry. Porter noted that firms facing intense competition in the domestic market are drilled through costs, quality, productivity and innovation to survive; the elements which are also needed in international markets. The types of strategy, structure and rivalry among firms vary across nations and they determine the growth of certain industries in a country to be capable to compete in the international platforms.

The above determinants together with all other necessary variables, such as the availability of resources and skills required in an industry; the information that shapes the opportunities that companies perceive; the directions in which they develop their resources and skills; the goals of the owners, managers, and individuals in companies; and the pressures on companies to invest and innovate, determine the fulfilment of international competitive advantage. Porter also maintains that firms are most likely to succeed in industries or industry segments where the sources of competitive advantage are more favourable; an important point which justifies the importance of the industry structure not only in directing the investment activities of firms but also in creating pressures for innovation through intensive domestic rivalry.

In addition, Porter includes two other exogenous variables that can influence the national system in important ways. These are chance and government. Chance is defined as "occurrences that have little to do with circumstances in a nation and are often largely outside the power of firms (and often the national government) to influence" (Porter, 1990, page 124). According to Porter:

> "chance events are important because they create discontinuities that allow shifts in competitive position. They can nullify the advantages previously established competitors held and create the potential that a new nation's firm can supplant them to achieve competitive advantage in response to new and different conditions." (Porter, 1990, page 124).

Some examples of chance events are: acts of pure invention, major technological discontinuities (biotechnology, microelectronics), discontinuities in input costs such as the oil shocks, significant shifts in world financial markets or exchange rates, surges of world or regional demand, political decisions by foreign governments, or wars (Porter, 1990, page 124). Unexpected shifts in any of these issues can become a force to generate new mechanisms to cope with selective factor disadvantages.

While most of the previously reviewed theories do not visit the role of the government in their analysis, Porter justified the role for the government at all levels. Government, as stated by Porter, can improve (or detract from) the national advantage of the nations by influencing the four determinants of competitive advantage. Government's new regulations and policies, for example, can change the previous home demand and factor conditions. They determine how firms compete within the boundaries governed by government and enforce within a economy (Nishimura and Okamuro, 2011; Sheng, Zhou and Li, 2011)

Porter's theory has spawned several inquiries that are the focus of debate. One of these is the meaning and measurement of 'competitiveness' or 'competitive advantage' and the relationship between the competitiveness of an economy and that of the industries and firms that operate within it. Although studies such as Sagebien (1990) declare Porter's definition of competitiveness as a breakthrough as it equates with national productivity, other studies such as Eilon (1990) argue that this proposition is confusing and misleading. Productivity, according to Eilon, is different from competitiveness, as one is an efficiency measure of resources use while the other refers to competency in gaining market share. This explanation clarifies why Porter's theory does not offer guidance on how competitive advantage should be defined and measured.

The term of competitiveness or productivity of a nation was also examined by Clark (1991) who provided evidence that this term was not actually similar to the competitiveness of its industries. Porter (1990) asserted that the competitiveness or productivity of a nation is essentially the competitiveness or productivity of any industries located in that country. Evidence such as Japanese auto-makers that established factories in Britain and outperformed local firms by using the same factors of production or American electronic companies that gained a high level of productivity in other countries (Reich, 1990), have shed a light on the difference between the national and industrial context of productivity. Porter argued that a nation is essentially an aggregation of industries and its economic performance is determined by the competitiveness of those industries for which it is the home base and the appropriate level of analysis should therefore be the industry. Congdon (1990) maintained that this description confounds the context of analysis of nation, industry and firm levels.

From the above accounts, it can be concluded that Porter's theory represents a combination of the distinguishing characteristics of comparative advantage and new trade theory. Hill (2002) noted that if Porter's theory is right, then a country's export pattern needs to reflect the presence of the four main components mentioned in the diamond model. Furthermore, countries will import goods from industries where some or all the components are missing domestically. The extent to which Porter's theory can explain many aspects of internationalisation at the firm level, however, remains limited, since the basis of Porter's diamond model is the nation/industry level of analysis. His emphasis on industry level was reflected in his explanation of each industry's diamond that captures the relative attractiveness of each particular industry. Porter (1990), in addition, attempted to identify a nation's 'competitive' industries and measured them based on their export-share statistics. Although, this measurement was considered flawed, for it was measuring companies located in the nation regardless of their home base, the focus of measurement was the industry within a nation. Thus, Porter's theory is incapable of explaining differences that may exist at the individual firm level, and it is necessary to extend the analysis to other relevant export theories to explain factors affecting firm's engagement in international markets.

3.5 A Review of Empirical Studies - Export Behavioural Models

In contrast to the international theories as presented earlier, export behaviour models attempt to explain *why* and *how* individual firms engage in export activities as part of the internationalisation process, and how the dynamic nature of such activities can be conceptualized. Export behaviour is defined both as the probability of being an exporter and export intensity for the exporting firm (Wakelin 1998, Basile, 2001). The focus is explicitly on determinants of export engagement. Perceived export benefits, perceived export barriers, firm size, and managerial characteristics are among important determinants found in export behaviour. Companies engaging in foreign marketing activities are often driven by the firm's expectations relative to their short term and long term objectives but they usually lack prior knowledge, experience, marketing information, and so on, which hinders their ability to initiate, develop, or sustain business operations in overseas markets.

3.5.1 Internal Determinants of Export Development

To act as an engine of development, international trade through exports must lead to steady improvements in managerial and organisational skills by developing performance at individual, team, and organisational levels. From this perspective, exports and a country's development cannot be seen simply as the aggregate of its economic growth and export performance. Exports represent a synthesis of the interaction between people's choices and trade with a view to improve their living standards, particularly through export engagement. The extent of such choice, in turn, depends on the interplay between internal and external factors that determine export outcome.

Several empirical studies have attempted to provide a quantitative indication of export behaviour by systematically accounting for factors governing export behaviour. Reviews by Bilkey (1978), Miesenbock (1988), Aaby and Slater (1989), Chetty and Hamilton (1993), Leonidou and Katsikeas (1996), Zou and Stan (1998), and Coviello and McAuley (1999) are those that are mostly cited in the literature. The empirical studies have included a wide range of industries for their analysis including the services industry. Most of the studies, however, dealt with SMEs from developed countries with only a few from newly industrialized and developing countries.

A substantial body of literature on this subject had been developed as early as the 1960's (see Mintz, 1967). But the fragmented nature of the research and the lack of consensus on the findings, have meant that the field suffers from a lack of proper synthesis and assimilation (Leonidou and Katsikeas, 1996). Despite this growing critique, a careful review of these empirical studies suggests that combination and interaction between external and internal factors (Brooks and Rosson, 1982; Aaby and Slater, 1989; Leonidou, 2004) plays a complementary role in influencing export behaviour and can lead to the direction of change over time, including to initiate or withdrawal from exports.

Unlike Porter's theory that included "entrepreneurship" as an inseparable factor in the diamond framework, most of the empirical research above were carried out explicitly seeking the relevant attributes that distinguish exporters from non-exporters and identifying the attributes correlating with success in exporting. A number of decision maker's characteristics are highlighted in the export behaviour literature and, as per Suarez-ortega and Alamo-vera (2005), include:

1. Perceptions of the barriers to exporting
2. Perceptions of the benefits associated with exporting
3. Age group
4. Level of education
5. International experience
6. Knowledge of foreign language
7. Professional and general business experience

Source: Suarez-ortega, Alamo-vera, 2005.

3.5.1.1 Perception of barriers to exporting

Barriers to exporting are defined as attitudinal, structural, operational, and related constraints which hinder or prohibit the firm's ability to initiate, expand or sustain export operations (Leonidou, 1995a, 2004). They are also called obstacles, impediments, hindrances, disincentives or problems (Leonidou, 1995a, 2004) that can exist at different stage of the internationalization process (Ahmed et al., 2004; Leonidou, 2004; Suarez-Ortega, 2003). Since exporting involves collective attitudes, opinions, and perceptions of a firm's management (Abdel-Malek, 1978), top management's insight and determination play a significant role in establishing the strategy to enter international markets.

The negative impacts that export barrier perceptions can have, particularly on SMEs' export behaviour, have been outlined in numerous pieces of research. To set a clear-cut analysis of various export barriers found in the literature, Leonidou (1995b, 2004) classified export barriers broadly into internal and external ones. While internal barriers are associated with organisational capabilities and a company's approach to export business, external barriers deal with home and host environments within which the firm operates. Although the findings indicate that there are differences by country in managers' perceptions of export barriers, the most common export barriers cited in the literature are:

1. Lack of government assistance and incentives/ lack of knowledge of government assistance (see for example: Ahmed et al., 2004; Da Silva and Da Rocha, 2008; Leonidou, 2004; Suarez-Ortega, 2003).
2. Insufficient knowledge about export opportunity/locating potential markets/ limited information to locate and analyse foreign markets/difficulty collecting accurate information on foreign markets (see for example: Ahmed et al., 2004; Da Silva and Da Rocha, 2008; Moini,1997; Suarez-Ortega, 2003).
3. Unavailability of finance/lack of financial assistance/shortage of working capital to finance exporting (see for example: Ahmed et al., 2004; Da Silva and Da Rocha, 2008; Morgan and Katsikeas, 1997; Suarez-Ortega, 2003).
4. Insufficient production capacity (see for example: Ahmed et al., 2004; Fillis, 2002; Leonidou, 2004; Suarez-Ortega, 2003;)
5. Lack of personnel and expertise to perform tasks associated with exporting (see for example: Da Silva and Da Rocha, 2008; Fillis, 2002; Leonidou, 2004; Suarez-Ortega, 2003).
6. High cost/risk involved in selling abroad/risk of variations in exchange rates/risk of losing money in selling abroad (see for example: Crick et al., 1998; Da Silva and Da Rocha, 2008; Fillis, 2002; Suarez-Ortega, 2003).

7. Strong international competition/inability to offer competitive price (see for example: Ahmed et al., 2004; Altintas et al., 2007; Leonidou, 2004; Suarez-Ortega, 2003)
8. Difficulties in collecting payments from abroad/honouring letters of credit (see for example: Ahmed et al., 2004; Altintas et al., 2007; Barker and Kaynak, 1992; Da Silva and Da Rocha, 2008).

Since the number and the types of barriers generated by each study vary, some studies have attempted to classify barriers based on their collective characteristics (Morgan, 1997). One such attempt was made by Cavusgil (1984) who distinguished barriers based on the internal and external environments of the firm. Another attempt was made by Ramaswami and Yang (1990) who classified barriers according to export knowledge, internal resources, procedural matters, and exogenous factors. Leonidou (2004) formulated a comprehensive structure to identify export barriers, particularly those perceived and experienced by SMEs, by integrating findings from previous studies (see Table 3.3).

Table 3.3 shows that there are three main categories of problems within the internal environment of the firm. They are informational, functional, and marketing categories. Four main categories of problems originated from the external environment of the firm and they are procedural, governmental, task, and environmental. Based on Leonidou's (2004) review, the internal barriers which consistently rated very high due to their critical impact on export decisions were: limited information to locate/analyse markets; inability to contact overseas customers; identifying foreign business opportunities; difficulty in matching competitors' prices; and excessive transportation and insurance costs. Meeting export product quality standards/specifications and lack of excess production capacity for exports, were revealed as having a low influence on management decisions to export. External barriers regarded to have a serious impact on export decisions were different foreign customer habits or attitudes; poor or deteriorating economic conditions abroad; and political instability in foreign markets. Verbal/nonverbal language differences were reported as having a low impact on export behaviour.

Table 3.3: Classification of Export Barriers based on Leonidou's Integrative Review

Barriers Hindering Small Business Export Development

Internal

- Informational
  - Limited information to locate/analyse markets
  - Problematic international market data
  - Identifying foreign business opportunities
  - Inability to contact overseas customers
- Functional
  - Lack of managerial time to deal with exports
  - Inadequate/untrained personnel for exporting
  - Lack of excess production capacity for exports
  - Shortage of working capital to finance exports
- Marketing
  - Product
    - Lack of expertise and/or resources and/or technology to:
      - Develop new products for foreign markets
      - Adapt export product design/style
      - Meet export product quality standards/specs
      - Meet export packaging/labelling requirements
      - Offer technical/after-sales service
  - Price
    - Lack of expertise and/or resources and/or technology to:
      - Offer satisfactory prices to customers
      - Match competitors' prices
      - Grant credit facilities to foreign customers
  - Distribution
    - Lack of expertise and/or resources and/or technology to:
      - Address the complexity of foreign distribution channels
      - Access export distribution channels
      - Obtain reliable foreign representation
      - Maintain control over foreign middlemen
      - Supply inventory abroad
  - Logistics
    - Lack of expertise and/or resources and/or technology to:
      - Access warehousing facilities abroad

Meet excessive transportation/insurance costs Develop export promotional activities
External
Procedural
Unfamiliarity with exporting procedures/paperwork Problematic communication with overseas customers Slow collection of payments from abroad
Governmental
Lack of home government assistance/incentives Unfavourable home rules and regulations
Task
Different foreign customer habits/attitudes Keen competition in overseas markets
Environmental
Economic
Poor/deteriorating economic conditions abroad Foreign currency exchange risks
Political-legal
Political instability in foreign markets Strict foreign rules and regulations High tariff and non-tariff barriers
Socio-cultural
Unfamiliar foreign business practices Different socio-cultural traits Verbal/nonverbal language differences

Source: Leonidou (2004).

Based on the export barriers literature, it can be concluded that perceived strength of export barriers varies depending on the demographic characteristics, resources and capabilities, and market destination of each firm. Different industries, for example, have been found to be different in their perception of the barrier types to exporting (Da Silva and Da Rocha, 2001). Firms with different market destinations also perceive barriers to exporting differently (see for example Bodur, 1986). The "cultural distance" between the home market and the international market has been highlighted by Shoham and Albaum (1995) as a factor that significantly influences the perceived severity of the problem. The importance of cross-cultural competency and management is evident in international business where cooperation and integration between companies in many countries is on the increase and challenges may be encountered when companies are working together (Browaeys and Price, 2015). Therefore, it is advisable to avoid market destinations with large psychic distance from the home market.

3.5.3 The Internationalization Stages: Export Development of a Firm

Most companies usually choose export operation as an initial mode of entry into international markets (Albaum et al., 1998; Cinquetti, 2009). This mode of entry to international markets is commonly used by SMEs (Hanson et al., 2017). There are evidences that firms only gradually develop their business in international markets (Boter and Holmquist, 1996). The concept of the export development process, that is part of the internationalisation process of a firm, has not been uniformly defined by authors (Johansen and Vahlne, 1977; Welch and Luostarinen, 1988). From the viewpoint of SMEs, the internationalization process can be seen as an evolutionary process of development in their international engagement (Rialp and Rialp, 2001). In this sequential process, a firm gathers foreign experience and accumulates organizational learning over time. The increase in the firm's level of international involvement will also lead to a change in their methods of serving foreign markets. The greater the international involvement a firm has, the deeper and more diverse its offering to foreign markets will be.

Several models have been applied to conceptualize the process of export development. Most of these models highlight the process as a series of incremental decisions, rather than large, dramatic foreign investments. Firms are believed to move through stages as their commitment to foreign markets increases (Hanson et al., 2017). This section provides a review of the existing staged models and their relevance in explaining how the individual firm is engaged in export activities.

According to Gankema et al. (2000) and Chetty and Campbell-Hunt (2004), there are two major approaches dominating the incremental internationalisation perspective: the Uppsala internationalisation model (U-model) and Innovation-related models (I-models). Although one model was developed in Sweden and the other in the USA, they both share the same concept that firms engage in international activities in incremental steps and through distinct stages (Hammoudi, 2005).

The U-model or the Uppsala model was introduced by Johanson and Wiedersheim-Paul (1975). The model is based on the study of four major Swedish firms – Sandvik, Atlas Copco, Facit and Volvo. The conclusions drawn from this study, show that the successive stages represent higher degrees of international involvement and therefore a greater commitment of resources to overseas markets. In this model, Johanson and Wiedersheim-Paul chose to distinguish between four different stages, with regard to the degree of involvement of the firm in international operations. The stages in this model are:

1. No regular export activities
2. Export to psychologically close countries via independent representation (agent);
3. Exporting to psychologically distant countries/establishment of an overseas sales subsidiary;
4. Overseas production/manufacturing units are established in the foreign country.

In this study, the most important obstacles to internationalization are lack of knowledge and resources. These obstacles are reduced through incremental decision making and learning about the foreign market and operations. Then, as the perceived risk of market investment decreases, the internationalization process is furthered by the increased need to control sales, by exposure to offers and demands, and to extend overseas operations (Johanson and Wiedersheim-Paul, 1975). According to Leonidou and Katsikeas (1996) the model emphasizes the critical role of information acquisition in every stage of internationalization. Knowledge acquired leads to reduced levels of uncertainty regarding foreign markets and operations.

In 1977, Bilkey and Tesar (1977) developed a stage hierarchy approach based on Roger's theory of diffusion of innovations, known as the I-model. The study took its data from a sample of small and medium-sized firms in Wisconsin, USA. The analytical methodology used requires treating each stage of the export development process as the dependent variable in a multiple regression equation; coefficients differing at each stage allowed for experience gained in preceding stages (Thomas & Araujo, 1985). The results of the study mainly conclude that: 1) The export development process of firms tends to proceed in stages; 2) Considerations that influence a firm's progression from one stage to another tend to differ by stage; 3) Within the size range of firms studied, size was relatively unimportant when account was taken of the quality and dynamism of management. The Bilkey and Tesar (1977) study divided the process into a six-staged model that consists of:

1. Management is not interested in exporting and will not even fill unsolicited orders.
2. Management is willing to fill unsolicited orders but makes no effort to explore the feasibility of actively exporting.
3. Management actively explores the feasibility of exporting (this stage may be omitted if a firm receives unsolicited orders).
4. The firm exports experimentally to one or a few psychologically close countries.

5. The firm is an experienced exporter to the country/ies it exports to and will make optimal export adjustments based on changes in environmental factors.
6. Management explores the feasibility of exporting to additional markets that are psychologically further away.

In 1982, Cavusgil proposed a model consisting of four stages. The criteria used in distinguishing firms in various stages include management level of awareness of foreign opportunities; the nature of search processes for information; decision-making mode of management; typical decision-making skills utilised; and the nature of international marketing involvement. The stages proposed are as follows:

1. Non-exporting firms. Not interested in gathering export-related information.
2. Non-exporting firms. Interested in gathering export related information. (These two stages may be grouped as the "pre-involvement stage").
3. Exporting firms. Export less than 10 per cent of their output. (Referred to as the limited/experimental involvement stage).
4. Exporting firms. Exports more than 10 per cent of their output (Referred to as the active involvement stage).

The study's findings primarily conclude that: 1) During the pre-involvement stage, non-exporting firms are not interested in gathering export related information. 2) New product development capability and product quality are the main impetus of the progression from stage one to stage two. 3) Second stage firms were found to be more active in gathering export related information than stage-one firms. 4) Managers in stage-two firms are more likely to be younger and more educated than those of stage-one firms. 5) Stage-three firms are more likely to enjoy management expertise in marketing and finance than those of stage-two firms. 6) Progression to stage four is facilitated more by the presence of a technologically intensive product.

Meanwhile, Wortzel and Wortzel (1981) developed a five-stage model based on their study in five Asian countries: three newly industries countries and two least developed countries. The five stages were based on marketing mix elements and the degree of control exerted by the exporter in overseas operations. The stages are as follows:

1. Importer pull – At this stage the firm has not made an explicit decision to seek exports, their export business is initiated by an importer who therefore dominates in various operations such as appearance, packaging, shipping, and quality control. The local producer is simply a seller of production capacity.
2. Basic production, capacity marketing – At this stage there is some commitment to exporting and "exporter push" has started. Some internal design skills are developed, but the firm's most powerful weapon is low prices. The firm is still a seller of production capacity rather than product.
3. Advanced production, capacity marketing – At this stage the products satisfy consumer expectations. The firm begins to be more dominant in gaining control over the elements of marketing mix. Its marketing organisation becomes more skilled. A firm in this stage is a supplier of know-how as well as of production capacity. However, price is still its major competitive weapon.
4. Product marketing, channel push – At this stage the firm produces for its own inventory rather than for customers only. The firm's investments and operations are considerably higher than that of firms in stage 3. With regard to the product, the firm is more dominant than its importer, and the responsibility in designing the product belongs to the firm. The firm may perform some marketing functions such as promotion. The firm has access to the technology levels of its competitors so that the limitations are more to do

with marketing than production. Price is still an important competitive advantage.

5. Product marketing, consumer pull – This is the stage the marketing efforts shift from "channel push" to "consumer pull". The firm differentiates its offerings either through branding or distinctive fashion and style. The price is no longer the most important factor but product features. The firm in this stage will be actively engaged in trade promotion, in advertising to consumers, and in product design.

The findings of this study conclude that: 1) Stage 5 was theoretical in the newly industrialized and less developed countries where the study was carried out. 2) There are four main factors that help to determine the stage in which particular exporters are found. They are firms' experiences with the product; product marketing requirements; structure of distribution; and the existence of trade barriers imposed either by actions of market participants or by regulations.

Following the development of the above stage models, several researchers have also attempted to develop their own staged models. A brief review of those models is as follows: 1) A study by Reid (1981) has further developed the Bilkey and Tesar model. Based on the findings of the study, it is concluded that "decision maker's attitudes towards and preferences for foreign markets and export entry, together with his perception and expectations of the results from such entry, are major determinants of the subsequent export behaviour" (Reid, 1981:110); 2) A study by Czinkota (1982) has generated a six-stage model consisting of a completely uninterested firm; partially interested firm; experimental exporter; experienced small exporter and final stage, experienced large exporter; 3) A study by Moon and Lee (1990) develops a three-stage model. The stages proposed are lower, middle, and higher stages; 4) A four-stage model was developed by Lim et al. (1991). The model consists of awareness, interest, intention, and adoption stages; 5) Rao and

Naidu (1992) offer a four-stage model consisting of non-exporters, export intenders, sporadic exporters, and regular exporters.

In their review of empirical models, Leonidou and Katsikeas (1996) suggested that despite differences among the various models as to number, nature, and content of the stages, the export development process can be divided into three broad phases of pre-engagement, initial and advanced stages. The review concluded that the pre-engagement phase includes three types of firms: those selling their goods in the domestic market and not interested in exporting; those involved in the domestic marker but seriously considering exporting; and those that used to export in the past but no longer do so. Firms in the initial phase were defined as those involved in sporadic export activity. In this phase, companies were classified as those having the potential to increase their overseas involvement, and those unable to cope with the demands of exporting, leading to marginal export behaviour or withdrawal from selling abroad altogether. Firms in the advanced phase were classified as regular exporters with extensive overseas experience and frequently consider more committed forms of international business.

Apart from the general acknowledgment of these stage models in the existing literature, many other studies have cast doubt on and criticized them. Some authors such as Diamantopoulos and Inglis (1988), Sullivan and Bauerschmidt (1990), argued that the underlying assumption that firms develop through stages in their internationalization process is far from universal in time and sequence. This can be observed in the description of the models and the variability in the number of stages, commonly ranging from three to as many as six. Andersen (1993) also noted that the stage models lack explanatory power as to how the process takes place or how movements between stages can be predicted. The boundaries between stages are claimed to be not clearly defined, leading to confusion as to when a specific stage begins and ends.

It is also claimed that most models do not readily accommodate the reality of reversals in the direction of change and sufficiently take into consideration the transition phases from one stage to another; some firms may even omit some of the stages making the adoption process much quicker (Cannon and Willis, 1981). Other researchers argue that some firms are international at their inception (see for example Harveston et al., 2000; Moen, 2002; Oviatt and McDougall, 1994), indicating that internationalization patterns and purposes of individual firms are quite unique and highly situation specific (Reid, 1983). Significant progress in various aspects of technology as well as the shifting mind-set of international markets has been claimed to be the reason for the international at inception phenomenon (Harveston et al., 2000; Moen, 2002; Oviatt and McDougall, 1994). The variation in knowledge and experience of firm's top management is also maintained to be a critical resource that contributes to an early adoption of export and internationalization (Reuber and Fischer, 1997). This reasoning indicates that firms may skip or compress stages in the export development process through well-planned engagement and commitment.

Due to the criticisms above, other researchers suggest an alternative "network" approach to export development models. According to Hanson et al. (2017), there are two types of alliance networks, ie. Stable alliance networks and dynamic alliance networks. Stable alliance networks are built among mature industries with long-term relationships where demand is relatively constant and predictable. The objective of this network is to exploit the economies of scale and scope available between the firms. On the other hand, dynamic alliance networks are established among firms that engage in rapid technological change which lead to short product life cycle. The objective of this network is to exploit new ideas among firms in the network to stimulate value-creating product innovation and opportunity to enter new or existing profitable markets. The focus of this approach is on the relationships that develop amongst firms which help to increase their knowledge and other resources needed to successfully internationalize (Berry and Brock, 2004; Coviello and Munro, 1995, Coviello and Munro, 1997). An assumption used in the network model is that the firm's export development varies according to the resources controlled by other firms. A firm usually gains access to these external resources due to their network positions. Although the network approach of export development offers an important element of understanding key issues involved in cooperation in industrial systems and of global industry competition, this approach has drawn criticism for having limited strength in understanding the internationalization pattern, and not offering very precise conclusions while including too many variables (Bjorkman and Forsgren, 2000). It is also criticized for not offering a satisfactory model for predictions (Bjorkman and Forsgren, 2000) and ignoring the way firms overcome the problems within their network relationship (Chetty and Blankenburg Hol, 2000). Thus, since the network model focuses mainly on larger firms and rarely explains how SMEs use networks in their internationalization (Nummela, 2002), the model simply adds to the consensus that the whole internationalization process is much more complex and less structured than was suggested by earlier theories and models.

3.6 The Conceptual Framework

The earlier sections have been devoted to reviewing a wide range of literature on determinants of export behaviour and the development of export in the firm. This section turns to a model development which attempted to conceptualize the relationship between managerial and organisational determinants of export behaviour and export development in the firm. The determinants of export behaviour are expected to vary along with the differences in a firm's level of export development.

Following the pioneering Uppsala model of Johansen and Vahlne (1977), a number of studies have concentrated almost exclusively on finding the relationship between market environmental/behavioural variables and foreign activities. Most of the studies, however, according to Cavusgil and Nevin (1981), lacked systematic empirical analysis. In 1978, Wiedersheim-Paul, Olson and Welch developed a model that stresses the role of a firm's "pre-export' activities in its export initiation. The model concentrates on three main factors namely the decision maker, the environment of the firm and firm itself. The model assumed that all firms are non-exporters in the beginning and sell to local markets and that there is only one decision maker in the firm who makes all important decisions.

The decision maker in this model is subject to different kinds of attention evoking factors or those factors that can trigger a firm to consider exporting as a possible strategy. The type and amount of attention and how it is perceived by the decision maker is contingent upon the characteristics of the decision maker, the environment of the firm and the firm itself, as well as the interaction between these factors. The decision maker characteristics include such aspects as international outlook, degree of international orientation and perception of uncertainty. The environment of the firm was defined in relation to the location of the firm in the domestic market. Location is considered significant in reducing transportation costs and fostering information flows. Firm characteristics such as its goal and degree of realisation, type of product line, history of the firm, and degree of extra-regional expansion were considered influential in determining pre-export behaviour of a firm.

Figure 3.1: Factors Affecting the Pre-export Activities of the Firm

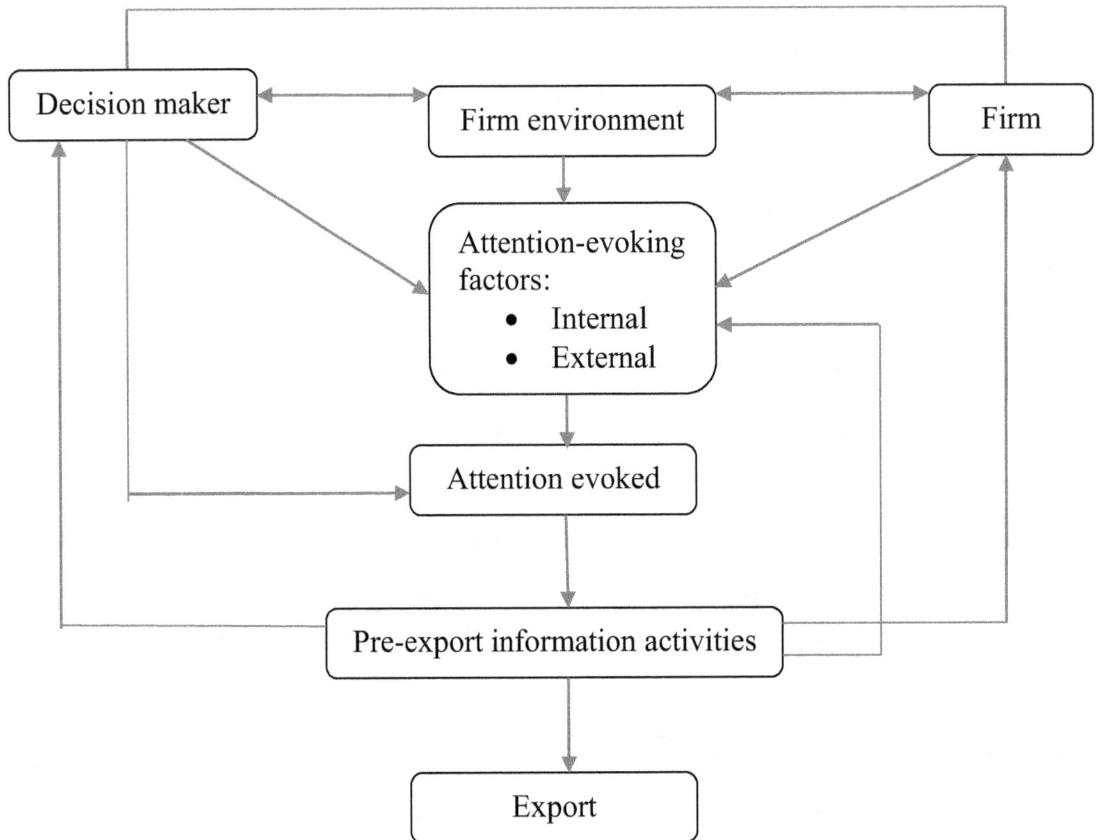

Source: Wiedersheim-Paul, Olson and Welch, 1978.

Attention-evoking factors in this model can be broadly classified into internal and external to the firm. Internal factors include such factors as differential firm advantage like the possession of unique competencies, and excess capacity in the resources of management, marketing, production, or finance. Under external-evoking factors, fortuitous orders from foreign customers, competition stimuli arising either from domestic or foreign competitors, market opportunities, and government export stimulation activities were identified.

In 1981, Cavusgil and Nevin proposed a model that emphasized a number of background and intervening variables (see Figure 3.2). Their model described export-marketing behaviour as a merging of two background variables namely differential firm advantages and managerial aspirations for business goals. Differential firm advantages are derived from the firm's products features, technological orientation and resources. The managerial aspirations variables underscore such dimensions as growth, profits, and market development. Cavusgil and Nevin's (1981) findings put the view that the reluctance of a firm to export is a consequence of the lack of determination of management and that management requires a long-range commitment in order to achieve success in export markets.

Figure 3.2: The Path Model of a Firms' Export Behaviour

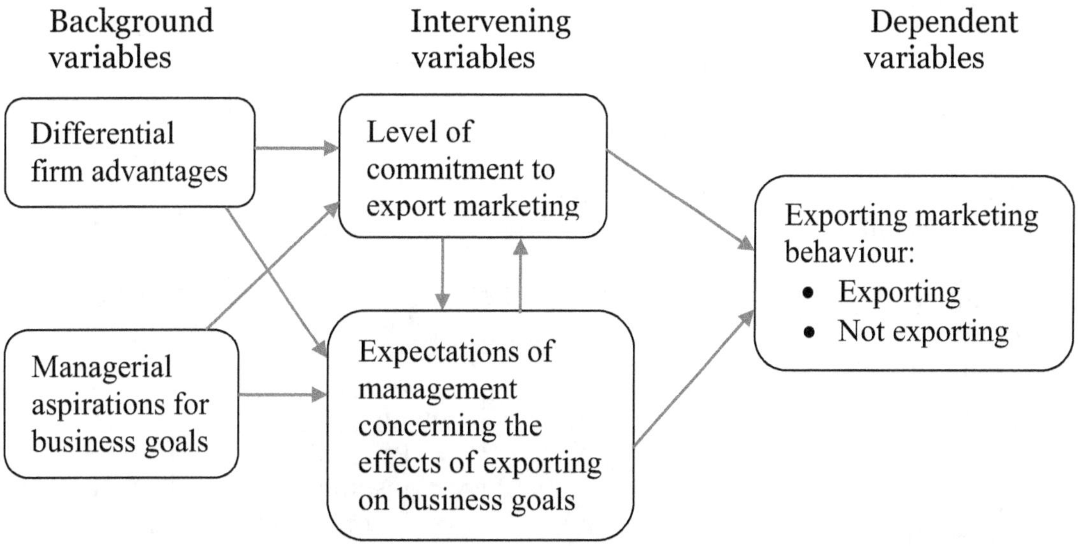

Source: Cavusgil and Nevin, 1981.

Figure 3.3: The Export Entrepreneurial Model

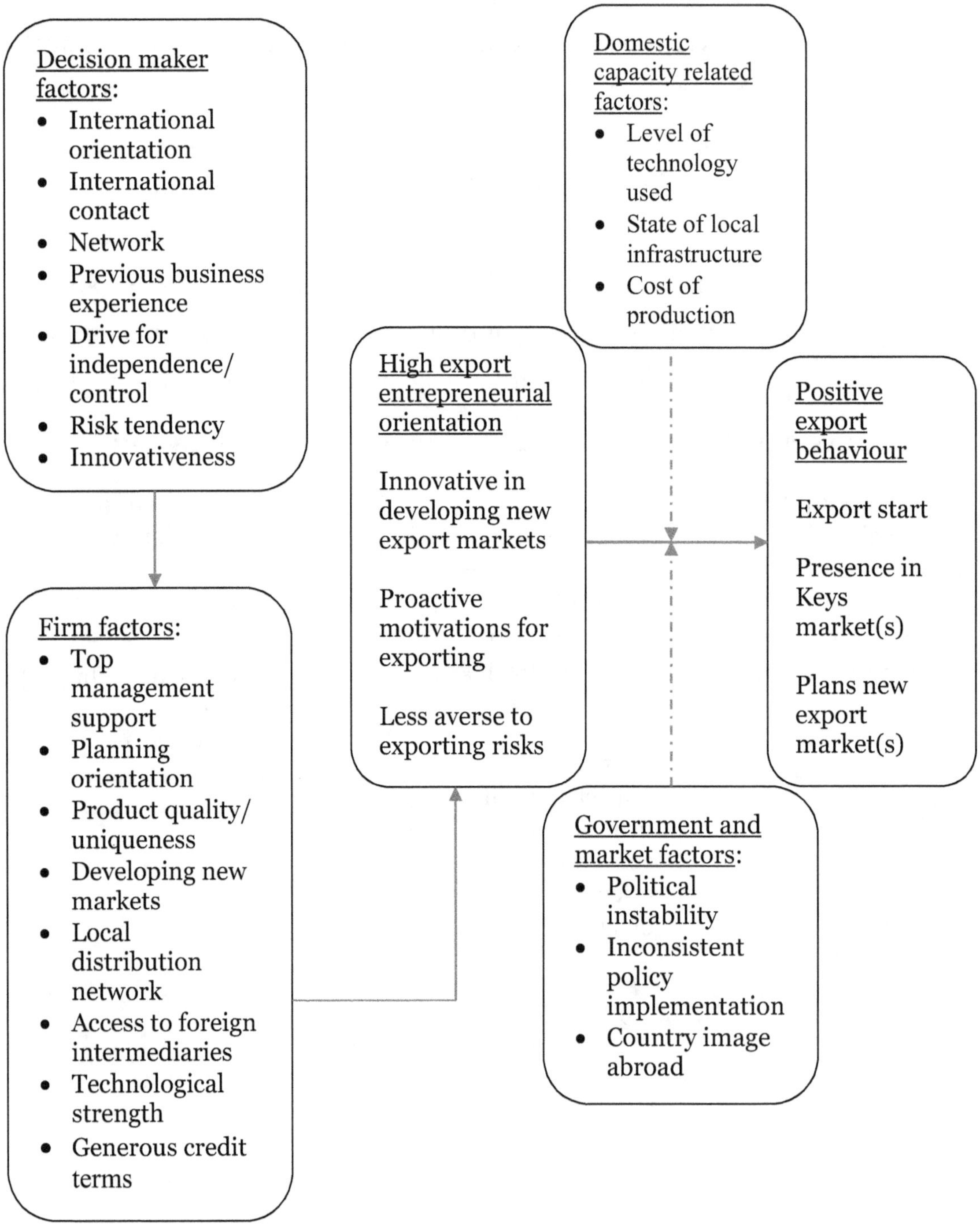

Decision maker factors:
- International orientation
- International contact
- Network
- Previous business experience
- Drive for independence/ control
- Risk tendency
- Innovativeness

Firm factors:
- Top management support
- Planning orientation
- Product quality/ uniqueness
- Developing new markets
- Local distribution network
- Access to foreign intermediaries
- Technological strength
- Generous credit terms

High export entrepreneurial orientation

Innovative in developing new export markets

Proactive motivations for exporting

Less averse to exporting risks

Domestic capacity related factors:
- Level of technology used
- State of local infrastructure
- Cost of production

Government and market factors:
- Political instability
- Inconsistent policy implementation
- Country image abroad

Positive export behaviour

Export start

Presence in Keys market(s)

Plans new export market(s)

Source: Ibeh and Young, 2001.

Ibeh and Young (2001) conceptualized the export entrepreneurial model from the perspective of Nigerian firms (see Figure 3.3). Their model was based on the notion that exporting is an 'entrepreneurial act'. The authors maintained that this concept of the entrepreneurial act is particularly useful in developing countries due to environmental problems and the increasing need for an entrepreneurial orientation which is often lacking in small sized and resource-deficient firms. They recommend strengthening firms' entrepreneurial foundations in order to improve export behaviour or performance. They also suggested some kind of assessment of entrepreneurial orientation in order to have better insights into the export potential of non-exporting firms.

Figure 3.4: Internal Determinants of Export Involvement

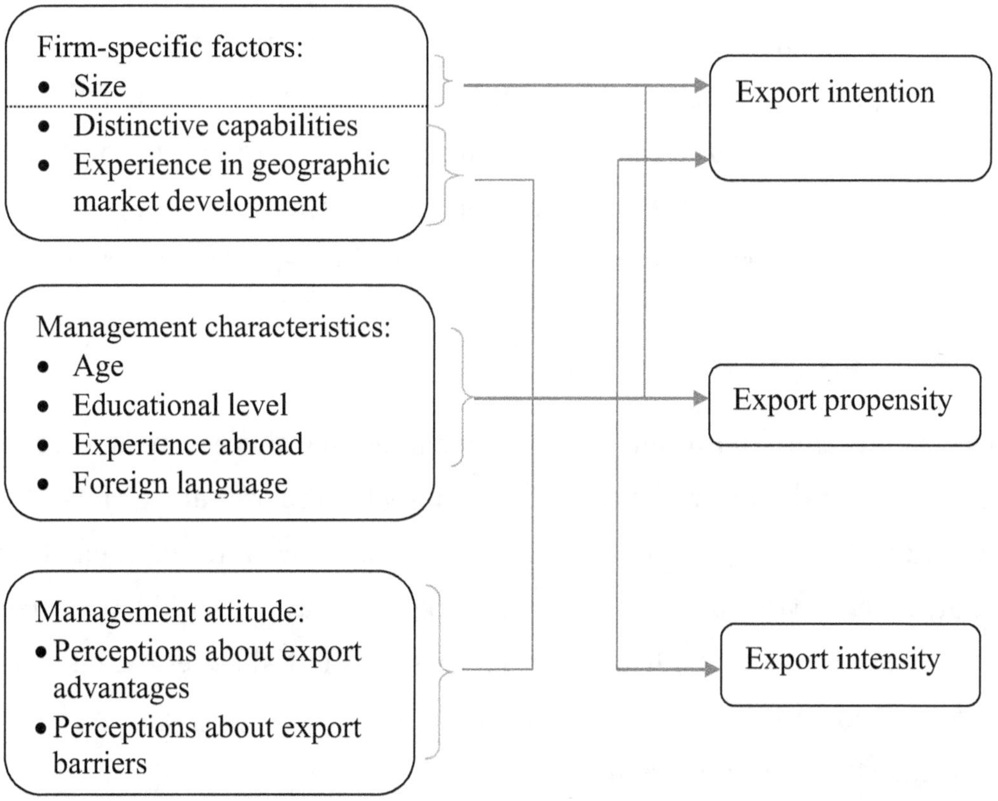

Firm-specific factors:
- Size
- Distinctive capabilities
- Experience in geographic market development

Management characteristics:
- Age
- Educational level
- Experience abroad
- Foreign language

Management attitude:
- Perceptions about export advantages
- Perceptions about export barriers

Export intention

Export propensity

Export intensity

Source: Suarez-Ortega and Alamo-Vera, 2005.

In examining export development behaviour in the Spanish wine industry, Suarez-Ortega and Alamo-Vera proposed a model with three distinct categories of resources and capabilities that influence export behaviour: 1) firm specific resources and capabilities; 2) management characteristics; and 3) management attitude and perceptions (see Figure 3.4). All dimensions, except size, under these three broad categories influence non-exporters and exporters in the export development proxies of export intention, export propensity, and export intensity.

The model suggests that the main driving forces motivating internationalization are found within the firm, and therefore they are based on management's strengths and weaknesses. Rather than the external environment, the pool of resources and capabilities within the firm that might be appropriately combined is the main influence on the internationalization endeavour. The authors further recommend assistance programmes aimed at enhancing managers' skills and capabilities in order to accelerate and support the internationalization process. Export promotion programmes should emphasize activities that increase managers' awareness of export advantage in order to get more non-exporters interested in exporting.

3.7 Chapter Summary

The review of literature in this chapter has concluded that there were at least four theoretical bases at the macro level as the grounds for this research. Most of the theories attempted to provide economic reasons for international trade, international trade patterns, and product-market evolution. Within this macro understanding of trade, it is obvious that there are potential benefits that can be gained from exporting. None of these theories alone, however, can explain all aspects of trade flows between countries.

In the micro considerations, there are a number of possible taxonomies to distinguish the degree of a firm's export development. This micro approach is selected on the grounds that the macro approaches were inadequate in describing the export behaviour of the individual business unit where managerial and organizational characteristics of each individual firm greatly impact on export behaviour. The decision to get involved in export activities and the likelihood of succeeding in export markets have been found to be strongly related to management's positive perceptions as well as distinct managerial and organizational background characteristics.

In addition to the internal characteristics of the firm, export behaviour models have also studied the impact of external determinants on a firm's involvement in exporting. There are two major classifications covered under external determinants, they are domestic external determinants and the foreign external determinants. Under the domestic external determinants, there are size and state of the domestic market and export promotion programme; while foreign external determinants include level of competition, tariff and non-tariff barriers, and physical and psychological distance. It is generally noted that favourable external conditions are more preferred by firms than adverse external conditions as the latter can inhibit a firm's progression along the internationalization path. Although it is pivotal to consider the external determinants in the analysis, the complexity and dynamism of these factors have constrained this current research to focus on factors internal to the firm. External factors will be incorporated as part of managerial perception variables which represent external barriers to export development.

The final part of this chapter has reviewed several conceptual frameworks explaining the relationship between managerial and organisational determinants of export behaviour and export development in the firm. Despite differences among the models regarding the determinants of export behaviour, it can be concluded that different sets of organizational and managerial determinants influence the different stages of the export development process and these dimensions are expected to recur over time due to the common characteristics of this internationalized mode of entry.

****

CHAPTER FOUR
METHODOLOGICAL FRAMEWORK

4.1 Introduction

The literature review in Chapters 2 and 3 highlighted a number of preconditions to support the need to examine manufacturing SMEs' behaviour in Indonesia. Some important findings showed that most of the government policies to promote SME development in Indonesia were evidently not effective due to the lack of a systematic plan and government capabilities (World Bank in Wie, 2006). Further studies of Indonesian manufacturing SMEs' export behaviour were inadequate to the extent where it is deemed necessary to develop an empirical model to help understand and confirm critical variables affecting SMEs development in overseas markets (Leonidou, 1995).

This chapter serves as the methodological chapter where the specification of managerial factors related to the firm's export development are conceptualized and operationalized. The structure of this chapter is as follows. Section 4.2 describes the critical linkage between the model specification of all predictors and export development. Section 4.3 elaborates the way each variable is made operational within the model. Data source descriptions and collection methods are discussed in Section 4.4. The major statistical techniques used in the data analysis are presented in Section 4.5. The chapter draws its conclusion in Section 4.6.

4.2 Managerial Characteristics and Export Development - the Linkages

The literature review discussed in Chapter 3 illustrates the need for an overview in a developing county context such as Indonesia. The most recent review of empirical studies (Suarez-Ortega and Alamo-Vera, 2005) revealed an absence of export behaviour studies carried out in developing countries. Furthermore, most studies focus on the managerial characteristics and direct effects of exporting without trying to construct a framework that investigates the relationships and interactions between the variables. Therefore, there is a need for a new approach that incorporates the most common factors of managerial characteristics that is managerial perceptions of export barriers, and that explores and understands their relationship and interaction in different stages of the export development process.

Building upon the review discussed, this current study uses four categories to build the conceptual model: managerial characteristics; export development; export propensity; and export intensity. All managerial perceptions about internal and external export barriers are considered as predictor variables. Since Indonesia has been pursuing an incremental approach in its economic development policy by initially focusing on import substitution, most Indonesian SMEs are assumed to have been following a gradualist approach to entering foreign markets. For measurement purposes, the study follows the generic export development stages of Leonidou and Katsikeas' (1996) study. That study also used proxies of export propensity and export intention to support the export development classification.

Figure 4.1: Managerial determinants of Export Development

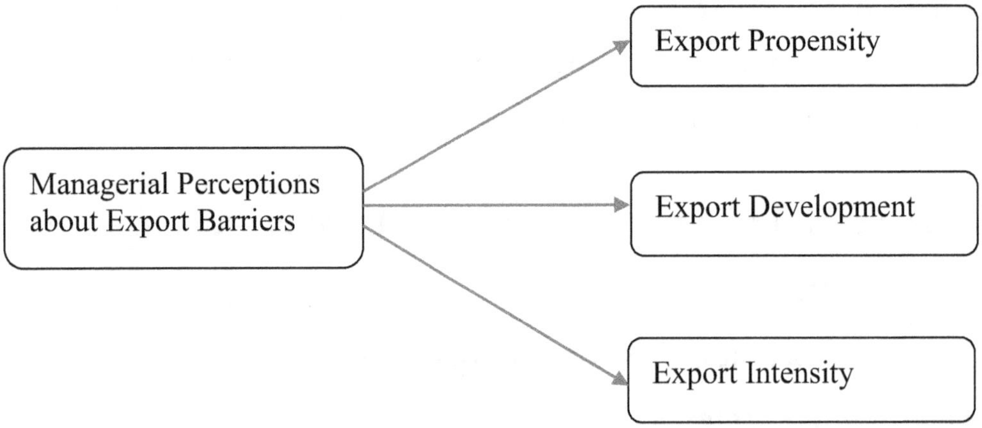

The proposed conceptual framework of this study, as depicted in Figure 4.1, shows perception variables that stem from managerial aptitude assessment are classified in managerial characteristics. The correlation between each management perception variables will determine the firm's level of export development, export propensity, and export intensity. To sum up, the concepts used to develop the proposed conceptual framework resemble Suarez-Ortega and Alamo-Vera's (2005) research closely but improve on the older technique by using factor analysis and structural equation approaches to solve the multidimensional correlations and relationships between each perception variable in the model.

4.3 Operationalisation of Variables and Research Hypothesis

4.3.1 Independent Variables - Perceived Export Barriers

Several studies (see for example: Kedia and Chhokar, 1986; Cheong and Chong, 1988; Yaprak, 1985) found that the cumulative nature of these barriers tends to differ between exporting firms and non-exporting firms. Some studies such as Barker and Kaynak (1992) and Cheong and Chong (1988) confirmed that non-exporting firms placed greater importance on problems associated with the initial engagement in export activity. While exporting firms were primarily experiencing operational problems as they have previously been engaged in export operations (Keng and Jiuan, 1989; Samiee and Walters, 1990).

The review of literature on the association between overall perceptions of export barriers and export development level shows that empirical studies have reached somewhat contrasting conclusions. Some of the studies concluded that non-exporting firms with the smaller export experience, may overstate, and therefore baulk at, export barriers (see for example: Leonidou, 1995, Madsen, 1989 and Yaprak, 1985). While other researchers (see for example, Bilkey and Tesar, 1977;

Keng and Jiuan, 1989) argued that non-exporting firms may perceive fewer barriers to exporting, when compared with exporting firms, due to a lack of knowledge of exporting. Based on the above results, however, it can be concluded that firms who perceive greater barriers to exporting are more likely not to export. Therefore, it can be hypothesized that:

H1: Non-exporters are perceived to rate export barriers higher than do exporters.

H2: There are significant differences between exporter and non-exporter groups in relation to the factors they perceive as important barriers to exporting.

In order to measure the impediments to exporting, respondents will be asked to indicate on a five-point Likert scale the extent to which they regard certain factors to be serious impediments to their export development. The problem items examined will be based on recent research carried out by Leonidou (2004), who developed a comprehensive theoretical classification of the perceived barriers hindering small business export development. The items include informational, functional, and marketing for barriers originating within firms and procedural, governmental, task, and environmental for those derived from outside the firm (see Table 3.3).

In order to shed light on the significance of possible differences in perceptions of export barriers among the groups of non-exporters and exporters and to identify the differences in relation to the factors they perceive as important barriers to exporting, independent sample t-test will be utilized. The reason for using these tests is that they allow for the analysis of rank data used in measuring this variable.

4.3.2 Dependent Variables

4.3.2.1 SMEs Export Development

This study defines exporting as the transfer of goods across national boundaries using direct and indirect methods (Leonidou and Katsikeas, 1996). The definition includes 'indirect method' because, as highlighted by other studies (see for example Hassler, 2003; Berry et al., 2002; Sjoholm, 2003; Lecraw, 1993), most Indonesian manufacturing SMEs tend to rely on distribution channels or foreign networks in initiating export operations. Therefore, firms engaged both in direct exporting by using their own export departments or divisions, and indirect exporting by relying on distribution channels are considered as exporters in this study.

As supported in the literature, the most effective and viable approach in studying the export behaviour of firms is to classify them by their stage of export development (Bilkey and Tesar, 1977; Czinkota and Johnston, 1981; Reid, 1981). A review of literature on the export development process shows that a wide range of studies has examined the differences between firms based on different stages of export development. However, it also reveals wide inconsistencies in terms of the number of stages of export development proposed by researchers. The number of stages varies from as low as two to as many as six. At the broadest level firms are divided into two main categories, namely non-exporter and exporter (see for example: Westhead, 1995; Keng and Jiuan, 1989; Yaprak, 1985; Kedia and Chhokar, 1985; Malekzadeh and Nahavandi, 1985). In a cross-sectional study, this division does not discriminate effectively between firms at different stages of the process. Leonidou and Katsikeas (1996), however, take the middle stream by concluding that the export development process can be broadly classified into three major phases. The first phase is the pre-engagement phase, where firms are not exporting. The second phase is the initial phase, where firms are exporting on a marginal basis. The third phase is the advanced phase which includes firms that export on a regular basis and are considering more committed forms of international involvement.

Drawing on the Leonidou and Katsikeas (1996) and Suarez-Ortega (2003) research, this study divides firms into four levels of export development: two levels of non-exporting firms (according to their intention to engage in export activity) and two of exporting firms (according to their levels of export intensity). This segmentation encompasses the following types of firms:

1. The uninterested non-exporters
2. The interested non-exporters
3. The initial exporters
4. The experienced exporters.

The above segmentation scheme supports the generally accepted proposition that exporting is a gradual sequential process with discernible differences between firms at different stages of export development and this process has been shown to be empirically valid across a wide range of studies and within the context of selected firm and managerial characteristics (Yaprak, 1985; Sharkey et al., 1989; Leonidou et al., 1998). Thus, because there is a sufficient number of small and medium sized enterprises involved in exporting in Indonesia, by grouping them into more specific segments, important information or attributes such as intention to initiate or expand export operations (see for example: Gipsrud, 1990; Reid, 1983; Yang et al., 1992) and their propensity to become exporters can be incorporated (Suarez-Ortega and Alamo-Vera, 2005).

In order to categorise firms into the above groups, firstly, the respondents will be asked to choose among five possible states (Leonidou and Katsikeas, 1996; Suarez-Ortega, 2003) that best described their company with respect to export activity, following a self-clustering process (see Table 4.3). Suarez-Ortega argued that this first question is useful in separating the firms based on their self-assessment and it is useful to cross-check the response reliability of any dependent variables used. Secondly, firms have to indicate their export intensity – export sales to total sales ratio- in the last three years. Finally, all firms will be asked whether their company has any intention of initiating or expanding their export operations over the next two years, with 'yes' or 'no' being the two alternative responses. These responses will be dummy coded (1 = if "yes", and 2 = if "no").

Note that the specification of export intention in this study follows that of Yang et al. (1992) in using an intention within a two-year period rather than as an immediate course of action. The logical explanation for such classification is that some firms may become involved in exporting fortuitously by responding to unsolicited enquiries from buyers abroad and show no obvious signs of commitment or intention to become an exporter (Suarez-Ortega, 2005). Using this type of classification also accommodates the apparent inconsistency between export attitude and behaviour (Eshghi, 1992).

Table 4.3: Firms Export Situation

Export situation statements:
1. Your firm has never exported and has no intention to do so in the near future
2. Your firm has never exported but is interested in starting to export
3. Your firm has exported marginally, but the experience has been somewhat disappointing
4. Your firm has had profitable export experiences, but is only taking the first steps towards international markets
5. Your firm is an experienced exporter

The responses to the above questions will be used to sort firms into four groups representing four different levels of export commitment. First, exporters are those firms in states 4 and 5, plus firms in state 3 who have nominated an intention to expand export activity in the next two years. The remaining firms are considered non-exporters. Second, among exporters, the study distinguishes between intensive exporters as those firms with an export-to-total sales ratio equal to or greater than 50 per cent, and non-intensive exporters as being the rest (Leonidou, 1998). Finally among non-exporters, the study distinguishes between uninterested and interested non-exporters. Uninterested non-exporters are those firms in state 1 plus firms in state 3 that nominate no intention to engage in exporting in the next two years. Interested non-exporters are those firms in state 2 that nominate an intention to engage in exporting in the next two years.

4.3.2.2 SMEs' Export Intensity

Export intensity is a measure used to quantify the contribution made to a firm's total business by exports (Kirpalani and Balcome, 1987). This ratio is repeatedly used in the export literature as an indicator of a firm's export performance or success (Aaby and Slater, 1989; Leonidou, 1998). It is concluded that the higher the export intensity, the greater the degree of internationalisation. For this study's purpose, and drawing on Leonidou's work (1998), firms with an export-to-total sales ratio equal or greater than 50 per cent will be designated as intensive exporters, and the remaining as non-intensive exporters.

Export intensity will be measured by two items: 1) the percentage of annual sales derived from exports in the most recent financial year; and 2) the percentage of annual sales derived from exports over the last three financial years. According to Anderson (1993), the increase in sales is an indicator of an increased commitment to export markets (Anderson, 1993).

4.3.2.3 SMEs' Export propensity

Many studies have attempted to explain why some firms do not export while others are engaged in exporting by finding a number of differences between exporters and non exporters. Similarly the present study will analyse the propensity for non-exporter SMEs to become exporters by comparing mean values differences of interested non-exporters and initial exporters.

Built on Patterson et al.'s (1999) and Lages and Montgomery's (2004) approaches, export propensity in this study is measured by means of three items focusing on:

1. The likelihood that the company will be exporting its product(s) in the next two years.
2. The desire for the company to export its product(s) in the next two years.

The variable of export propensity will be measured by evaluating the likelihood of a firm to export its product within the next two years. A five-points Likert scale from "Very unlikely" (1), "Unlikely" (2), "Moderate chance" (3), "Likely" (4), to "Very likely" (5) will be used to analyse the variable.

4.4 Data Sources and Description

The secondary data used in the analysis was obtained mainly from Industry and Trade Services in the provinces of Jakarta, West Java, Central Java, and D.I. Yogyakarta; Indonesian Ministry of Cooperative, Small and Medium Enterprises (MOCSME); and the National Agency for Export Development (NAFED). Other sources of secondary data were from Indonesian Board of Statistics (*Badan Pusat Statistik* in Indonesian), the business directory of the Indonesian Coordination Board of Investment (*Badan Koordinasi Penanaman Modal* in Indonesia) and the Indonesian yellow pages.

4.4.1 Survey Area

The study focused on four areas of Java Island being: the capital of DKI Jakarta province; West Java province, with the capital of Bandung situated very close to the Indonesian capital, Jakarta; Central Java, with the capital of Semarang; and East Java with the capital of Surabaya.

Table 4.4: Number of Firms Registered with Industry and Trade Services, 2007

	PROVINCE	NUMBER OF FIRMS
1	BALI	605
2	BANTEN	1893
3	BENGKULU	20
4	CENTRAL JAVA	3771
5	CENTRAL KALIMANTAN	80
6	CENTRAL SULAWESI	53
7	D. I. YOGYAKARTA	404
8	D. K. I. JAKARTA	2172
9	EAST JAVA	4941
10	EAST KALIMANTAN	133
11	JAMBI	129
12	LAMPUNG	250
13	MALUKU AND PAPUA	88
14	NORTH SULAWESI	82
15	NORTH SUMATRA	993
16	RIAU AND KEPULAUAN RIAU	371
17	SOUTH EAST SULAWESI	99
18	SOUTH KALIMANTAN	137
19	SOUTH SULAWESI	287
20	SOUTH SUMATRA	282
21	WEST JAVA	4911
22	WEST KALIMANTAN	161
23	WEST NUSA TENGGARA	155
24	WEST SUMATRA	282

Source : NAFED's website, 2007.

These areas were chosen based on the consideration that they represented some of most densely concentrated areas of SMEs in Indonesia. If these four provinces are combined together, they represent around 48 per cent of all SMEs listed by the Central Board of Statistics and contribute 50.29 per cent of the total US$79.6 billion (IMI, 2009) non-oil exports in 2007. Of firms with legal entities and registered with Industry and Trade Services through license or permit to establish a firm and business tax file number, the four chosen provinces represent 70.8 per cent of all firms.

Table 4.5: Number of Exporters in All Provinces, 2007

	PROVINCE	NUMBER OF FIRMS
1	BALI	61
2	BANTEN	28
3	BENGKULU	5
4	CENTRAL JAVA	136
5	CENTRAL KALIMANTAN	1
6	CENTRAL SULAWESI	1
7	D. I. YOGYAKARTA	54
8	D. K. I. JAKARTA	234
9	EAST JAVA	70
10	EAST KALIMANTAN	19
11	JAMBI	4
12	LAMPUNG	20
13	MALUKU	8
14	NORTH SULAWESI	5
15	NORTH SUMATRA	39
16	PAPUA	12
17	RIAU	10
18	RIAU ISLAND	11
19	SOUTH EAST SULAWESI	14
20	SOUTH KALIMANTAN	7
21	SOUTH SULAWESI	16
22	SOUTH SUMATRA	12
23	WEST JAVA	139
24	WEST KALIMANTAN	4
25	WEST NUSA TENGGARA	4
26	WEST SUMATRA	16

Source : NAFED's website, 2007.

4.4.2 Population and Sampling Frame

The sample population in this study is small and medium sized firms dealing in exportable manufactured products. The types of industries included are food and beverages, garments and footwear, furniture and wood products. The main reason for targeting these industries is because most of the small and medium sized firms involved in exporting in Indonesia fall under these three industries (Berry et al., 2001). These industries can also be generalized as light industries or consumer goods industries which can offer a better platform for export initiation, particularly in the context of developing countries (Ibeh and Young, 2001; and Tybout, 2000; Wade, 2003).

The sampling frame is developed based on the multiplicity of sources, mentioned in Section 4.4 introduction and 4.4.1, in order to achieve the most comprehensive list possible. Any duplication in the listings was noted and deleted in order to come up with a complete list of SMEs from the three industries and to avoid double counting. However, due to inconsistency in definitions between the Indonesian public agencies and this study, the total number of SMEs has not been categorically identified. The number of firms of all sizes currently registered in the four provinces chosen was 11,258 units (2,172 firms in DKI Jakarta; 4,911 firms in West Java; 3,771 firms in Central Java; and 4941 firms in East Java). The following criteria are used to select firms into the final sampling frames:

1. Firms must have at least 5 employees. All other sizes below this number will be considered as either micro or cottage enterprises.
2. Firms must be producing and/or trading in an exportable product and come from the garments or footwear or wood products sub-sectors. All firms engaged in sub-sectors other than the abovementioned three, as well as firms in the service sector, are excluded.
3. Firms must be privately owned and the owners must be actively involved in the running of the business. Government owned enterprises are not included in the sample.
4. Firms must have been in operation for at least three years.

4.4.3 Sampling Method and Sample Size

Stratified random sampling was used to come up with the final sample population. Malhotra et al. (2002) defined stratified sampling as a two-step process in which the population is partitioned into sub-populations or strata. The strata should be mutually exclusive and collectively exhaustive in that every population element should be assigned to one and only one stratum and no population elements should be omitted. In this study, firms of all sizes currently registered in the four provinces and three industries selected will be firstly stratified along a small, medium, and large sizes stratum, and then through an exporter and non-exporter stratum, and then finally, a simple random sample was taken from each stratum. The two main reasons for using this mixed method are: a) to make the sample more representative and hence improve the precision of the results; b) to achieve greater statistical significance in a smaller sample and reduce the standard error (Malhotra et al., 2002). The same sampling fraction or proportional allocation was taken from each stratum (Cavana et al., 2001). The total number of exporters registered by NAFED is 930 with 408 inclusive of the four provinces and three industries chosen.

The decision on the final size of independent observations (N) required to obtain a sample pattern that is stable and approximates the population involves several issues of consideration. Some researchers typically recommend that the necessary sample size is determined by a set of observed variables (p) involved in the research problem (See for example: Baggaley, 1982; Brislin et al., 1974; Cattell, 1978; Gorsuch, 1983; Hair et al., 1998; Kunce et al., 1975; Lindeman et al., 1980; Marascuilo and Levin; Nunally, 1978). These sources suggest N-to-p ratios which vary from 2:1 to 20:1. A minimum N of 100 to 200 observations is also frequently suggested (Comrey, 1978; Gorsuch, 1983; Guilford, 1954; Hair et al., 1998; Lindeman et al., 1980; Loo, 1983). Velicer et al. (1982), in a simulation study, compared the solutions obtained from three types of factor analysis procedures (principal-components analysis, image-component analysis, and maximum likelihood factor analysis) to determine under what conditions the methods produce different patterns. A comparison of sample factor and component patterns suggested that "with only moderate sample sizes (N = 144), the fit of the pattern to the population target was quite good" (Velicer et al., 1982, p. 386).

In addition to the number of observed variables and the proposed data analysis, Miaoulis and Michener (1976) point out the importance of the level of precision, the level of confidence or risk, and the degree of variability in the attributes being measured. The level of precision or sampling error is defined as the range in which the true value of the population is estimated to be. This range is often expressed in percentage points (for example, ±5 per cent). The confidence level or risk level is based on the key concept encompassed in the Central Limit Theorem. According to this theorem, when a population is repeatedly sampled, the average value of the attribute obtained by those samples is equal to the true population value. The values obtained by these samples are distributed normally about the true value, with some samples obtaining a higher value and some gaining a lower score than the true population value. In a normal distribution, approximately 95% of the sample values are within two standard deviations of the true population value. The degree of variability refers to the distribution of attributes in the population. The more heterogeneous a population, the larger the sample size required to obtain a given level of precision. The more homogeneous a population, the smaller will be the requisite sample size. The degree of variability of 50%, however, suggests a greater level of variability than either 20% or 80%, because 20% or 80% indicate that a large majority do not or do, respectively, have the attribute of interest. The maximum variability of 0.5, therefore, is often used to determine a more conservative sample size which requires a larger sample in order to fit the true variability of the population.

The above criteria are used by various studies developed to estimate sample size. Cochran (1963:75), for example, developed an equation [1] to obtain a representative sample for proportions from a population that is large,

$$n_0 = \frac{Z^2 pq}{e^2} \qquad [1]$$

where n_o is the sample size, Z^2 is the abscissa of the normal curve that cuts off an area at the tails (the desired confidence level, for example, 95%), e is the desired level of precision, p is the estimated proportion of an attribute that is present in the population, and q is 1-p. Thus, suppose this study intends to estimate the sample from a large population of which variability is unknown, therefore, it is assumed that p=0.5 (maximum variability), and if the study desires a 95% confidence level and ±5% precision, then the sample size will be:

$$n_0 = \frac{Z^2 pq}{e^2} = \frac{(1.96)^2(0.5)(0.5)}{(0.05)^2} = 385$$

If the population is small then the sample size can be reduced slightly. The reduction is carried out when the sample size provides proportionately more information for a small population than a large population, as in the case of an homogeneous population. The sample size (n_o) can be modified using equation [2]:

$$n = \frac{n_0}{1 + \left(\frac{n_0 - 1}{N}\right)} \qquad [2]$$

Given that the evaluation of this study will only affect 816 exporters and non-exporters, then the sample size would be:

$$n = \frac{n_0}{1 + \left(\frac{n_0 - 1}{N}\right)} = \frac{385}{1 + \left(\frac{385 - 1}{816}\right)} = 261$$

Based on the above result, this study aims to interview 262 exporting and non-exporting firms. However, due to the possibility of a non-response rate which is typically between 60 and 50 per cent for personally administered questionnaires (Groves, 1989; Ornstein, 1998; Massey et al., 1997), then 435 identified exporters and non-exporters in the three industries in the four selected provinces will be targeted for final data collection. This is obtained from the following equation:

$$n^a = \frac{n \times 100}{re\%} = \frac{261 \times 100}{60} = 435$$

Where n^a is the actual sample size required, n is the minimum sample size and re% is the estimated response rate expressed as a percentage (Saunder et al., 2003).

4.4.4 Data Collection Methods

4.4.4.1 Personally Administered Questionnaire Approach

For primary data, a personally administered questionnaire was employed to achieve higher respondent participation and better-quality data. During the process of data collection, it is important to select the most appropriate individual in each participant firm to provide the information needed. Most knowledgeable individuals or key informants will be either the export manager (especially in larger firms) or the owner/director (mainly in smaller firms) in order that they have access to the information required by the study. The questionnaire administration was conducted by the author, and emphasis was given to minimising the chance of interviewer bias by designing and implementing a structured questionnaire which was based mainly on a scale format for participant responses.

4.4.4.2 Data Collection Procedure

The data was collected using a personally administered questionnaire. The questionnaire was designed based on the information needed to test the hypothesis put forward in this study, as well as other issues closely related to exporting. A single questionnaire was designed for both exporters and non-exporters. Most of the questions in the questionnaire make use of five-point Likert and itemised scales, where respondents were asked to tick their responses on clearly outlined alternatives. Such questions make it easier for respondents to fill in the questionnaire and are also faster than other methods of data collection. The questionnaire also facilitated analysis of data regarding respondent attitudes and opinions using statistical tools such as Statistical Package for Social Science (SPSS) and Analysis of Moment Structure (AMOS).

An information letter was sent before the researcher's visit and administration of the questionnaire. This provided information to the potential respondents regarding the general purpose of the research, as well as inviting their participation and cooperation in the data collection process. It assured them that they would remain anonymous as personal and business identification details were not required. They were informed that, as a requirement of the University of Newcastle Research Ethics Clearance, they could withdraw from the research project at any stage without penalty or register any complaint via the contact details provided in the covering letter.

During the pilot study, the questionnaire was given to officials from the National Agency for Export Development in order to solicit their comments and observations on the questionnaire in general and the issues covered. The aim was to ensure the agency was apprised of those issues and considered them to be of real concern and worthy of addressing in the development and promotion of export in small and medium sized firms. The questionnaire was pre-tested on a small sample of 24 firms (12 exporters and 12 non-exporters). The pre-testing aimed to determine if the questionnaire was easily understood by the respondents and to determine the average length of time taken to complete a questionnaire. Personally administered questionnaire interviews were used to perform the pre-testing and the actual administration of the questionnaire. This not only helped in reducing misunderstood questions and inappropriate or incomplete responses, but also in gaining greater control over the environment in which the survey was administered. In order to help improve the face and content validity of the measures and the study as a whole, respondents in the pre-testing stage were asked to provide comments on the questions. All the observations obtained during the pre-testing stage were taken into account when developing the final questionnaire, which was used in this study.

In administering the final questionnaire, each of the potential respondents was contacted and personally interviewed based on the structured questions in the questionnaire. Personal physical presence was considered important because it was strongly believed that most of the respondents would not be keen to fill out the questionnaire without help and guidance from the interviewer. Physical presence, therefore, was expected to improve the response rate. The over-reliance on mail out surveys by most of the previous studies (Bell and Young, 1998), which achieved low response rates, also justifies the use of a mixed methods approach.

4.5 Statistical Techniques for Data Analysis

All the data collected in this study was subject to statistical analysis using Statistical Package for Social Science (SPSS) and Analysis of Moment Structure (AMOS). The five-point Likert and itemised scales were treated as interval scales. Diamantopoulos and Schlegelmilch (1997) pointed out that Likert scales, semantic differential scales, itemised rating scales, as well as Stapel scales, can be considered interval scales, especially in social research. Cavana et al. (2001) noted that, in some cases, numbers can be assigned to the different categories in a categorical scale and as long as the intervals between each category are equal, then the scales can be treated as interval. The scales were tested for their reliability and validity before using them in the analysis.

4.5.1 Factor Analysis and Testing Reliability of a Construct

Squared multiple correlations will be used in order to test for item reliabilities. The preferred value for item reliability was equal to or higher than 0.50, although values exceeding 0.30 are usually adopted as standard (Cunningham, 2007). In addition to item reliabilities, two other model-based estimates: 1) composite reliability and 2) the variance extracted estimate (Bollen, 1989), will also be presented. The purpose of composite reliability is to measure the internal consistency of a set of measures and the variance extracted estimate is to reflect the overall amount of variance in the indicators accounted for by the latent construct (Fornell and Larcker, 1981). The multi-item scales that will be subject to reliability tests, for example, are: perceived barriers of export and perceived benefits of exporting.

Factor analysis with maximum likelihood estimation (Hair et al, 1998) will be run to examine the structure of the relationships among the items of latent variables such as the 39 items of perceived export barriers and the 6 items of perceived export benefits. This test is also useful in addressing the double-counting issue (e.g. Miniard and Cohen, 1979). The results of this analysis will be presented in the form of loading factors, eigenvalues, and per cent of variance explained (Hair et al., 1998). Factorial analysis is necessary when a study has 20 or more variables to be analysed (Nunnaly and Bernstein, 1994).

4.5.2 Bivariate and Multivariate Data Processing and Analysis

Data processing and analysis techniques will include:

1. Factor Analysis – Factor analysis will be used in the study for the main purpose of finding latent variables or factors among observed variables. In other words, if the data contains many variables, factor analysis can be used to reduce the number of variables. Factor analysis examines the structure of inter-

correlations among a large number of observed variables and groups them into a set of common underlying dimensions, known as factors (Hair et al., 1998). With factor analysis, the researcher can first identify the separate dimensions of the structure and then determine the extent to which each variable is explained by each factor. When these dimensions and the explanation of each variable have been determined, the two primary uses for factor analysis – that of summarizing and data reduction - can be achieved.

There are three stages in factor analysis (Francis, 1999):

a. First, a correlation matrix that shows the correlation coefficients of the variables in relation to each other is generated for all the variables.
b. Second, factors are extracted from the correlation matrix based on the correlation coefficients of the variables in order to estimate how closely an observed distribution matches an expected distribution – it is usually referred to as the goodness-of-fit-test
c. Third, the factors are rotated in order to maximize the relationship between the variables and to test whether two random variables are independent.

In addition to the chi-square test, a number of other model fit indices will be used to determine whether the observed data supports the hypothesized model in this factor analysis. An assessment of model fit determines the degree to which parameter estimates of the proposed model are able to reproduce the sample data variance and covariance. Usually, model evaluation is assessed by the chi-square test and its accompanying significance test. If the associated p value *is not significant*, one can conclude that there is no significant difference between the sample variance/covariance matrix and the model-implied variance/covariance matrix and hence the data fits the model well.

The most common indices found in the literature are CMIN/DF, the Standardized Root-Mean-Square Residual (SRMR), the Root Mean Square Error of Approximation (RMSEA), the Goodness-of-fit Index (GFI), the Adjusted Goodness-of-fit Index (AGFI), the Normed Fit Index (NFI), the Tucker-Lewis index (TLI), and the Comparative Fit Index (CFI). The properties of these fit indices will be briefly discussed in the following sub-sections.

a. CMIN/DF is the minimum discrepancy divided by its degrees of freedom. Several writers (see for example Wheaton et al., 1977; Carmines and McIver, 1981; Marsh and Hocevar, 1985) suggested ratios in the range of 2 to 1 or 3 to 1 as indications of an acceptable fit between the hypothetical model and the sample data.
b. The Standardized Root-Mean-Square Residual (RMR) measures the average difference between corresponding elements of the sample and model-implied correlation matrices. Because the units of measurement are in standardized form, a model may be considered to fit the data well when this average value is less than 0.05 (Hu and Bentler, 1999). Large values of the SRMR may indicate outliers in the data.
c. The Root-Mean-Square Error of Approximation (RMSEA) – The logic underlying RMSEA is that no model will ever fit exactly in the population and one can only rely on a close approximation to reality (Browne and Cudeck in Bollen and Long, 1993). The RMSEA computation requires the chi-square statistic, degrees of freedom, and sample size for the target model (Rigdon, 1996). The RMSEA has a lower bound of zero which indicates a perfect fit with values increasing as model fit deteriorates. Browne and Cudeck in Bollen and Long (1993) suggested that a RMSEA value of about 0.05 or less indicates a model of close fit, while values between 0.05 and 0.08 indicate reasonable fit.
d. The Goodness-of-fit index (GFI) and the Adjusted Goodness-of-fit index (AGFI) provide an indication of the relative amounts of the covariance

among the latent variables that are accounted for by the model (Mathieu et al., 1992). The GFI is based on a ratio of the sum of the squared differences between the observed and reproduced matrices to the observed variances. The AGFI is the GFI adjusted for the degrees of freedom of the model relative to the number of variables. Both the GFI and AGFI should be between 0 and 1 with values exceeding 0.95 considered to be an indication that the data fits a model well.

e. NFI or normed fit index incorporates the minimum discrepancy of the model being evaluated and the minimum discrepancy of the baseline model (Bentler and Bonett, 1980). Models with overall fit indices of less than 0.90 can usually be improved substantially.

f. TLI or Tucker-Lewis index estimates the relative improvement per degree of freedom of the target model over an independence model (Hu and Bentler, 1998). For a good fitting model, values exceeding 0.95 are preferred.

g. CFI or comparative fit index measures the improvement in going from a target model to an independence model. The CFI has a range of 0-1 and values greater than 0.95 are generally considered satisfactory fit of the model to the data (Hu and Bentler, 1999).

2. Correlation Analysis – Using correlation coefficients, correlation analysis will be used to test for statistical association of variables. It allows for measurement of a linear association between two variables. Values of the correlation coefficient are always between -1 and +1. A correlation coefficient of +1 indicates that the two variables are perfectly related in a positive linear sense; a correlation coefficient of -1 indicates that the two variables are perfectly related in a negative linear sense; and a correlation coefficient of 0 indicates that there is no linear relationship between the two variables.

For simple linear regression, the sample correlation coefficient is the square root of the coefficient of determination. Correlation analysis will be extensively used in testing the correlation between each independent variable and dependent variable in the proposed model. The firm size variable, for instance, will be tested to investigate whether it has a positive or negative correlation with the level of export development.

3. Path Analysis – Path analysis will be used to examine multiple relationships in a single model. Path analysis will be used as an alternative to multiple regressions which can estimate a single relationship. However, path analysis in AMOS can estimate many equations at once (Hair et al., 1998).

   Other advantages of path analysis compared to multiple regression include more flexible assumptions (particularly allowing interpretation even in the face of multicollinearity), use of confirmatory factor analysis to reduce measurement error by having multiple indicators per latent variable (Loehlin, 1992), the support of path analysis' graphical modelling interface, the desirability of testing models overall rather than coefficients individually (Madigan and Raftery, 1994), the ability to test models with multiple dependents, the ability to model mediating variables, the ability to model error terms (Kline, 1998), the ability to test coefficients across multiple between-subjects groups, and the ability to handle difficult data (time series with autocorrelated error, non-normal data, incomplete data) (Olsson et al., 2000).

   Nevertheless, path analysis, using AMOS software, remains limited to continuous dependent variables. The non-metric character of a dichotomous dependent variable is accommodated by making predictions of group membership based on Z scores. AMOS approaches this task in a manner similar to that found in logistic regression and multiple regression analysis. Structural equation modelling also cannot itself draw causal arrows in models or resolve causal ambiguities. Theoretical insight and judgment by the researcher, therefore, are still of utmost importance (Hair et al., 1998).

4.6 Chapter Summary

In this chapter, the research design and methodology of the study have been discussed and the focus has been on making operational the independent and dependent variables as well as constructing the hypotheses that will be tested by the study. The chapter also outlines the sampling plan, data collection methods, and statistical techniques used for analysing the data.

The export development construct is presented as a categorical variable consisting of four categories; the uninterested non-exporters, the interested non-exporters, the initial exporters, and the experienced exporters. To validate this segmentation approach, other dependent variables of export intention, export propensity, and export intensity are also utilised. The proposed export development model and its mathematical equation form are aimed at understanding the relationships of perceived export barriers associated with the export development process of a firm.

Due to a lack of a readily available sampling frame in the chosen industries, a sampling frame is developed with the help of lists from Industry and Trade Services in the provinces of West Java, Central Java, and Special Province of Yogyakarta; plus the Ministry of Cooperative, and Small and Medium Enterprises; the National Agency for Export Development; and the Central Board of Statistics.

A personally administered questionnaire was the instrument used to collect data. The questionnaire was initially pre-tested on a group of 12 exporting firms and 12 non-exporting firms. In addition, in-depth interviews with the respondents were held at the same time in order to collect more information on issues covered in the questionnaire. Only the owner/part owner managers of the firms were allowed to fill in the questionnaire.

In the following chapters the analysis of the data will be reported. This analysis uses Statistical Package for Social Science (SPSS) and Analysis of Moment Structure (AMOS). A number of statistical techniques are employed including crosstab analysis, chi-square test, standard t-test, correlation, factor analysis and path analysis.

****

CHAPTER FIVE
EMPIRICAL ANALYSIS OF PERCEIVED OF EXPORT BARRIERS

5.1 Introduction

This chapter investigates managerial perceptions of export barriers amongst manufacturing SMEs in Indonesia. A review of the literature in Chapter 2 revealed that in recent times the Indonesian government has implemented a series of policies aimed at minimizing or reducing export barriers facing SMEs. An understanding of the interrelationships between managerial perception of export barriers, as part of managerial characteristics, and export development of manufacturing SMEs is important in informing the formulation and implementation of policies that will promote the export performance of firms in Indonesia.

The rest of the chapter is organized as follows: Section 5.2 examines the perceptions of managers of manufacturing SMEs about export barriers; and Section 5.3 reports and discusses the empirical analysis of differences in perceptions between exporters and non-exporters about export barriers. Section 5.4 summarizes the findings of the chapter.

5.2 Confirmatory Factor Analysis of Export Barriers

5.2.1 Internal Barriers

Confirmatory factor analysis (CFA) was performed to determine whether the number of factors and the loadings of measured (indicator) variables are consistent with the hypothesized factor or latent construct on the basis of pre-established theory. A series of one-factor congeneric models, each of which represents the regression of a set of observed variables on a single latent variable, was used for testing and evaluating each factor that consists of four or more indicators. Constructs with two or three indicators were tested in pairs. In each step of the testing, if the chi-square statistic is unsatisfactory, changes, indicated by factor retention or factor free estimation, are made to the model. These changes are processed one at a time, provided that the changes are statistically and theoretically justifiable. When the data does not support the model, indicated by a significant chi-square, a model may be rejected or, alternatively, respecified based on theoretical considerations and magnitudes of the standardized residuals and/or modification indices (Joreskog in Bollen and Long, 1993).

Traditionally, the Cronbach alpha test was used to examine the reliability of the scales. Due to the fact that the Cronbach alpha has inherent weaknesses, such as the assumption of parallelity in which all factor loadings and error variances are constrained to be equal (Bollen, 1989), and the possibility of underestimating or overestimating the reliability of congeneric measures (Raykov, 1997, 1998), this study uses the composite reliability (see Fornell and Larcker, 1981) and variance extracted tests (Bollen, 1989; Anderson and Gerbing, 1988; Bagozzi, 1991). The composite reliability test assesses the internal consistency (Fornell and Larcker, 1981 and Joreskog and Sorbom, 1993), while the variance extracted test measures the amount of variance captured by a construct in relation to the variance due to random measurement error (Bollen, 1989). The CFA was performed by the maximum likelihood method.

The first stage of the analysis is to indicate to what extent the participants considered various export barriers to be a hindrance to their firms' export activities. Table 5.1 displays the first 22 internal barriers according to respondents' perceptions.

Table 5.1: Perceived Difficulty of Internal Export Barriers

Export barriers	Perceived difficulty					Mean	s.d.
	1	2	3	4	5		
	%	%	%	%	%		
Limited information to locate/analyse markets (Info1)	16.5	13.5	30.5	11.5	28.0	3.21	1.41
Problematic international market data (Info2)	17.0	13.5	24.5	17.5	27.5	3.25	1.43
Lack of knowledge to identify foreign business opportunities (Info3)	14.5	11.5	26.5	19.0	28.5	3.36	1.38
Lack of access to any potential overseas customers (Info4)	15.5	13.0	22.0	19.0	30.5	3.36	1.43
Domestic market takes all managerial time; no time to deal with exports (Func1)	59.5	17.5	12.5	4.0	6.5	1.81	1.20
Lack of trained personnel (Func2)	47.0	18.0	14.0	11.0	10.0	2.19	1.39
Lack of excess production capacity (Func3)	44.5	15.5	18.5	9.0	12.5	2.30	1.43
Lack of working capital (Func4)	20.5	14.0	17.0	14.5	34	3.28	1.55
Lack of resources to develop new products for foreign markets (Prod1)	34.0	14.5	23.0	14.0	14.5	2.61	1.44
Lack resources to adapt export product design/style (Prod2)	41.0	17.5	16.5	11.5	13.5	2.39	1.45
Lack of resources to meet export product quality standards/specs (Prod3)	36.5	16.0	17.5	13.0	17.0	2.58	1.51
Lack of resources to offer technical/after-sales service (Prod4)	37.0	17.0	16.0	13.0	17.0	2.56	1.51
Difficulty in matching competitors' price due to higher	23.0	8.0	28.5	16.5	24.0	3.11	1.46

unit costs and other additional costs (Price1)							
Inability to grant credit facilities to foreign customers due to fear of risk (Price2)	24.0	7.5	17.5	16.0	35.0	3.31	1.59
Complexity of foreign distribution channels (Place1)	47.5	8.0	17.0	9.0	18.5	2.43	1.58
Difficulty in accessing export distribution channels (Place2)	48.5	10.0	14.0	11.5	16.0	2.37	1.55
Difficulty in obtaining reliable foreign representation (Place3)	45.5	8.5	15.5	10.5	20.0	2.51	1.61
Difficulty in maintaining control over foreign middleman due to geographic and cultural distance (Place4)	49.5	6.0	11.5	15.5	17.5	2.46	1.62
Difficulty in supplying inventory abroad due to transportation delays, demand fluctuations, and unexpected events (Log1)	30.0	16.0	17.5	17.0	19.5	2.80	1.51
Unavailability of warehousing facilities abroad (Log2)	58.5	6.0	11.5	10.0	14.0	2.15	1.53
Excessive transportation/insurance cost for export (Log3)	57.5	6.5	13.5	11.5	11.0	2.12	1.47
Inability to adjust export promotional activities (Log4)	62.0	6.0	12.5	10.0	9.5	1.99	1.42

Notes: 1 = 'no effect at all'; 2 = 'make somewhat difficult'; 3 = 'make difficult'; 4 = 'make very difficult'; 5 = 'make extremely difficult'

Source: Derived from survey data.

From the research findings illustrated in Table 5.1, it is evident that manufacturing SMEs perceived Informational barriers (Info1, Info2, Info3, and Info4), Price barriers (Price1 and Price2) and one Functional barrier (Func4) as being of the 'make difficult' to cope type. The problems with information gathering and communication transmissions, as well as with working capital to support export activities, have been discussed widely by the literature. This stated, non-exporting firms consistently perceive these concerns as more problematic than exporting firms (see for example: Da Silva and Da Rocha, 2008; Katsikeas and Morgan, 1994; Suarez-Ortega, 2003). In order to formulate effective export strategies, including pricing strategies for the product, it is necessary for firms to elicit suitable market intelligence (Leonidou, 2000). It is also a must for a firm to have sufficient capital to finance research of overseas markets, as this can act as a push factor to initiate or continue to adapt to overseas market product standards and specifications (Da Silva and Da Rocha, 2001; Leonidou, 2004; Altintas et al., 2007).

A confirmatory factor analysis was carried out to determine whether all 37 of the internal and external barriers (see Table 5.2) studied could be grouped under a smaller number of underlying dimensions. The eigenvalues, composite reliability and variance extracted for each factor were calculated and are reported in Table 5.2 which represents the outline of one-factor congeneric models for each factor of the internal barriers.

From Table 5.2, two dimensions, Func4 (shortage of working capital to finance exports) and Price2 (inability to grant credit facilities to foreign customers due to fear of risk), have standardized loadings less than 0.4 and hence have been dropped from the analysis (Cunningham, 2007). All Chi-square statistics and p-values, except for the informational barriers where coefficients were found to be significant at the 0.05 level, were insignificant suggesting that the model and the data set were a good fit. Given that the standardized residuals of the internal barriers in Table 5.2, except for the dropped items of Func4 and Price2, were less than 2 standardized deviations from the correct model, this implies that the model is able to account for much of the shared variance between the particular item pairs, so the study retained them for the multi-factor analysis (Joreskog and Sorbom, 1984).

Table 5.2: Outline of One-Factor Congeneric Models of Internal Barrier Factors

Factor Barrier	Observed Variables	Chi-square (dof[1])	p-value	Factor(s) omitted or freely estimated	Eigen-values ≥ 1	Composite reliability (variance extracted[2])
Informational Barriers	Info1	14.623 (2)	0.001	None	1	0.909 (0.717)
	Info2					
	Info3					
	Info4					
Functional Barriers	Func1	1.347 (2)	0.510	Func4	1	0.761 (0.525)
	Func2					
	Func3					
	Func4					
Product and Price Barriers	Prod1	2.926 (6)	0.818	Price2	1	0.815 (0.534)
	Prod2					
	Prod3					
	Prod4					
	Price1					
	Price2					
Distribution Barriers	Place1	5.855(2)	0.054	None	1	0.971 (0.893)
	Place2					
	Place3					
	Place4					
Logistic Barriers	Log1	1.574 (2)	0.455	None	1	0.833 (0.508)
	Log2					
	Log3					
	Log4					

Notes: 1= number of distinct sample moments minusnumber of distinct parameters to be estimated, 2= As a general rule, reliabilities exceeding 0.50 and corresponding to an approximate factor loading of 0.70 are preferred, although values of reliabilities exceeding 0.30 are usually regarded as acceptable (Fornell and Larcker, 1981; Bollen, 1989)

Source: Derived from survey data.

Figure 5.1: Model Re-specification of Perceived Internal Barriers

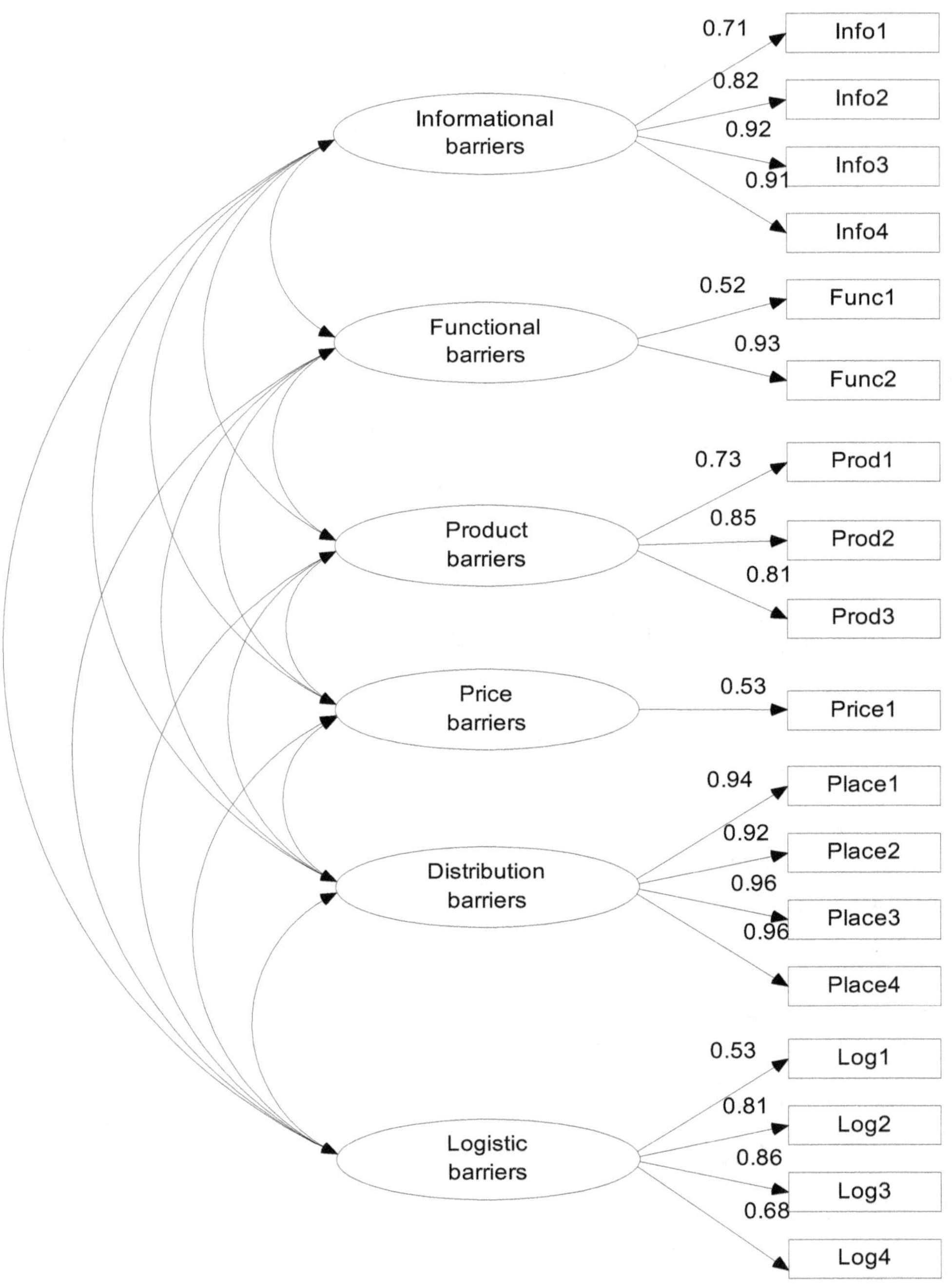

Source: Derived from survey data.

The model re-specification of internal barrier is presented in Figure 5.1. After extracting Prod4 and Func3, the model's p–value became insignificant. Hence the data fit the model well at the 5 per cent significance level, $\chi^2(122) = 144.763$, $p = 0.078$. Standardized loadings ranged from a low of 0.52 to a high of 0.96. Given that these coefficients are of reasonable magnitude that exceed at least 0.40 (see MacCallum et al., 1996; Hayduk, 1996; Hayduk and Glasser, 2000), all items are retained as they exhibit insignificant difference between the data and the model.

5.2.2 External Barriers

Table 5.3 presents the means and standard deviations of managerial responses on the 15 items of external export barriers. The Table 5.3 indicates that manufacturing SMEs perceive governmental barriers (Gov1 and Gov2), one task barrier (Task2), economic barriers (Econ1 and Econ2), and political-legal barriers (Poleg1 and Poleg2) as being of the 'make difficult' to cope type. Government rules and regulations have created problems for Indonesian SMEs for a long time (Wengel and Rodriguez, 2006). These impediments are often viewed unfavourably by Indonesian SMEs due to their high-cost consequences on SMEs' export ventures. The high mean value attached to Gov1 (government assistance and export promotion programmes) indicates the possibility of lack of efficacy and lack of accessibility to government services in Indonesia (SMECDA's website, 2010b). Keen competition in overseas markets and foreign politico-economic conditions were also problematic to most respondents. Although these barriers are subject to rapid change and are very difficult to predict and control, they should be approached effectively in order to reduce their impact on SMEs' export ventures.

Table 5.3: Perceived Difficulty of External Export Barriers

Export barriers	Perceived difficulty					Mean	s.d.
	1	2	3	4	5		
	%	%	%	%	%		
Unfamiliarity with exporting procedures/paperwork (Proc1)	47.0	10.5	17.5	10.0	15.0	2.36	1.51
Problematic communication with overseas customers due to poor communication infrastructure (Proc2)	49.5	14.5	12.5	12.0	11.5	2.22	1.45
Slow collection of payments from abroad (Proc3)	30.0	12.0	17.5	13.0	27.5	2.96	1.60
Lack of domestic government assistance/incentives (Gov1)	18.0	8.0	18.0	18.0	38.0	3.50	1.50
Unfavourable domestic rules and regulations (Gov2)	25.0	9.5	18.5	15.0	32.0	3.20	1.58
Inability to adjust to foreign customer habits/attitudes (Task 1)	35.0	19.5	21.5	13.5	10.5	2.45	1.36
Keen competition in overseas market (Task2)	14.0	11.5	20.5	15.0	39.0	3.54	1.45
Poor/deteriorating economic conditions in foreign markets (Econ1)	13.5	9.0	20.0	20.0	37.5	3.59	1.41
Foreign currency exchange risks (Econ2)	20.0	13.5	22.0	14.5	30.0	3.21	1.50
Political instability in foreign markets (Poleg1)	20.0	12.0	15.0	20.0	33.0	3.34	1.53
Strict foreign rules and regulations (Poleg2)	23.5	11.0	20.0	20.0	25.5	3.13	1.51
High tariff and non-tariff barriers (Poleg3)	32.0	11.0	17.5	17.5	22.0	2.87	1.56
Unfamiliar foreign business practices (Socul1)	32.5	19.5	18.5	9.5	20.0	2.65	1.51

Different socio-cultural traits (Socul2)	43.5	19.5	15.0	12.0	10.0	2.26	1.38
Verbal/non-verbal language differences (Socul3)	39.0	18.5	21.0	11.0	10.5	2.36	1.37

Notes: 1 = 'no effect at all'; 2 = 'make somewhat difficult'; 3 = 'make difficult'; 4 = 'make very difficult'; 5 = 'make extremely difficult'
Source: Derived from survey data.

Table 5.4 summarizes a number of one-factor congeneric models on the 15 items of the external barriers, and demonstrates that no item has been extracted from the factors, as p-values are insignificant at the 5 per cent significance level, suggesting that the data is an adequate fit to each model.

Following the earlier procedure adopted for internal barriers, a multi-factor measurement model analysis is performed on the external barriers and is depicted in Appendix 5.2. Its associated p-value was significant, implying the unfitness of the data to the model at the 5 per cent significance level, $\chi^2(75) = 165.019$, $p = 0.000$. A four-factor solution to the model is suggested by the eigenvalues. Two items, Task2 (Keen competition in overseas market) and Poleg1 (political instability in foreign markets), were indicating large standardized residuals; standardized residual covariance that exceeds a magnitude of 2 standard deviations suggests the model is not accounting for associations in the data. Thus, in order to improve the model fit, these two items are extracted from each of their constructs.

Table 5.4: Outline of One-Factor Congeneric Models of External Barrier Factors

Factor Barrier	Observed Variables	Chi-square (dof[1])	p-value	Factor(s) omitted or freely estimated	Eigen-values ≥ 1	Composite reliability (variance extracted[2])
Procedural/ Government Barriers	Proc1	1.946 (4)	0.746	None	2	0.790 (0.444)[2]
	Proc2					
	Proc3					
	Gov1					
	Gov2					
Task/ Economic Barriers	Task1	0.110 (1)	0.740	None	1	0.732 (0.410)
	Task2					
	Econ1					
	Econ2					
Political-legal/Socio-cultural Barriers	Poleg1	3.250 (8)	0.918	None	2	0.897 (0.599)
	Poleg2					
	Poleg3					
	Socul1					
	Socul2					
	Socul3					

Notes: 1= number of distinct sample moments – number of distinct parameters to be estimated, 2= As a general rule, reliabilities exceeding 0.50 and corresponding to an approximate factor loading of 0.70 are preferred, although values of reliabilities exceeding 0.30 are usually regarded as acceptable (Fornell and Larcker, 1981; Bollen, 1989)
Source: Derived from survey data.

The extraction of items Task2 and Poleg1 from the model yields an insignificant p-value (see Figure 5.2). The model, therefore, has achieved a model fit at the 5 per cent significance level, $\chi^2(52) = 61.384$, $p = 0.175$. Standardized loadings ranged from a low of 0.48 to a high of 0.99 and the eigenvalues indicate a three-factor solution to the model.

Figure 5.2: Model Re-specification of Perceived External Barriers

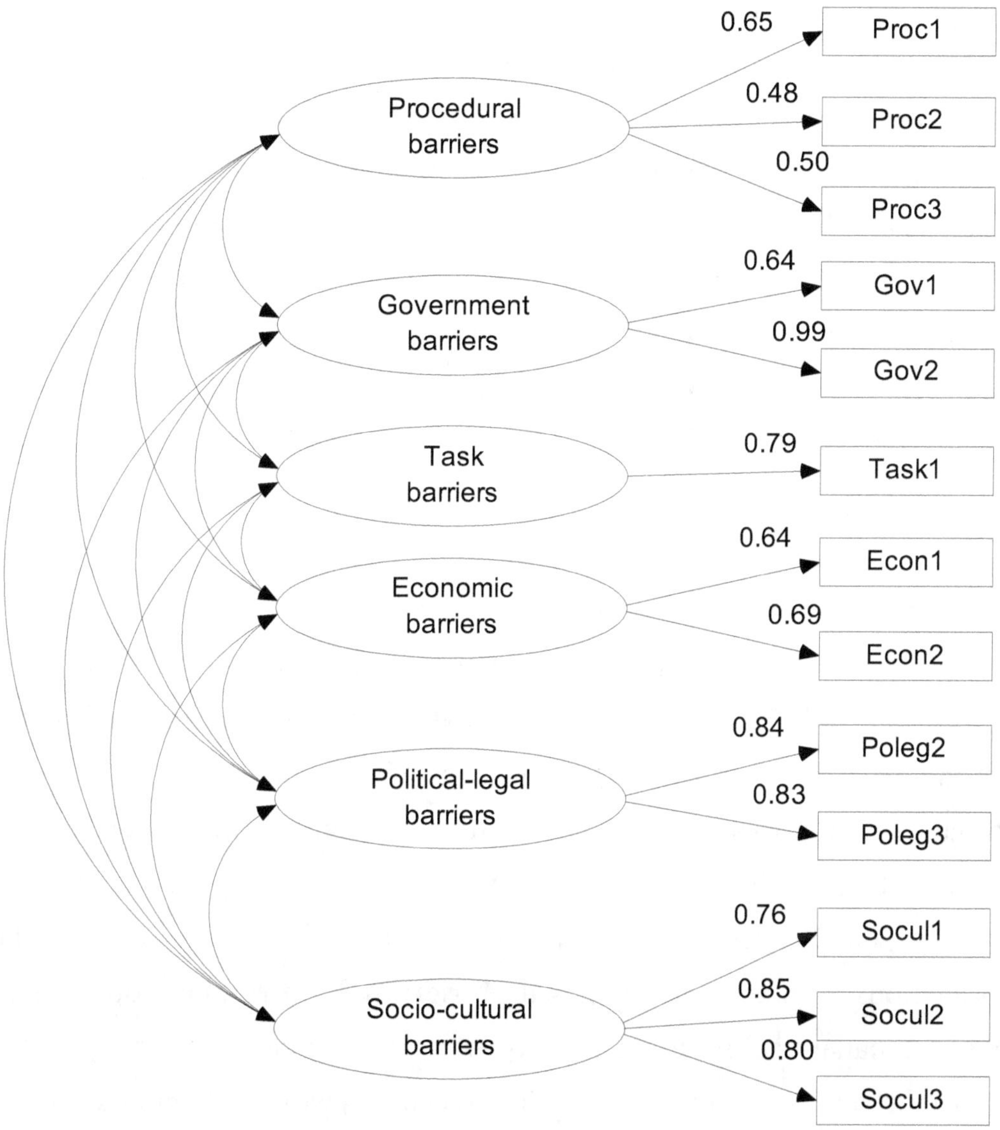

Procedural barriers
0.65 Proc1
0.48 Proc2
0.50 Proc3
Government barriers
0.64 Gov1
0.99 Gov2
Task barriers
0.79 Task1
Economic barriers
0.64 Econ1
0.69 Econ2
Political-legal barriers
0.84 Poleg2
0.83 Poleg3
Socio-cultural barriers
0.76 Socul1
0.85 Socul2
0.80 Socul3

Source: Derived from survey data.

5.2.3 Integrating Internal and External Barriers

Internationalisation process literature is maintained to have been relying on internal factors as the key driving forces of that process (Suarez-Ortega and Alamo-

Vera, 2005). Previous literature was also criticized as having failed to examine the full set of managerial and organisational factors simultaneously (Leonidou, 1998a; Zou and Stan, 1998). Thus, as this study adopts a multidimensional approach, it is necessary to combine internal and external factors of perceived export barriers under one structural model and measure for their relationships. This will render the proposed model a proper instrument for measuring the export activities of Indonesian SMEs. Therefore, the remaining items of internal and external barriers, not eliminated in the previous analysis, were integrated and examined simultaneously in one model. The chi-square statistic for the multi-factor model of perceived barriers to exporting, however, suggested an unfitness of the data to the model at the 5 per cent significance level, $\chi^2(372) = 507.994$, $p = .000$ (see Appendix 5.3).

From standardized residual covariance it is noted that misfits consistently occurred with Log1 (difficulty in supplying inventory abroad due to transportation delays, demand fluctuations, and unexpected events), Log2 (unavailability of warehousing facilities abroad), and Proc3 (Slow collection of payments from abroad) items in their associations with other items in the model. Furthermore, cross-loading of items was evident with Socul1 (unfamiliar foreign business practices) and Place2 (difficulty in accessing export distribution channels) in their associations with the Informational barrier; and with Func1 (domestic market takes all managerial time to deal with export) and Place2 (difficulty in accessing export distribution channels) in their associations with the Socio-cultural barriers (items that load with more than one factor may cause problems when interpreting the factor solution: Byrne, 2009) In addition, a very low item reliability (indicated by low squared multiple correlations) was attached to Proc2 (problematic communication with overseas customers due to poor communication infrastructure item) item. The extraction on these items was, therefore, necessary in order to improve the model fit.

A model re-specification of perceived internal and external export barriers is presented in Figure 5.3. After dropping problematic items of Log1, Log2, Proc2, Proc3, Socul1, Place2, and Func1 from each of its constructs, the p-value became insignificant suggesting the model finally fits to the data at the 5 per cent significance level, $\chi^2(194) = 195.272$, $p = 0.461$. Standardized residuals were all less than 2 suggesting that the model is now able to account for much of the covariation that exists among items. Squared multiple correlation, as an indicator of item reliability, ranged from as low as 0.30 to as high as 0.99. Item reliabilities exceeding 0.30 are usually deemed acceptable (Cunningham, 2007). In addition to item reliability, two other model-based estimates of reliability, by Fornell and Larcker (1981) and Bollen (1989) are reported for cross validation.

Based on Table 5.5, only the Price1 (difficulty in matching competitors' prices due to higher unit costs and other additional costs) item showed a value exactly equal to 0.30. The item, however, was kept due to the obtained model fit. All other coefficients were deemed acceptable as they exceeded 0.30 (Cunningham, 2007).

All estimates in the standardized regression weights met the requirements to satisfy model fit by having values more than 0.40. In addition to the chi-square test, a number of other measures of model fit are displayed in Table 5.6 to determine whether the data generally supports the hypothesized model. From the model fit summary, it is noted that the data generally corresponds to the model well with a slightly less than required value for AGFI.

Figure 5.3: Model Re-specification of Perceived Internal and External Barriers

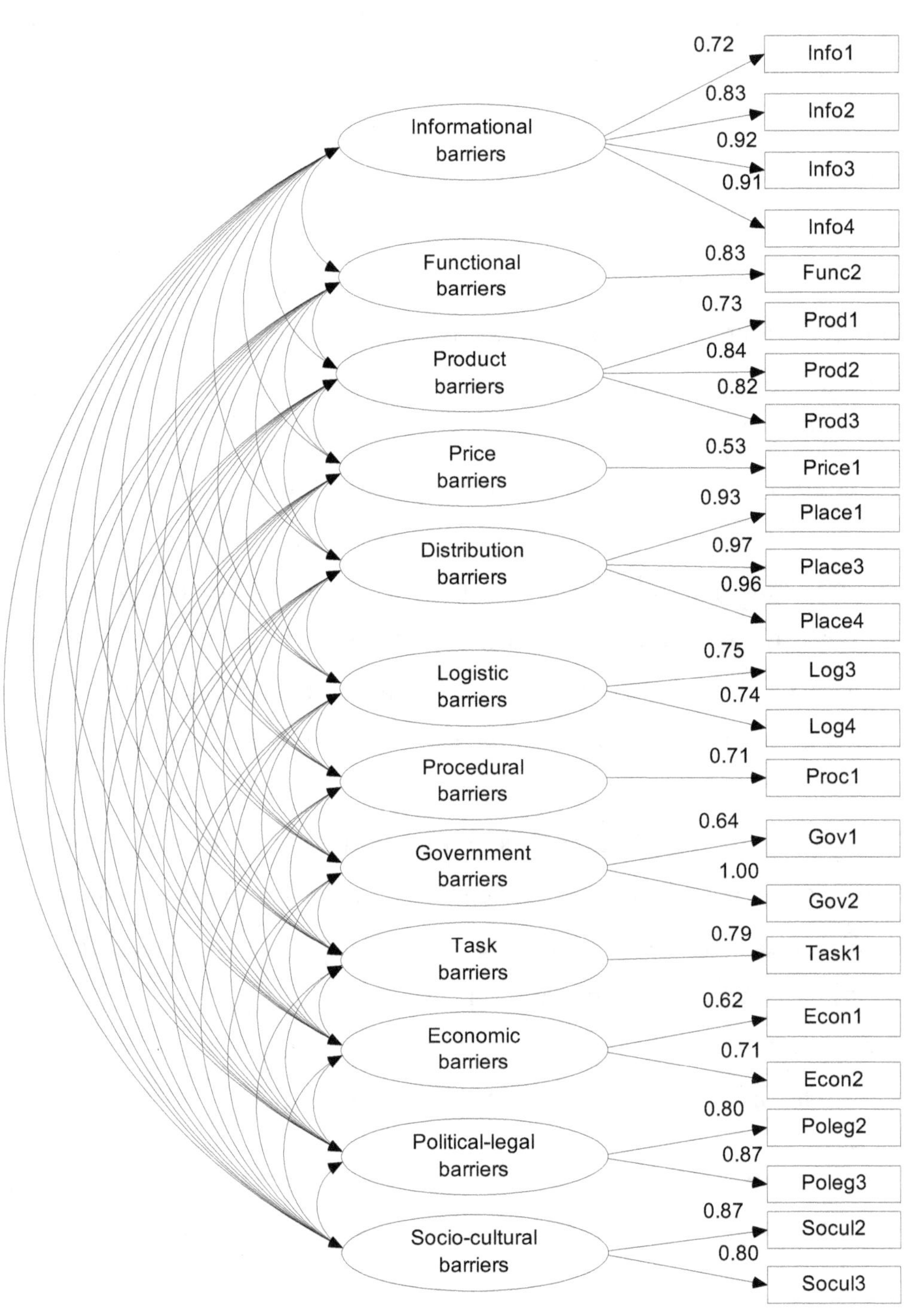

Source: Derived from survey data.

Table 5.5: Item reliability, Composite Reliability, and Variance Extracted of Perceived Export Barriers

Factor	Squared Multiple Correlation	Composite reliability	Variance extracted
Info1	0.515	0.909	0.716
Info2	0.681		
Info3	0.845		
Info4	0.825		
Func2	0.687	0.687	0.687
Prod1	0.535	0.848	0.637
Prod2	0.707		
Prod3	0.670		
Price1	0.300	0.300	0.300
Place1	0.870	0.967	0.908
Place3	0.934		
Place4	0.920		
Log3	0.560	0.715	0.557
Log4	0.554		
Proc1	0.511	0.511	0.511
Gov1	0.406	0.818	0.702
Gov2	0.990		
Task1	0.622	0.622	0.622
Econ1	0.387	0.614	0.444
Econ2	0.502		
Poleg2	0.635	0.821	0.697
Poleg3	0.759		
Socul2	0.756	0.822	0.698
Socul3	0.638		

Source: Derived from survey data.

Table 5.6: Further Indices of Model Fit of Impact of Perceived Export Barriers to Exporting

Measurement model	Overall model fit							
	Model fit					Model comparison		
Model fit indices	CMIN/DF[1]	SRMR[2]	RMSEA[3]	GFI[4]	AGFI[4]	NFI[5]	TLI[6]	CFI[7]
Level of acceptable model fit	<2	<.05	<0.08	>0.90	>0.90	>0.90	>0.90	>0.90
Perceived Barrier to Exporting	1.007	.0323	.006	.925	.885	.934	.999	1.000

Notes:
1. CMIN/DF is the minimum discrepancy divided by its degrees of freedom. Suggested ratios in the range of 2 to 1 or 3 to 1 (Wheaton et al., 1977; Carmines and McIver, 1981; Marsh and Hocevar, 1985);
2. SRMR is the average difference between corresponding elements of the sample and the model-implied correlations matrices. A model is fit when SRMR is less than 0.05 (Hu and Bentler, 1999);
3. RMSEA is a fit index that uses the confidence interval to indicate the precision of the estimate of fit. RMSEA value should be about 0.05 or less (Browne and Cudeck in Bollen and Long, 1993)
4. GFI/AGFI give an indication of the relative amount of the covariances among the latent variables that are accounted for by the model and it should be exceeding 0.95 (Mathieu et al., 1992);
5. NFI calculates the minimum discrepancy of the model and the value should be less than 0.90 (Bentler and Bonett, 1980);
6. TLI estimates the relative improvement per degree of freedom of the target model over an independence model and the value should be exceeding 0.95 (Hu and Bentler, 1998);
7. CFI measures the improvement of a target model and an independence model. Its value should be greater than 0.95 (Hu and Bentler, 1999).

Source: Derived from survey data.

The findings show a difference between the data-set's factor structure and the original factor structure as suggested by the literature. From 37 barriers presented in the literature, 13 were extracted due to:

1. Considerable difference between the sample variance and the model-implied variance. With a correct model, most standardized difference should be less than two in absolute value for a factor to be able to account for much of the covariation that exists between incompatible items (Joreskog and Sorbom, 1984);
2. Low loading items. Standardized loading estimates should be at least .4 in magnitude to be highly associated with the latent construct (MacCallum et al., 1992; Hayduk, 1996; Hayduk and Glasser, 2000);
3. Cross loading items. Items that have strong relationships with more than one factor may cause problem when interpreting the factor solution (Byrne, 2009).

The remaining 24 items suggest actual factors hindering Indonesian small and medium sized firms from involvement in export operations as they have a relatively good fit to the data. Although there is a continuing debate surrounding model-generating or staged approaches to data analysis in structural equation modelling, changes to this model have been made in sequence and only if such changes are theoretically justifiable.

5.3 Differences in Perceptions between Exporters and Non-exporters

Having identified the factor structure of perceived export barriers of Indonesian manufacturing SMEs, this section adopts a bivariate approach to test for the presence of significant difference on each item or perceived export barrier based on firms' level of export development. The tests will be carried out to address the second research objective of investigating the perception of manufacturing SMEs on export barriers based on their level of export development. Research hypotheses which have been developed to achieve this research objective are:

H1: Non-exporters are perceived to rate export barriers higher than do exporters.

H2: There are significant differences between exporting and non-exporting SMEs in relation to the factors they perceive as important barriers to exporting.

Table 5.7 demonstrates that in nearly all the model items significant differences do exist between non-exporting and exporting manufacturers. The exceptions are Prod1 (lack of expertise, resources, and technology to develop new products for foreign markets); Prod2 (lack of expertise, resources and technology to meet export product design/style); Prod3 (lack of expertise, resources, and technology to meet export product quality standard/specifications); Price1 (difficulty in matching competitors' price due to higher unit costs and other additional costs); Gov1 (lack of domestic government assistance/incentives); Task1 (inability to adjust with foreign customer habits/attitudes); Econ1 (poor/deteriorating economic conditions in foreign markets); and Econ2 (foreign currency exchange risks). Non-exporting firms, in particular, strongly perceive more difficulty in relation to all informational, distributional, logistic, procedural, politico-legal, and socio-cultural dimensions as opposed to exporting firms. These results provide full support to the first hypotheses (H1) that non-exporters perceive significantly higher export barriers than do exporters.

Table 5.7 identifies four items where the mean perception of difficulty of exporters exceeds that of non-exporters, namely Prod1 (lack of expertise, resources, and technology to develop new products for foreign markets), Prod3 (lack of expertise, resources, and technology to meet export product quality standard/specifications), Price1 (difficulty in matching competitors' price due to higher unit costs and other additional costs) and Econ1 (poor/deteriorating economic conditions in foreign markets). The mean differences between exporters and non-exporters on these dimensions, however, were not significant. Hence, what had been hypothesized in H2 is only partially supported as non-exporters do rate a set of factors as being more of a barrier than do exporters and the differences are significant. However, the set of factors that exporters rate as being more of a barrier than non-exporters, do not show significant differences.

Table 5.7: Perceived Export Barriers of the Export Development Process

Export barriers	Mean values		Statistic	Differences by two independent groups
	Non-exporting firms (n =88)	Exporting firms (n=109)		
Info1	3.48	3.00	t = 2.369**	NE > E
Info2	3.51	3.04	t = 2.300**	NE > E
Info3	3.73	3.06	t = 3.470***	NE > E
Info4	3.68	3.11	t = 2.875***	NE > E
Func2	2.40	2.03	t = 1.890*	NE > E
Prod1	2.50	2.69	t = 0.912	
Prod2	2.43	2.36	t = 0.360	
Prod3	2.53	2.62	t = 0.382	
Price1	2.93	3.24	t = 1.494	
Place1	2.94	2.03	t = 4.241****	NE > E
Place3	2.95	2.16	t =3.568****	NE > E
Place4	2.99	2.04	t = 4.320****	NE > E
Log3	2.45	1.86	t = 2.873***	NE > E
Log4	2.24	1.79	t = 2.176**	NE > E
Proc1	2.83	1.98	t = 4.092****	NE > E
Gov1	3.60	3.42	t = 0.852	

Gov2	3.44	3.00	t = 1.982**	NE > E
Task1	2.50	2.41	t = 0.459	
Econ1	3.45	3.70	t = 1.215	
Econ2	3.32	3.13	t = 0.900	
Poleg2	3.50	2.84	t = 3.199***	NE > E
Poleg3	3.35	2.48	t = 4.061****	NE > E
Socul2	2.56	2.02	t = 2.784***	NE > E
Socul3	2.72	2.07	t = 3.396***	NE > E

Notes: $^{*}p < 0.10$; $^{**}p < 0.05$; $^{***}p < 0.01$; $^{****}p < 0.001$.
NE = Non-exporters; E = Exporters.
Source: Derived from survey data.

In summary, Table 5.7 finds that non-exporting firms perceive significantly higher difficulty with the internal barriers of informational, functional, distributional and logistic items than those of exporting firms. These results are consistent with the study conducted by SMEs Resource Assessment Division of Ministry of Cooperation and SMEs in 2004 (SMECDA's website, 2010b). The study's findings maintained that most SMEs are still experiencing difficulties in penetrating export markets and, particularly for Indonesian SMEs, third party facilitation to improve their accessibility to export markets is required. Most SMEs obtained access to export markets through participation in trade shows/exhibitions and information from their business partners. Only a small number of SMEs got their information independently from mass media, internet, or other sources (SMECDA's website, 2010b). The reliance on a limited number of information sources is probably due to SMEs unfamiliarity with national and international sources of information, and even when they are aware of these, accessing them might prove difficult due to limited knowledge, language proficiency, and/or resources or lack of a clear idea as to the specific information required for foreign market entry (Leonidou, 2004). These impediments have also led some Indonesian SMEs to respond to unsolicited orders from foreign customers on a trial and error basis in an attempt to gain opportunities from overseas markets.

Functional barriers specified in the model suggest internal organisation functional inefficiencies (Altintas et al., 2007). Particularly, the results imply that most non-exporting SMEs do not have skilled and knowledgeable personnel to deal with the particular work demanded by an export operation (Gomez-Mejia, 1988). Human resource problems in the Indonesian context arise from insufficient specialized knowledge and expertise to deal with such export business tasks as documentation handling, logistical arrangements, and communicating the specifications of the products with foreign customers. The results from SMECDA's study (SMECDA's website, 2010b) showed that the majority of Indonesian SMEs are experiencing difficulty in generating product specifications in accordance with the development of foreign consumers' tastes and standards. This, to a large extent, can be attributed to inadequate training and development of company personnel in export business issues.

Distribution and logistic barriers represent parts of the problematic marketing elements for non-exporting firms in this study. Although some studies have found distribution and logistic barriers to be equally an impediment for exporting firms (Kedia & Chhokar, 1986; Leonidou, 2004), the results of this study identify the dimensions as more problematic for non-exporting firms than their exporting counterparts. Since foreign distribution systems vary considerably in their characteristics such as purchasing power or quality of the services offered in the channels, exporting firms, with their assumed experiences, may be able to cope better with these variations than their non-exporting counterparts who perceive them as being significantly more problematic.

Significant differences attached to procedural problem was also found between exporting and non-exporting firms. Despite the extrinsic nature of procedural barriers that largely depend on the ability to act expediently on rules and regulations, the results in Table 5.5 reveal that non-exporting firms witnessed greater difficulty than exporting firms in areas of bureaucratic procedures and export documentation requirements (e.g. export licences, import certificates, and letters of credit). As stated in the literature, there are two main reasons why these problems often stack up against non-exporting or less experienced exporting firms. Lack of knowledge on procedures to handle administrative demands (Kedia and Chhokar, 1986; Moini, 1997; Terpstra and Sarathy, 2000), as well as time pressure to oversee these procedural complexities, were maintained to be the main reasons that hinder non-exporting firms to pursue their exporting endeavour (Ogram, 1982). In the Indonesian context, these problems are aggravated by associated red tape which then encourages a negative attitude towards handling exports (Moini, 1997). Although the Indonesian government has introduced a number of measures to reduce the bureaucracy of exporting procedures, they still need to monitor their implementation at the operational level and provide some assistance through consultative services or agencies particularly for SMEs.

Consistent with the view that the perception of problems is coloured by the incremental nature of decision making and learning about the foreign market and its operations, this study has found significant differences between non-exporting and exporting firms in relation to some procedural, governmental, political-legal, and socio-cultural external barriers. Different socio-cultural traits are among the socio-cultural issues which constitute serious difficulties, particularly for non-exporting firms. According to Cateora and Graham (2001), the significance of this dimension might greatly affect consumer behaviour, targeting approaches, and marketing programmes. Some ways that are suggested to accommodate this issue include the appointment of managers with an international outlook and foreign language proficiency which might be very helpful in export information gathering and market evaluation (Terpstra and Sarathy, 2000).

Domestic government rules and regulations have been a problem for both non-exporting and exporting firms and are often considered to be an obstacle for their export development. The role of the home government may also become an impediment through a number of restrictions imposed on indigenous SMEs exporters. In the case of Indonesia, the inconsistent regulatory framework and lack of dissemination of the new government rules and regulations are maintained to be major problems to most respondents. Despite possible losses, SMEs are expected to comply with these rules and regulations in order to maintain support from government agencies for their export endeavours (Leonidou, 2004). A higher mean in the politico-legal aspects suggests that non-exporters perceive that foreign governments might, in addition, impose unfavourable controls such as entry restrictions, price controls, or special tax rates on companies that export goods into their markets. These unfavourable issues turn export endeavour into a tiresome and expensive process which discourages small firms to pursue their export tasks. Import tariffs are also indicated as a serious obstacle, particularly for non-exporting SMEs, in their consideration of intention to export in the near future. Serious difficulties caused by numerous tariff barriers imposed by some countries have urged the World Trade Organisation (WTO) to gradually reduce the impact of tariff and non-tariff barriers by liberalizing international trade in a number of countries.

5.4 Chapter Summary

The findings in this chapter show differences between the observed counts' factor structure and the overall structure suggested by the literature. From 37 barriers presented in the literature, 13 items are eliminated mostly due to considerable standardized residual covariance; cross loadings to other factors; low item reliability, and multicolilnearity issues. The original models of export benefits and distinctive capabilities have also been re-specified due mainly to standardized residual covariance and item reliability issues.

The remaining 24 items were used as a basis to test two hypotheses, H1 and H2. The results from an independent sample t-test indicated full support for H1 (non-exporters perceive significantly higher export barriers than do exporters) and a partial support for H2 (there are significant differences between exporter and non-exporter groups in relation to the factors they perceive as important barriers to exporting). Non-exporting firms, in particular, significantly perceived more difficulty in relation to all informational, distributional, logistical, procedural, political-legal, and socio-cultural dimensions as compared to exporting firms. Table 5.5, however, indicates that exporters have higher, but not significant at 5 per cent significance level, means in the four dimensions of Prod1, Prod3, Price1 and Econ1. Hence, what has been hypothesized in H2 is partially supported as non-exporters do rate a set of factors as being more of a barrier than do exporters and the differences are significant. However, the set of factors that exporters rate as being more of a barrier than non-exporters, do not show significant differences.

Following factor analysis of latent constructs, an examination of dependence relationships among dependent and independent variables developed in the conceptual model will be carried out in subsequent Chapter 6. AMOS programme will be used to simultaneously estimate the conceptual model proposed in chapter 4.

CHAPTER SIX
EMPIRICAL ANALYSIS OF THE CAUSAL RELATIONSHIPS

6.1 Introduction

An attempt has been made in Chapter 5 to test the validity of the factor structure of managerial perceptions of export barriers. The findings have also highlighted the differences between the observed factor structure and the overall structure suggested by the literature. Model changes, as a result, have been conducted in order to achieve a model fit for export barriers. Chapter 5, in addition, has established that non-exporting firms view significant more difficulty regarding informational, functional, distributional, logistical, procedural, governmental, politico-legal, and socio-cultural dimensions as compared to exporting firms.

The study also aims to address interaction effects, the question of causality, and an assessment of external determinants excluded from previous studies (Madsen, 1987), this chapter will combine and measure all perceived export barriers concurrently in path analysis and measure for their regression weights on the export development, export propensity, and export intensity variables. The weight of relationships is expected to change according to the extent to which the inclusion of other variables contributes adversely to the existing individual results.

The present chapter reflects the need to extend the bivariate analyses conducted in Chapters 5. In this second stage of analysis, the causal relationships between criterion and predictor variables, developed in the conceptual framework, is performed in an attempt to test H3 that an export barrier is perceived to have a negative effect on the level of export development, thus having a negative effect on export propensity and intensity. The structural model, with predictor variables of managerial perception of export barriers will be analysed to evaluate their relationships with export development, export propensity, and export intensity. A conventional path analysis was used to examine this relationship. Path analysis has the ability to incorporate latent and measured constructs into the analysis (Cunningham, 2007; Hair et al., 1998). Path analysis has been used to study consumer behaviour, psychology, and management. Hair et al. (1998) maintained that path analysis provides a simple way of dealing simultaneously with multiple relationships and is capable of assessing these relationships.

The organisation of the chapter is as follows: Section 6.2 examines the magnitude of perceptions of export barriers affecting export development. Section 6.3 presents an analysis on perceptions of export barriers affecting export propensity. Section 6.4 investigates the magnitude of perceived export barriers influencing export intensity. Section 6.5 summarizes the key findings of the chapter.

6.2 Managerial Perceptions of Export Barriers and Export Development

Path analysis is an approach that extends regression analysis by providing a way of testing the adequacy of a model through examination of the differences or residuals between the sample and model implied correlations (Asher, 1983). A regression is done for each variable in the model as a dependent or criterion on others which the model indicates as causes or predictors. The regression weights predicted by the model are then compared with the observed correlation matrix for the variables, and a goodness-of-fit statistic is calculated (Cunningham, 2007). Path analysis, in addition, requires the usual assumptions of regression.

Appendix 6.1 displays the initial saturated model for all possible paths and correlations of organisational and managerial factors affecting the level of export development. The chi-square statistic was once again used to judge the fit of the model to the data. If the chi-square test is not significant, then the data is not significantly different from the hypothesized model.

The initial model was not a good fit to the data at 5 per cent significance level as $\chi^2(503) = 726.633$, $\rho = 0.000$. The results indicate a consistent misspecification between export development and export intensity as well as between export development and export propensity. The model is re-specified by including the direct path from export development to export intensity and from export development to export propensity. The paths imply that export development functions as a proxy that can help explain the level of export intensity and export propensity. All paths that have standardized residual covariance larger than 2 in absolute value were extracted to improve the model fitness.

All managerial perceptions about export barriers were retained as they indicated a good fit to the data. Other independent variables were extracted due to large standardized residuals and low item reliabilities. In general, large standardized residuals overall are indicative of a poorly fitting model. As maintained by Cunningham (2007), examining the standardized residuals is the most reliable method of identifying the source of model misspecification. When the structural and measurement models are estimated, the standardised regression weight or standardised loading coefficients provide an estimate of the reliabilities of the indicators and the overall constructs. The model in this study consisted of multiple paths into export development, export propensity, and export intensity, being the three endogenous or criterion variables.

After extracting the paths with large standardized residuals and low reliabilities as well as adding direct paths from export development to export intensity and export propensity, the model fits the data well, $\chi^2(427) = 463.053$, $\rho = 0.111$. The goodness of fit indices for the adjusted model are presented in Table 6.1. The interpretation of these indices is informed by SME literature (see for example: Schumacker and Lomax, 1996; Hu and Bentler, 1998; Hutchinson and Olmos, 1998).

Table 6.1: Model Fit Indices of Factors Affecting Export Development

Measurement model	Overall model fit							
	Model fit					Model comparison		
Model fit indices	CMIN/DF[1]	SRMR[2]	RMSEA[3]	GFI[4]	AGFI[4]	NFI[5]	TLI[6]	CFI[7]
Level of acceptable model fit	<2	<.05	<0.08	>0.90	>0.90	>0.90	>0.90	>0.90
Factors Affecting Export Development	1.084	0.0314	0.021	0.906	0.810	0.895	0.981	0.990

Notes:
1. CMIN/DF is the minimum discrepancy divided by its degrees of freedom. Suggested ratios in the range of 2 to 1 or 3 to 1 (Wheaton et al., 1977; Carmines and McIver, 1981; Marsh and Hocevar, 1985);
2. SRMR is the average difference between corresponding elements of the sample and the model-implied correlations matrices. A model is fit when SRMR is less than 0.05 (Hu and Bentler, 1999);
3. RMSEA is a fit index that uses the confidence interval to indicate the precision of the estimate of fit. RMSEA value should be about 0.05 or less (Browne and Cudeck in Bollen and Long, 1993)
4. GFI/AGFI give an indication of the relative amount of the covariances among the latent variables that are accounted for by the model and it should be exceeding 0.95 (Mathieu et al., 1992);
5. NFI calculates the minimum discrepancy of the model and the value should be less than 0.90 (Bentler and Bonett, 1980);
6. TLI estimates the relative improvement per degree of freedom of the target model over an independence model and the value should be exceeding 0.95 (Hu and Bentler, 1998);
7. CFI measures the improvement of a target model and an independence model. Its value should be greater than 0.95 (Hu and Bentler, 1999).

Source: Derived from survey data.

All indices, in general, indicate that the model provides an adequate fit to data. Of the seven model-fit measures, AGFI and NFI were slightly below the required level of 0.90 but they still suggest a reasonable model fit (Hu and Bentler, 1998). Once the overall model fit was confirmed, focus moved to the testing of hypotheses. Maximum likelihood estimation is adopted. This estimate is obtained by means of an iterative procedure that minimizes a definite fitting function by successively improving the parameter estimates starting with the initial estimates (Joreskog and Sorbom, 1982).

The hypotheses were tested by determining the statistical significance of the path coefficients. To evaluate the estimated causal relations, the actual size of each parameter was assessed in terms of the standardized β coefficients and ρ-values. In order to ease the analysis, the regression weights for perceptions of export barriers in predicting each of export development, export propensity, and export intensity are presented in separate figures and tables. The following Table 6.2 present the regression weights for managerial perceptions of export barriers in predicting export development. While the regression weights for managerial and organisational factors in predicting export propensity can be found in Appendices 6.2 and for export intensity in Appendices 6.3. In the discussion that follows the results by export development, export intensity and export propensity will be covered contiguously.

The results establish that the relationships between the three dependent variables and each of perceived export barriers is weakly linear. The correlation coefficients for all export barrier items indicate weak correlations with export development and its proxy measures. The coefficients range from as low as 0.006 to as high as 0.430.

A number of items are found to be significantly different from zero at the 0.05 significance level in predicting the level of export development. Info3 (lack of knowledge to identify foreign business opportunities); Prod1 (lack of expertise, resources, and technology to develop new products for foreign markets); Place4 (difficulty in maintaining control over foreign middleman due to geographic and cultural distance); and Socul3 (verbal/non-verbal language differences), in particular, have negative relationships with export development. The results imply that the lesser the difficulty perceived in each of these barriers, the more developed SMEs are in their export operations.

Other items that are found significant in predicting proxy measures of export propensity are Place1 (complexity of foreign distribution channels); Log4 (inability to adjust export promotional activities); and Socul2 (different socio-cultural traits). The negative relationship between each of these items and export propensity suggests that as perceived difficulty in Place1, Log4, and Socul3 reduces, the more the likelihood of SMEs to export in the near future. Func2 (inadequate/untrained personnel to deal with exports); Proc1 (unfamiliarity with exporting procedures/paperwork); and Poleg3 (high tariff and non-tariff barriers), in addition, are found significant at the 0.05 significance level in predicting the proxy measure of export intensity. The negative relationship between each of these items and export intensity means that the lesser the difficulty perceived by SMEs in Func2, Proc1, and Poleg3 areas, the higher SMEs' export-to-total sales ratio. Based on these accounts, H7 (export barriers are perceived to have negative effects on the level of export involvement and on export propensity and intensity) is partially accepted as, although barrier items have negative associations with the level of export development and its proxies, only a few items show significant weights in affecting these criterion variables.

Table 6.2: Managerial and Organisational Determinants of Export Development

	r^b	Unstandardized Coefficients		Standardized Coefficients	t	Sig.
		B	S.E.[c]	βeta		
Export devt[a] ‹— Informational1	-0.167	-0.020	0.044	-0.029	-0.458	NS[d]
Export devt ‹— Informational2	-0.158	0.082	0.052	0.119	1.572	NS
Export devt ‹— Informational3	-0.290	-0.132	0.067	-0.185	-1.973	**
Export devt ‹— Informational4	-0.250	0.035	0.063	0.051	0.559	NS
Export devt ‹— Functional2	-0.261	-0.026	0.042	-0.036	-0.618	NS
Export devt ‹— Product1	0.006	0.133	0.042	0.194	3.122	***
Export devt ‹— Product2	-0.135	0.044	0.048	0.066	0.932	NS
Export devt ‹— Product3	-0.080	-0.640	0.045	-0.097	-1.413	NS
Export devt ‹— Price barrier1	0.064	0.045	0.037	0.066	1.201	NS
Export devt ‹— Distributional1	-0.404	-0.037	0.072	-0.06	-0.523	NS
Export devt ‹— Distributional3	-0.390	0.126	0.084	0.206	1.500	NS
Export devt ‹— Distributional4	-0.430	-0.199	0.081	-0.327	-2.460	**
Export devt ‹— Logistic3	-0.311	0.010	0.042	0.015	0.234	NS
Export devt ‹— Logistic4	-0.333	-0.035	0.045	-0.05	-0.777	NS
Export devt ‹— Procedural1	-0.378	-0.069	0.042	-0.107	0.726	NS
Export devt ‹— Governmental2	-0.150	-0.005	0.034	-0.008	-0.139	NS
Export devt ‹— Task barrier1	-0.175	0.033	0.046	0.046	0.726	NS
Export devt ‹— Economic1	0.009	0.051	0.037	0.073	1.367	NS
Export devt ‹— Economic2	-0.01	-0.033	0.038	-0.05	-0.876	NS
Export devt ‹— Political-legal2	0.253	-0.030	0.043	-0.046	-0.695	NS
Export devt ‹— Political-legal3	-0.308	-0.049	0.044	-0.078	-1.117	NS
Export devt ‹— Socio-cultural2	-0.322	-0.010	0.052	-0.014	-0.186	NS
Export devt ‹— Socio-cultural3	-0.353	-0.113	0.049	-0.157	-2.321	**

Notes: a) Export development; b) r = correlation coefficient; c) S.E. = Standard error; d) NS = Not significant; * $\rho < 0.10$; ** $\rho < 0.05$; *** $\rho < 0.01$; **** $\rho < 0.001$
Source: Derived from survey data.

6.3 Chapter Summary

To summarize, investigations using path analysis have developed a full model of multiple regressions which examined the relationships between dependent or criterion variables, and a number of independent or predictor variables. Criterion variables that were tested individually in previous chapters using crosstab, chi-square, and the standard t-test, were regressed simultaneously onto all criterion or endogenous variables in one structural model.

The first saturated model for all possible paths and correlations revealed large differences or residuals between the sample and model implied correlations. The significant χ^2 statistic was used to justify the model unfitness. Additional paths from export development to export intensity and from export development to export propensity and removal of paths with a standardized residual covariance (larger than 2 in absolute value) improved the model fitness.

The adjusted first model indicated that the 28 managerial perceptions about export barriers should be retained due to their consistent fit to the model. All model fit indices also suggested a general fit of the model. The correlation between export development and/or its proxies and each of the barrier perceptions suggested a very weak relationship. The path analysis indicated that export development and/or its proxies was significantly predicted by Prod1 (lack of expertise, resources, and technology to develop new products for foreign markets); Func2 (inadequate/untrained personnel to deal with exports); Place1 (complexity of foreign distribution channels); Place4 (difficulty in maintaining control over foreign middleman due to geographic and cultural distance); Log4 (inability to adjust export promotional activities); Proc1 (unfamiliarity with exporting procedures/paperwork); Poleg3 (high tariff and non-tariff barriers); Socul2 (different socio-cultural traits) and Socul3 (verbal/non-verbal language differences). When other factors in the model are controlled, perceived export barrier is expected to cause export development and/or its proxies to fall respectively by some amount when increased by a unit.

****

CHAPTER SEVEN
SUMMARY, CONCLUSIONS AND IMPLICATIONS

7.1 Policy Background, Research Objectives and Industry Review

Since the end of the Suharto era, as part of the industrial development strategy, the Indonesian government has implemented policies aimed at stimulating and sustaining growth in exports of small and medium sized enterprises. A series of five-year development plans which were intended to establish development priorities and set specific growth targets, have explicitly espoused government commitment toward SMEs. The Indonesian government effort to develop SMEs through various policies and deregulations, however, has largely been regarded as ineffective due to a lack of coordination between the agencies in charge of SME programmes, poor programme design, and inadequate monitoring and evaluation (Wie, 2006). The purpose of this research was to undertake an empirical study to investigate the nature and magnitude of relationships between export barriers and the level of export development of manufacturing SMEs in Indonesia

The specific objectives of the study were:

1. To develop a conceptual framework for explaining export behaviour of manufacturing SMEs in Indonesia.
2. To identify the importance of different export barriers faced by manufacturing SMEs in Indonesia.
3. To examine the interrelationships between managerial perceptions of export barriers and export development, export intensity and export propensity
4. To make recommendations to assist in policy formulation and implementation for improving manufacturing SMEs' export performance in Indonesia.

The present study has synthesized aspects from each of the existing determinants of export behaviour models and export intensity into the conceptual framework. The study employed a quantitative approach using multivariate data analysis.

The study, based on personally administered questionnaires on 197 SMEs owners or managers, identified that the export development of Indonesian manufacturing SMEs is explained by interrelated factors of perceived export barriers. Non-exporting firms, in particular, significantly perceived more difficulty in relation to all informational, distributional, logistical, procedural, political-legal, and socio-cultural barriers as compared to exporting firms. These findings contribute to a better understanding of the export development process of SMEs in a developing country context.

Three sub-sectors, namely textiles; garments, leather and footwear; and furniture and wood products, were selected for analysis because the sub-sectors contain a concentration of SMEs as the main players. The structure and performance of the sub-sectors over the last two decades was reviewed. Textile, garment and footwear industries began to grow in the 1970s and garments and footwear were significant exports from Indonesia in the 1980s. The number of establishments in these two sub-sectors, however, has decreased in the last two decades.

The garment and footwear sub-sectors were mainly controlled by domestic private producers, being around 90 per cent of all producers. Most firms from these two sub-sectors were situated in Java and locations in the Sumatera islands. The textile, garment, and footwear industries are major contributors to non-oil manufacturing GDP and export earnings in Indonesia; more than 50 per cent of SMEs' exports come from these three sub-sectors (Sandee and Ibrahim, 2002; Basri and van der Eng, 2004). The sub-sectors also accounted for substantial investment formation in the economy.

Furniture and wood products manufacturing was another sub-sector of interest. This industry has been growing rapidly since the Indonesian government imposed a ban on log exports and restrictions on processed wood exports in 1990. To compensate for plummeting domestic purchasing power in the 1997 Asian crisis, the industry increased its profits through export. The government through its foreign and domestic scheme directed this industry to focus on high added value finished products to increase the industry's revenue.

The total number of establishments of furniture and wood products in Indonesia also declined in the last two decades. Like the previous two sub-sectors, ownership here is dominated by the domestic, private producers. Most of the producers are concentrated in Java with furniture firms generally located in Central Java, Yogyakarta, and West Java provinces, while wood producers tend to be spread around Java and Bali. The majority of firms in this sub-sector are serving overseas markets. Their share of total non-oil exports, however, has been growing gradually since the Asian financial crisis.

Despite unfavourable global conditions, Indonesian SMEs still aspire to seize export opportunity and develop in terms of output and employment growth. Government policy seeks to promote an efficient and dynamic SME sector and create an environment which allows them to grow without long-term dependence on government support (Berry et al., 2001). The export response of SMEs during the crisis corroborates their potential and demonstrates that being less reliant on government support was an additional incentive to grow.

The remaining discussion in this chapter is organized around the four objectives stated earlier. The emphasis will be on drawing conclusions and outlining managerial and public policy implications. The study's contribution to the export literature, its limitations and suggestions for future research are scrutinized in the last two sections.

7.2 A Review of the Research Findings

7.2.1The Development of a Conceptual Framework

The industry review in Chapter 2 and the literature review in Chapter 3 identified problems and knowledge gaps that establish the need for further examination of manufacturing SMEs' behaviour in Indonesia. As already noted, deficiencies in government policies to promote SME development in Indonesia were known to exist (World Bank in Wie, 2006). Further studies of Indonesian manufacturing SMEs' export behaviour were inadequate, that is they lacked an empirical model that facilitated understanding and offered a confirmation of critical variables affecting Indonesian SMEs' export development in overseas markets. Evidence supporting this contention is found in the fact that, although the stream of research on export behaviour is growing, both the focus and actuality of the literature still calls for an overview in a developing country context. The recent empirical studies reviewed in Suarez-Ortega and Alamo-Vera (2005) reveal that export behaviour studies carried out in developing countries were almost non-existent. Furthermore, most studies focused on the managerial characteristics and direct effects without trying to bring them together into a framework where the relationships and interactions between the variables could be observed. Hence, there is a need for a new approach to incorporate the most common factors of firm and managerial characteristics including managerial perceptions about export operations and to explore their relationship to different stages of the export development process.

Building upon the review of literature, the study uses four categories to investigate the determinants of export behaviour: managerial perceptions of export barriers;

export development; export propensity; and export intensity. All managerial perceptions about internal and external export barriers are included under managerial characteristics and are considered as predictor variables (Suarez-Ortega and Alamo-Vera, 2005). Since Indonesia has been pursuing an incremental approach in its economic development policy by initially focusing on import substitution and gradually embracing outward oriented policy, most Indonesian SMEs are assumed to have been following a gradualist approach to enter foreign markets. For measurement purposes, the study follows the generic types of export development stages set out by Leonidou and Katsikeas (1996). The study also uses the proxies of export propensity and export intention to support the export development classification.

The proposed conceptual framework of this study is depicted in Figure 4.1. All perception variables that stem from managerial assessment are classified in managerial characteristics. The correlation between managerial perception of export barriers and export development determines the firm's level of export development, export propensity, and export intensity.

7.2.2 Perceptions of Export Barriers Based on Level of Export Development

Of 37 barriers identified in the literature and originally adopted in this research, 13 items had to be deleted. There were three grounds for exclusion of a factor. First, factors were deleted where considerable difference between the sample variance and the model-implied variance existed. With a correct model, the maximum standardized difference should be less than two in absolute value in order for a factor to be able to account for much of the covariation that exists between incompatible items (Joreskog and Sorbom, 1984). Second, some factors were withdrawn as they were low loading items. Standardized loading estimates should be at least 0.4 in magnitude to be highly associated with the latent construct

(MacCallum et al., 1992; Hayduk, 1996; Hayduk and Glasser, 2000). Finally, some factors were excluded as they were cross-loading items. Items that have strong relationships with more than one factor may cause problem when interpreting the factor solution (Byrne, 2009).

The remaining 24 items suggest the actual factors hindering Indonesian small and medium sized firms from involvement in export operations. In the context of the sample, Indonesian non-exporting manufacturing SMEs consistently perceived internal exporting problems, represented by informational, functional, distributional, and logistic items, as being of the 'make difficult' to cope type. The barriers perceived to be difficult by respondents, particularly non-exporting firms, suggest significant internal inefficiencies being experienced by the majority of this group.

Consistent with the findings of a study conducted by SMEs Resource Assessment Division, Ministry of Cooperation and SMEs (2010), most SMEs were found to be experiencing difficulties in penetrating export markets and required third party facilitation to improve their access to export markets. The study carried out in several provinces in Indonesia indicated that the majority of SMEs obtained access to export markets through participation in trade shows/exhibitions and information from their business partners. Only a small number of SMEs got the information independently from mass media, internet, or other sources (SMECDA, 2010). The reliance on a limited number of information sources is probably due to SMEs unfamiliarity with national and international sources of information. Even when they are aware of and have access to them, they might encounter difficulties with data retrieval due to limited knowledge, language proficiency, resources or unclear ideas as to the specific information required for foreign market entry. Tesform et al. (2006) suggested that although some problems can be solved through individual action by the firms, other problems are more intractable, for instance overcoming the lack of market information, the preparation of proper designs, and the fulfillment of minimum quantity requirements.

The results of the current research identify functional barriers as a source of significant internal organisational inefficiencies (Altintas and Tokol, 2007). Specifically, the results imply that the majority of respondents, particularly non-exporting SMEs, do not have skilled and knowledgeable personnel to deal with the particular work demanded by export operations (Gomez-Mejia, 1988). Human resources problems in Indonesia arise from insufficient specialized knowledge and expertise to deal with such export business tasks as documentation handling, logistical arrangements, and communicating the specifications of the products to foreign customers. The SMECDA study (2010) concluded that the Indonesian SMEs failure to generate product specifications in accordance with the development of foreign consumers' tastes and standards, to a large extent, could be attributed to inadequate training and development of company personnel particularly in export business issues.

Turning to the distribution and logistic barriers, although some studies found distribution and logistic barriers to be a serious problem for exporting firms (Kedia & Chhokar, 1986; Leonidou, 2004), this study identified the dimensions as more problematic for non-exporting firms than their exporting counterparts. Since foreign distribution systems vary considerably in their characteristics such as purchasing power, segmentation, or quality of the services offered, exporting firms with their assumed experiences may be able to cope better with the impact of these variations than non-exporting firms who perceive them as being significantly more problematic.

Complexity attached to procedural problems also rated highly as a perceived barrier, particularly by non-exporting firms. Despite the extrinsic nature of procedural barriers that are largely dependent on the ability to act expediently on rules and regulations, the results revealed that most non-exporting firms witnessed greater difficulty than exporting firms in areas of bureaucratic procedures and export documentation requirements (e.g. export licences, import certificates, and letters of credit). As stated in the literature, there are two main reasons why these problems are often exacerbated for non-exporting or less experienced exporting firms. Lack of knowledge on procedures to handle administrative demands (Kedia and Chhokar, 1986; Moini, 1997; Terpstra and Sarathy, 2000) as well as time pressure to oversee these procedural complexities were maintained to be the main reasons that hinder non-exporting firms in pursuing their exporting endeavour (Ogram, 1982). In the Indonesian context, these problems are aggravated by associated red tape which fostered a negative attitude towards handling exports (Moini, 1997). Although the Indonesian government has introduced a number of measures to address these issues, they still need to monitor their implementation at the operational level and provide some assistance through consultative services or agencies particularly for SMEs.

Consonant with the view that the perception of problems will depend on the incremental nature of decision making and learning about foreign markets and their operations, this study found considerable difficulty perceived by respondents, particularly non-exporting firms, in relation to governmental, political-legal, and socio-cultural barriers. Different socio-cultural traits were among the socio-cultural issues which constitute serious difficulties, particularly for non-exporting firms. According to Cateora and Graham (2001), the significance of this dimension might greatly affect consumer behaviour, targeting approaches, and marketing programmes. One way suggested to overcome this issue is to appoint managers with an international outlook and foreign language proficiency which might be very helpful in export information gathering and market evaluation (Terpstra and Sarathy, 2000).

Domestic government rules and regulations have been a problem for both non-exporting and exporting firms and are often considered to be an obstacle for their export development. The role of the home government may also become an impediment through a number of restrictions imposed on indigenous SME exporters. In the case of Indonesia, the inconsistent regulatory framework and unsystematic dissemination of information regarding the new government rules and regulation as well as government export schemes are maintained to be the major problems and are assumed to be the cause of the higher means in this dimension. Despite possible losses from compliance, SMEs should satisfy these rules and regulations in order to maintain support from government agencies for other export endeavours (Leonidou, 2004). A higher mean in the politico-legal aspects suggest that foreign governments might, in addition, impose unfavourable controls such as entry restrictions, price controls, or special tax rates, on companies that export goods to their markets. These unfavourable imposts might turn the export endeavour into a tiresome and expensive process that discourages small firms from pursuing their export tasks. Import tariffs are also indicated as a serious problem, particularly for non-exporting SMEs, and would deter their intention to export in the near future. The serious difficulties caused by numerous tariff barriers imposed by some countries have caused the World Trade Organisation (WTO) to urge the gradual reduction of tariff and non-tariff barriers and to promote the liberalisation of international trade.

Exporters exhibited higher means than non-exporters in four construct dimensions: Prod1 (lack of expertise, resources, and technology to develop new products for foreign markets); Prod3 (lack of expertise, resources, and technology to meet export product quality standard/specifications); Price1 (difficulty in matching competitors' price due to higher unit costs and other additional costs); and Econ1 (poor/deteriorating economic conditions in foreign markets). However, the mean differences between exporters and non-exporters on these four dimensions were not significant at the 0.05 significance level. Hence, the exporter group did not really have particular factors that they perceived more significantly as barriers than the non-exporter group.

7.2.4 Policy Implications of the Findings

This section presents the implication of the findings and in so doing addresses the study's last objective of providing recommendations for promoting the export endeavour of SMEs in Indonesia. Several implications both for the management decision maker and the public policy maker in their tasks to promote export activity within their respective spheres of influence are raised for discussion.

7.2.4.1 Managerial Policy Implications of the Findings

Managerially, the study provides SME managers with the information to recognize the determinants affecting their level of export development. From the 24 retained factors hindering Indonesian SMEs involvement in export operations, managerial perception of export barriers is found to be significant. By looking at it closely, it is evident that Indonesian SME owners or managers have typical internal and external problems associated with lack of training and experience, lack of access to market information, technological challenges, and impractical government rules and regulations. Specific implications are detailed below.

Lack of training and experience - Functional and distribution inefficiencies of significant magnitude are explained, to some extent, by the low skilled labour force in Indonesian SMEs. Since SMEs are required to be able to produce products according to customer taste or market demand which are subject to fast-changing trends, they need to have skilled and educated labour that can absorb knowledge and meet the market demand. This limitation needs to be addressed by owner-managers through their commitment to provide training and apprenticeships in order to improve skills and knowledge of labourers. A number of government and private bodies' initiatives have attempted to facilitate this necessity by providing a wide range of technical assistance and capacity building programmes. The owner-manager, therefore, need to be receptive and proactive to these plans.

SMEs' difficulty in producing a product specification in accordance with consumer preferences or market trends also indicates a lack in technological expertise (SMECDA, 2010). The relatively short-cycle of market trends requires an adequate support of technological expertise and infrastructure in order to produce competitive and innovative products which are compatible with international standards. As a result of this limitation, most SMEs lacked ability to fulfil customer orders due to an absence of creativity, innovation and productive capacity.

Lack of access to market information - Indonesian SME owner-managers are also facing distribution inefficiency which is closely linked with their ability to build a marketing network both domestically and internationally. Since market access is a key success of export activities, owner-managers need to improve their access to export distribution channels. It can be inferred that the majority of respondents relied on their participation in trade show and/or exhibition and/or business partners' references to build their international network (SMECDA, 2010). This passive approach which waits for buyers to come knocking on the firm's door has led to inefficient and ineffective marketing strategies for the majority of respondents.

In parallel with distribution inefficiency, SME owner-managers also perceive informational obstacles to their export endeavour. Since the knowledge of a product market as a whole is also critical in export activities, owner-managers are required to have strong market research. The data acquired from the research can provide firms with a series of information inputs about their target segment, industry and competitors. For those firms in the initial stage of their export endeavour, market research can help in determining how feasible a business idea is. As firms increase their export commitment, market research can be used to improve marketing programmes, set goals and differentiate products or services, and/or seek new market opportunities. Nevertheless, the majority of Indonesian SMEs are still facing financial and communication infrastructure problems in their attempts to do market research. The most effective methods that might be suggested in the Indonesian context would be to use external resources that are freely available, such as market research projects conducted by local universities, references from public libraries, and information gathered regularly by trade associations, trade magazines, newspapers, and industry newsletters.

Impractical government rules and regulations - Among external factors that are found difficult to cope with by SMEs in their export endeavour are exporting procedures and domestic government rules and regulations. The majority of the sample firms found it difficult to complete documentation requirements that must be met as part of exporting procedures. Besides the complex bureaucracy of exporting in Indonesia, inadequate knowledge and understanding of the administration and export procedures might also be a contributor to the higher means of difficulty in this factor. Thus, owner-managers have to deal with this issue by attending and utilizing workshops, seminars, and training sessions held by government bodies and/or agencies to assist SMEs in processing export documentation.

Domestic government rules and regulations have been identified consistently as being problematic for manufacturing SMEs in Indonesia and are often considered to be a major external constraint for their export development. Various official and illicit fees as well as complicated rules and regulations were indicated by the majority of respondents. These come into force from stages as early as acquiring raw materials until initiating the export. These practices have led to a high cost economy and created unfavourable conditions for many respondents in all industries. The situation is exacerbated by the implementation of autonomous policy at the local government (regency) level which insist on their rights to impose levies in order to increase local government revenue. Although this problem is completely external to management, SME owner-managers are required to possess an up to date knowledge and understanding of current government rules and regulations. Information from trade associations or trade newsletters would help SMEs update and adjust to any alterations in government rules and regulations.

Barriers based on export development level - The results on perceived export barriers based on SMEs' export development level confirm the previous findings (Leonidou, 1995 and Madsen, 1989) that non-exporting firms perceive more difficulties in nearly all problem dimensions, than those of exporting firms. The clear implication, particularly to owner-managers in the initial stage of exporting endeavour, is that their increasing commitment to export markets will provide valuable experiences and can eventually help lessen their perceived export barriers. In addition, firms need to continuously improve their export capabilities by becoming familiar with their export weaknesses and alternative ways to solve them.

Since experienced exporters tend to have distinct export challenges, owner-managers in this stage of export development need to strengthen their managerial and technical capacities in order to maintain and expand their business in international markets. Improving the combination of industrial linkages, a well-educated and skilled workforce and technology adoption would be a strategic step in this level of export involvement (SMECDA's website, 2010; Berry et al., 2001).

The importance of export promotion programmes - SME owner-managers with strong intentions to tap into international markets need to take into account export promotion programmes as ways to introduce and market their products to potential buyers. SME owner-managers can also gain other network-related benefits from programmes attended. Owner-managers, therefore, are required to be accessible and responsive to export promotion activities.

Foreign language proficiency is found significant in determining the level of export development and should be acted upon positively by SME owner-managers. Investing in English or other foreign language courses or training would lead to a number of financial, marketing, and other benefits over time as implied earlier in the literature review (Burton and Schlegelmilch's, 1987; Dichtl et al., 1990; Holzmuller and Kasper, 1991; and Leonidou et al., 1998). Owner-managers are required to meet this necessity by willingly and persistently learning foreign language(s) in order to improve their business performance.

The causalities between perceived barriers and export development level - The significant strength of the linear relationship between export development level and managerial perceptions about export benefits and export impediments confirm that, in the context of this study, export development has been an important factor in determining the level of export barriers perceived by the firm. This result confirms previous evidence obtained by a number of studies in other countries that as the firm increases its commitment in the export markets, its perception of export barriers will decrease. This reinforcing effect of export barriers on export behaviour and vice versa, can provoke initiation of or withdrawal from exports. Although it is not always easy to alleviate export barriers, SMEs which have stayed relatively strong through the economic crisis should encourage owner-managers to continue transforming and improving their internal systems to face the challenges ahead.

7.2.4.2 Public Policy Implications of the Findings

Within the context of this study, public policy makers need to realize that perceived export barriers occur due the high risks, and costs, associated with export activities. Thus, in order to alleviate these barrier perceptions and promote exports amongst SMEs in Indonesia, public policy makers need to understand that the typical internal problems faced by SME managers are essentially related to their low quality of human resource, poor business management, low access to financial sources and markets, and low information technology. Public and private agencies' efforts to alleviate these barriers can operate by improving firms' financial and managerial capabilities, building strong marketing networks to promote export-oriented products, and providing necessary information technology supports to foster demand and supply of export in their target markets.

Government policies and regulations need to be conducive to reducing the difficulties faced by SMEs in their export endeavours. Any training, apprenticeship, or mentoring schemes need to be equally disseminated in order to provide equal opportunity to every business entity. In order to improve performance of training institutions and/or inter-network training, government need to develop incentive, accreditation, and certification systems. Government agencies, additionally, need to develop and revitalize training units and research and development (R & D) services, owned by various government agencies and regional centres, to serve as business development agencies.

SMEs' access to both investment and working capital has to be simplified and made affordable. Non-bank financial institutions that perform as alternative capital sources for SMEs need to strengthen their institutional competence and service quality. Government, as a regulator, needs to monitor and increase the role of these institutions by looking after their legal status, licensing, and accreditation.

Government agencies, in addition, need to provide assistance to reduce SMEs' barriers in accessing raw materials for production purposes. This can be done, not only through financial or managerial assistance, but also through simplification of documentation procedures and requirements.

Government needs to increase private sector and/or community involvement in providing information technology services and managerial consultancies for SMEs through incentive and establishment supports. By increasing the competition, the cost of acquiring these services is expected to level off to favour SMEs as end users.

It is also suggested that government agencies develop market intelligence systems to understand opportunities and demand challenges for SMEs' products and put them into a suitable market segment based on their product distinctiveness. Improvements in the quality and accessibility of information gathered through market intelligence will, in turn, solve informational barriers which were indicated by most non-exporting firms as costly to develop under their own budget.

Government agencies need to provide financial and technical assistance in strengthening SMEs' marketing network for both domestic and international markets. This can be done by assisting SMEs in developing their marketing divisions, including their business networks, business partnerships, and on-line business transaction systems.

In regard to the promotion of exports particularly for exporting firms, government-funded programmes need to focus on long-term targets. Government agencies need to ensure that SME producers are not only able to win export orders but also maintain their continuous long-term access to export markets by providing managerial and technical assistance in relation to their quality control, consistency in production volumes and products' time delivery. Most non-exporting SMEs indicated a hesitancy to attend a trade show due to cost-benefit considerations. Government agencies, therefore, need to provide subsidies, particularly for 'newcomers' who would like to participate in a domestic trade-exhibition or other export promotion programme for the first time. In addition, eligibility criteria for support of SME trade fair participation should be improved to ensure fair and equal sponsorships.

Although the programmes run by the Ministry's agency (NAFED) are relatively well rated by SMEs that have participated in the promotional activities, there is no attempt from national and local (cluster based) associations to combine their export promotion programmes. A concerted effort might actually enhance outreach, effectiveness, and sustainability of public interventions. Such a synergy would also encourage networking among firms, support joint marketing efforts, and be beneficial for the development of supporting industries.

Some respondents, during the data collection, commented on the importance of integrating all business aspects including market intelligence, R&D, export finance, infrastructure, human resources, and standardisation and certification policies under one-roof as it can be more cost effective and cost efficient for SMEs as the service users. Current export promotion policies within public agencies (Indonesian Ministry of Industry, National Agency for Export Development (NAFED), Ministry of Cooperatives and SMEs, Indonesian Investment Board, and Tourism Promotion Board), and between public and private sectors lack coordination and often lead to overlapping programmes and waste of funding. A closer integration, therefore, not only can facilitate interaction between agencies but also reduce overlap in promotion activities.

7.3 Major Contributions of the Current Study

This research has made a number of contributions to the field of export business theory and practice. These are:

The validation of export business theory, that has previously been tested in a developed country context, for a developing country's business environment via application to a sample of 197 manufacturing SMEs in Indonesia. The differences that exist between developed and developing countries make the findings significant by extending the scope of the theory and then confirming the previous results in a cross-sectional research design.

The formulation of a new approach to perceived export barriers by adopting a comprehensive export barrier structure deduced from export business literature. Leonidou's recent review (2004) that integrated export barriers from previous work formed the basis to define and validate factors perceived as significant by Indonesian manufacturing SMEs. Using the confirmatory factor analysis in AMOS, the study determined whether the data supported the hypothesized model by applying goodness-of-fit indices.

The adoption of path analysis using the AMOS platform made it possible to simultaneously examine the relationships between various perceived export barriers and export development in a single model and to quantify these relationships. The study has tested a number of particular hypotheses using multivariate data analysis where previously hypotheses were tested by ignoring interactions and using only bivariate data analysis.

The innovation of combining export development, export propensity, and export intensity as predictor or endogenous variables in the conceptual framework.

Conceptual models from previous studies were criticized for the unbalanced treatment given to the examination of different export development stages and for ignoring export propensity and export intensity as well as the failure to test concurrently the full set of managerial and organisational factors against the full range of export dimensions (Leonidou, 1998; Suarez-Ortega and Alamo-Vera, 2005).

7.4 Limitations of the Study

Some possible limitations that must be recognized before generalizing the findings to other contexts are:

- The cross-sectional research design involves the collection of data at a single point in time. Such an approach produces the difficulty of detecting respondent's patterns over time, as they might change due to new circumstances emerging.
- The sampling frame of this study is small and medium sized firms dealing in exportable products in three types of sub-sectors that were textiles, garments, footwear, and furniture and wood products. As maintained earlier, the main reason for selecting these industries is because of their concentration of small and medium sized firms involved in exporting from Indonesia (Berry et al. 2001). Thus, although the purpose of this study was to generally understand export behaviour of small and medium sized firms, irrespective of their type of industry, caution should be exercised in any attempt to generalize the findings due to differences at industry and country levels.

7.5 Suggestions for Future Research

- A qualitative approach based on indepth interviews with SME owners or senior managers is needed to confirm their views on all identified factors affecting SMEs export development in this study. By expanding the study to a longitudinal and qualitative research design, insight into dynamic processes could also be gained. Multiple case study methodology would be appropriate to investigate and chart the impact of internal factors on decision making within the firms and the consequent interaction with the level of export development.

- Given the volatile global economy and policy reforms in Indonesia, constant monitoring of these changes and their impact on export development and performance is pertinent.

REFERENCES

Aaby, N. & Slater, S. F. 1989, Management Influences on Export Performance: A Review of the Empirical Literature 1978-1988, *International Marketing Review*, Vol. 6, Issue 4, pp. 7-27.

Abdel-Malek, T. Export Marketing Orientation in Small Firms, *American Journal of Small Business*, Vol. 3, Issue 1, pp. 25-34.

Acs, Z. J. & Preston, L. 1997, Small and Medium-Sized Enterprises, Technology, and Globalisation: Introduction to a Special Issue on Small and Medium-Sized Enterprises in the Global Economy, *Small Business Economics*, Vol. 9, Issue 1, pp. 1-6.

ADB (Asian Development Bank) 2004, Asia Foundation, and Swiss Contact (forthcoming). *SMEs After the Crisis: The Role of Export-Oriented SMEs*. ADB: Indonesia Resident Mission, Jakarta.

ADB (Asian Development Bank) 2006, *Indonesia 2006-2009*, Country Strategy and Programme, viewed 18 January 2010, <http://www.aseansec.org/pdf/sme_policies_1.pdf>

Agarwal, S. & Ramaswami, S.N. 1992, Choice of Foreign Market Entry Mode: Impact of Ownership, Location and Internationalisation Factor, *Journal of International Business Studies*, Vol. 23, Issue 1, pp. 1-27.

Aggrey, N., Eliab, L. & Joseph, S. 2010, Determinants of Export Participation in East African Manufacturing Firms, *Current Research Journal of Economic Theory*, Vol. 2, Issue 2, pp. 55-61.

Ahmed, Z. U., Julian, C. C., Baalbaki, I. & Hadidian, T. V. 2004, Export Barriers and Firm Internationalisation: A Study of Lebanese Entrepreneurs, *Journal of Management & World Business Research*, Vol. 1, Issue 1, pp. 11-22.

Albaum, G., Strandskov, J. & Duerr, E. 1998, *International Marketing and Export Development*, Addison-Wesley Longman, England.

Alexandrides, C. B. 1971, How the Major Obstacles to Expansion can be Overcome, *Atlanta Economic Review*, Vol. 21, Issue 5, pp. 12-15.

Altintas, M. H., Tokol, T., & Harcar, T. 2007, The Effects of Export Barriers on Perceived Export Performance: An Empirical Research on SMEs in Turkey, *EuroMed Journal of Business*, Vol. 2, Issue 1, pp. 36-56.

Andersen, O. 1993, On the Internationalisation Process of the Firms, A Critical Analysis, *Journal of International Business Studies*, Vol. 24, Issue 2, pp. 209-231.

Anderson, K. 2005, Setting the Trade Policy Agenda: What Roles for Economists? *World Bank Policy Research Working Paper* No. 3560.

Anderson, J. C. & Gerbing, D. W. 1988, Some Methods for Respecifying Measurement Models to Obtain Unidimensional Construct Measurement, *Journal of Marketing Research*, Vol. 19, Issue 1, pp. 453-460.

Anonymous, 1996, The Miracle of Trade, *The economist*, 27 January 1996.

ANU, Australian National University, National Asia Pacific Economic and Scientific (NAPES) Database, viewed June 2009, http://napes.anu.edu.au.virtual.anu.edu.au/

Arthur, W. B. 1990, Competing Technologies, Increasing Returns, and Lock-in by Historic Events, *Economic Journal*, Vol. 99, pp. 116-131.

Asia Foundation 2009, Asia's Economic Recovery: Constrasting Narratives, viewed June 2009, <asiafoundation.org/...asia/.../asias-economic-recovery-contrasting-narratives/>.

Aswicahyono, H. & Feridhanusetyawan, T. The Evolution and Upgrading of Indonesia's Industry, viewed June 2007, <http://www.csis.or.id/papers/wpe073>

Athukorala, P. 2006, Post-crisis Export Performance: The Indonesian Experience in Regional Perspective, *Bulletin of Indonesian Economic Studies*, Vol. 42, Issue 2, pp. 177-211.

Aulakh, P. S. & Kotabe, M. 2000, Export Strategies and Performance of Firms from Emerging Economies: Evidencefrom Latin America, *Academy of Management Journal*, Vol. 43, Issue 3, pp. 342-361.

Axinn, C. N. 1988, Export Performance: Do Managerial Perceptions Make a Difference? *International Marketing Review*, Vol. 5, Issue 2, pp. 61-71.

Axinn, C. N. 1985, *An Examination of Factors that Influence Export Performance*, Unpublished PhD Dissertation, East Lansing, Michigan State University.

Axinn, C. N. & Matthyessens, P. 2002, Limits of Internationalisation Theories in an Unlimited World, *International Marketing Review*, Vol. 19, Issue 5, pp. 436-449.

Bappenas, Badan Perencanaan dan Pembangunan Nasional, viewed January 2010a, <http://els.bappenas.go.id/upload/kliping/Neraca-MI.pdf>

Bappenas, Badan Perencanaan dan Pembangunan Nasional, viewed January 2010b, <http://www.bappenas.go.id/get-file-server/node/1119/>

Bagchi-Sen, S. 1999, The Small and Medium Sized Exporters' Problems: An Empirical Analysis of Canadian Manufacturers, *Regional Studies*, Vol. 33, Issue 3, pp. 231-245.

Bagozzi, R. P. 1991, Further Thoughts on the Validity of Measures of Elation, Gladness, and Joy, *Journal of Personality and Social Psychology*, Vol. 61, Issue 1, pp. 98-104.

Barabba, V. P. & Zaltman, G. 1991, Competitive Advantage through Creative Use of Marketing Information, *Hearing the Voice of the Market*, Harvard Business School Press, Boston, MA.

Barker, A. T. & Kaynak, E. 1992, An Empirical Investigation of the Differences Between Initiating And Continuing Exporters, *European Journal of Marketing*, Vol. 26, Issue 3, pp. 27-36.

Barret, N. I. & Wilkinson, I. F. 1986, Internationalisation Behavior: Management Characteristics of Australian Manufacturing Firms by Level of International Development, in Turnbull P. W. & Paliwoda S. J., editors, *Research In International Marketing*, Croom Helm, London, pp. 213-233.

Bartlett, C. A. & Ghoshal, S. 2000, *Transnational Management: Text, Cases, and Readings in Cross-border Management*, Irwin/McGraw Hill, Boston.

Basile, R. 2001, Export Behaviour of Italian Manufacturing Firms Over the Nineties: The Role of Innovation, *Research Policy*, Vol. 30, Issue 8, pp. 1185-1201.

Basri, M. C. & Van der Eng, P. 2002 Business in Indonesia: New Challenges, Old Problems, Institute of SouthEast Asian Studies, Singapore.

Beamish, P. W., Craig, R. & McLellan, K. 1993, The Performance Characteristics of Canadian versus U.K. Exporters in Small and Medium Sized Firms, *Management International Review*, Vol. 33, Issue 2, pp. 121-137.

Bell, J. 1995, The Internationalisation of Small Computer Software Firms: A Further Challenge to 'Stage' Theories, *European Journal of Marketing*, Vol. 29, Issue 8, pp. 60-75.

Bell, J., McNaughton, R., Young, S. & Crick, D. 2003, Towards an Integrative Model of Small Firms Internationalisation, *Journal of International Entrepreneurship*, Vol. 1, Issue 4, pp. 339-362.

Benito, G. & Gripsurd, G. 1992, *The Expansion of Foreign Direct Investment: Discrete Rational Location Choices or a Cultural Learning Process*, Vol. 23, Issue 3, pp. 461-476.

Bentler, P. M. & Bonnet D. G. 1980, Significance Tests and Goodness of Fit in the Analysis of Covariance Structures, *Psychological Bulletin*, Vol. 88, Issue 1, pp. 588-606.

Berry, A. & Nugent J. B. 1999, *Fulfilling the Export Potential of Small and Medium Firms*, Kluwer Academic Publishers, Boston, MA.

Berry, A., Rodriguez, E. & Sandee, H. 2001, Small and Medium Enterprise Dynamics in Indonesia, *Bulletin of Indonesian Economic Studies*, Vol. 37, Issue 5, pp. 363-384.

Berry, A., Rodriguez, E. & Sandee, H. 2002, Firm and Group Dynamics in the Small and Medium Enterprise Sector in Indonesia, *Small Business Economics*, Vol. 18, Issue 1/3, 141-161.

Berry, M. M. J. & Brock, J. K. 2004, Marketspace and Internationalisation Process of the Small Firm, *Journal of International Entrepreneurship*, Vol. 2, Issue 3, pp. 187-216.

Bilkey, W. J. 1978, An Attempted Integration of the Literature on the Export Behavior of Firms, *Journal of International Business Studies*, Vol. 7, pp. 33-46.

Bilkey, W. J. 1970, *Industrial Stimulation*, Lexington, MA: Heath Lexington Books, D. C. Heath and Company, pp. 95-100.

Bilkey, W. J. & Tesar G. 1977, The Export Behavior of Smaller-Sized Wisconsin Manufacturing Firms, *Journal of International Business Studies*, Vol. 8, pp. 93- 98.

Bodur, M. 1986, A Study on the Nature and Intensity of Problems Experienced by Turkish Exporting Firms in Cavusgil, S. T., *Advances in International Marketing 1*, editor, Greenwich, JAI Press, pp. 205-232.

Bollen, K. A. 1989, *Structural Equations with Latent Variables*, John Wiley and Sons, New York.

Bollen, K. A. & Long, J. S. 1993, *Testing Structural Equation Models,* CA: Sage, Beverly Hills.

Bonaccorsi, A. 1992, On the Relationship between Firm Size and Export Intensity, *Journal of International Business Studies*, Vol. 23, Issue 4, pp. 605-635.

Boter, H. & Holmquist, C. 1996, Industry Characteristics and Internationalisation Processes in Small Firms, *Journal of Business Venturing*, Vol. 11, Issue 6, pp. 471-487Bourke, I.J. & Leitch, J. 1998, *Trade Restrictions and Their Impact on International Trade in Forest Products*, FAO, Rome.

Bourke, I. J. & Leitch, J. 1998, *Trade Restrictions and Their Impact on International Trade in Forest Products*, FAO, Rome.

BPS, 2010, *Berita Resmi Statistik*, Vol. 30, Issue 1.

BPS, 2008, *Berita Resmi Statistik*, Vol. 28, Issue 5.

Bollen, K. A. & Long, J. S. 1993, *Testing Structural Equation Modeling*, CA: Sage, Newbury Park.

Booth, A. 1998, *The Indonesian Economy in the Nineteenth and Twentieth Centuries: A History of Missed Opportunities*, Macmillan, London.

Bradley, F. 1995, The Service Firm in International Marketing, in Glynn, W.J. & Barnes, J.G., editors, *Understand Services Management*, John Wiley & Sons, New York, NY and Chichester, pp. 420-448.

Bradshaw, R. & Burridge, M. 2001, Practices of Successful Small and Medium-sized Exporters: The Use of Market Information, *Journal of Small Business and Enterprise Development*, Vol. 8, Issue 3, pp. 267-273.

Brooks, M. & Rosson, P. 1982, A Study of Export Behavior of Small and Medium-Sized Manufacturing Firms in Three Canadian Provinces in Czinkota, M. R. & Tesar, G., editors, *Export management - An International Context*, editors, Praeger Publishers, New York, pp. 39-54.

Burton, F. N. & Schlegelmilch, B. B. 1987, Profile Analysis of Non-exporters versus Exporters Grouped by Export Involvement, *Management International Review*, Vol. 27, Issue 1, pp. 38-49.

Byrne, B. M. 2009, *Structural Equation Modeling with AMOS: Basic Concepts, Applications, and Programmeming*, Routledge/Taylor & Francis, New York.

Calof, J. L. 1994, The Relationship Between Firms Size and Export Behavior Revisited, *Journal of International Business Studies*, Second Quarter, pp. 367-387.

Cannon, T. 1980, Managing International and Export Marketing. *European Journal of Marketing*, Vol. 14, Issue 1, pp. 34-49.

Cannon T. & Willis, M. 1981, The Smaller Firm in International Trade, *European Small Business Journal*, Vol. 1, Issue 3, pp. 45-55.

Cateora, P. R. & Graham, J. L. 1999, *International Marketing*, 10th edition, Irwin MCGraw-Hill, Boston, MA.

Cavusgil, S. T. & Nevin, J. R. 1980, A Conceptualisation of the Initial Involvement in International Marketing, in Lamb Jr., C. W. & P. M. Dunne, editors,

Theoretical Developments in Marketing, pp. 68-71, American Marketing Association, Chicago.

Cavusgil, S. T. 1984, Differences Among Exporting Firms Based on Their Degree of Internationalisation, *Journal of Business Research*, Vol. 12, Issue 2, pp. 195-208.

Cavusgil, S. T. 1982, On the Nature of Decision Making for Export Marketing, in Bush, R. F. & S. D. Hunt, *Marketing Theory: Philosophy of Science Perspectives*, editors, American Marketing Association, Chicago, pp. 117-180.

Cavusgil, S. T. & Nevin, J. N. 1981, Internal Determinants of Export Marketing Bevahiour: An Empirical Investigation, *Journal of Marketing Research*, Vol. 18, Issue 1, pp. 114-119.

Cavusgil, S. T. & Naor, J. 1987, Firm and Management Characteristics as Discriminators of Export Marketing Activity, *Journal of Business Research*, Vol. 15, Issue 3, pp. 221-235.

Chang, T. L. 1990, *The Competitive Strategies of Firms in Their Internationalisation Process: The Case of Taiwanese Firms in the Information Industry*, PhD Dissertation, The George Washington University, Washington DC.

Chen, M. J. 1996, Competitor Analysis and Interfirm Rivalry: Toward a Theoretical Integration, *Academy of Management Review*, Vol. 21, Issue 1, pp. 100-134.

Cheong, W. K. & Chong, K. W. 1988, Export Behavior of Small Firms in Singapore, *International Small Business Journal*, Vol. 6, Issue 2, pp. 34-41.

Chetty, S. K. & Hamilton, R. T. 1996, The Process of Exporting in Owner-Controlled Firms, *International Small Business Journal*, Vol. 14, Issue 2, pp. 12-25.

Chetty, S. K. & Hamilton, R. T. 1993, Firm-Level Determinants of Export Performance: A Meta-Analysis, *International Marketing Review*, Vol. 10, Issue 3, pp. 26-35.

Chowdhury, A. R. 1993, Does Exchange Rate Volatility Depress Trade Flows? Evidence from Error-Correction Models, *The Review of Economics and Statistics*, Vol. 75, Issue 4, pp. 700-706.

Christensen, C. H., da Rocha, A., & Gertner, R. K. 1987, An Empirical Investigation of the Factors Influencing Exporting Success of Brazilian Firms, *Journal of International Business Studies*, Vol. 18, Issue 3, pp. 61-77.

Clark, T. 1991, Review of the Competitive Advantage of Nations, by M. E. Porter, *Journal of Marketing,* Issue October, pp. 118-120.

Clarke, G. R. G. 2005, *Beyond Tariff and Quotas: Why Don't African Manufacturing Enterprises Export More*, World Bank Policy Research Working Paper 3617.

Comrey, A. L. 1978, Common Methodological Problems in Factor Analytic Studies, *Journal of Consulting and Clinical Psychology*, Vol. 46, Issue 1, pp. 648-659.

Congdon, T. 1990, Autumn books....should be made of Sterner Stuff: The Competitive Advantage of Nations, *Spectator*, Vol. 265, Issue 8463, pp. 41-42.

Corden, W. M. 1994, *Economic Policy, Exchange Rates, and the International System*. Oxford University Press, New York.

Coviello, N. E. & Munro, H. 1997, Network Relationships and the Internationalisation Process of Small Software Firms, *International Business Review*, Vol. 6, Issue 4, pp. 361-386.

Coviello, N. E. & Munro, H. 1995, Growing the Entrepreneurial Firm: Networking for International Market Development, *European Journal of Marketing*, Vol. 29, Issue 7, pp. 49-62.Crick, D. & Chaudry, S. 1997a, Small Businesses' Motives for Exporting; The Effect of Internationalisation, *Journal of Marketing Practice: Applied Marketing*, Vol. 3, Issue 3, pp. 156-171.

Crick, D. 1995, An Investigation into the Targeting of U.K. Export Assistance, *European Journal of Marketing*, Vol 29, Issue 8, pp. 76-94.

Crick, D., Al Obaidi, M. & Chaudry, S. 1998, Perceived Obstacles of Saudi-Arabian Exporters of Non-oil Products, *Journal of Marketing Practice: Applied Marketing Science*, Vol. 4, Issue 7, pp. 187-199.

Crick, D. & Chaudry, S. 2000, UK Agricultural Exporters' Perceived Barriers and Government Assistance Requirements, *Marketing Intelligence & Planning*, Vol. 18, Issue 1, pp. 30-38.

Crick, D. & Chaudry, S. 1997a, Small Businesses' Motives for Exporting; The Effect of Internationalisation, *Journal of Marketing Practice: Applied Marketing*, Vol. 3, Issue 3, pp. 156-171.

Crick, D. & Chaudry, S. 1997b, Export Problems and Government Assistance Required by UK Exporters: An Investigation into the Effect of Ethnicity, *International Journal of Entrepreneurial Behavior and Research*, Vol. 3, Issue 1, pp. 3-18.

Crick, D. & Chaudry, S. 1996, Export Behaviour of Asian and Indigenous-owned SMEs in the UK Clothing Industry: A Reseach Note, *International Journal of Entrepreneurial Behavior and Research*, Vol. 2, Issue 1, pp. 77-84.

Crick, D. & Czinkota, M. R. 1995, Export Assistance: Another Look at Whether We are Supporting the Best Programmes, International Marketing Review, Vol 12, Issue 3, pp. 61-72.

Cunningham, E. 2007, *Structural Equation Modeling Using AMOS*, Education and Statistics Consultancy, Statsline, Victoria, Australia

Cushman, D. O. 1988, Exchange-rate Uncertainty and Foreign Direct Investment in the United States, *Review of World Economics*, Vol. 124, Issue 2, pp. 322-336.

Czinkota, M .R. 1982, *Export Development Strategies: U.S. Promotion Policy,* Praeger Publishers, New York.

Czinkota, M. R. & Johnston, W. J. 1983, Exporting: Does Sales Volume Make a Difference? *Journal of International Business Studies*, Vol. 14, Issue 1, pp. 147-153.

Czinkota, M. R, Ronkainen, I. A., & Moffett, M. H. 2003, *International Business*, Dryden Press, Fort Worth.

Czinkota, M. R. & Ronkainen, I. A. 1998, *International Marketing*, Dryden Press, Fort Worth.

Czinkota, M. R, Ronkainen, I. A., & Rivoli, P. 1992, *International Business*, Dryden Press, Fort Worth.

Czinkota, M. R, & Ursic, M. 1991, Classification of Exporting Firms According to Sales and Growth into a Share Matrix, *Journal of Business Research*, Vol. 22, Issue 3, pp. 243-53.

Daniels, J. D. & Guyburo, J. 1976, The Exporter – Non-exporter Interface: A Search for Variables, *Foreign Trade Review*, Vol. 1, Issue 3, pp. 258-282.

Da Rocha, A., Christensen, C. H., & Cunha, C. E. 1990, Aggressive and Passive Exporters: A study in Brazilian Furniture Industry, International Marketing Review, Vol. 7 Issue 5, pp. 6-15.

Da Silva, P. A., & Da Rocha, A. 2008, Do Perceived Export Barriers Change over Time? A Longitudinal Study of Brazilian Exporters of Manufactured Goods, *American Business Review*, Vol. 9, Issue 1, pp. 102-128.

Da Silva, P. A., & Da Rocha, A. 2001, Perceptions of Export Barriers to Mercosur by Brazilian Firms, *International Marketing Review*, Vol. 18, Issue 6, pp. 589-610.

Davis, P. S. & Harveston, P. D. 2000, Internationalisation and Organisational Growth: The Impact of Internet Usage and Technology Involvement Among Entrepeneurled Family Businesses, *Family Business Review*, Vol. 13, Issue 2, pp. 107-120.

Deephouse, D. L. 1999, To be Different or to be the Same? It's a Question (and Theory) of Strategic Balance, *Strategic Management Journal*, Vol. 20, Issue 2, pp. 147-166.

De Toni A. F. & Nassimbeni, G. 2001, The Export Propensity of Small Firms: A Comparison of Organisational and Operational Management Levers in Exporting and Non-Exporting Units, *International Journal of Entrepreneurial Behaviour & Research,* Vol. 7, Issue 4, pp. 132-147.

Diamantopoulos, A. & Inglis K. 1988, Identifying Differences between High and Low Involvement Exporters, *International Marketing Review*, Vol. 5, Issue 2, pp. 52-60.

Diamantopoulos, A. & Schlegelmilch, B. B. 1997, *Taking the Fear Out of Data*, The Dryden Press, London, UK.

Diamantopoulos, A., Schlegelmilch, B. B. & Allpress, C. 1990, Export Marketing Research in Practice: A Comparison of Users and Non-users, *Journal of Marketing Management*, Vol. 6, Issue 3, pp. 257-274.

Diamantopoulos, A. Schlegelmilch, B.B. & Tse, K.Y. 1993, Understanding the Role of Export Marketing Assistance: Empirical Evidence and Research Needs, *European Journal of Marketing*, Vol. 27, Issue 4, pp. 5-18.

Diamantopoulos A. & Souchon, A.L. 1998, Information Utilisation by Exporting Firms: Conceptualisation, Measurement, and Impact on Export Performance, in Urban, S. et al., editors, *Information and Management: Utilisation of Technology* – Structural and Cultural Impact, Gabler, Wiesbaden, pp. 112-135.

Dichtl, E., Leibold, M., Koglmayr, H. & Muller, S. 1984, The Export Decision of Small and Medium-sized Firms: A Review, *Management International Review,* Vol. 24, Issue 2, pp. 49-60.

Dichtl, E., Koeglmayr, H. & Mueller, S. 1990, International Orientation as a Precondition for Export Success, *Journal of International Business Studies*, Vol. 21, Issue 1, pp. 23-40.

Dick, H, Houben, V. J. H., Lindblad, J. T. & Wie, T. K. 2002, *The Emergence of a National Economy: An Economic History of Indonesia, 1800-2000*, University of Hawai'I Press, Honolulu.

Dicken, P. & Lloyd, P. E. 1990, *Location in Space: Theoretical Perspectives in Economic Geography*, Harper Collins, New York.

Dollar, D. & Kraay, A. 2004, Trade, Growth, and Poverty, *The Economic Journal*, Vol 114, Issue 493, pp. F22-F49.

Dominguez, L. V. & Sequeira, C. G. 1993, Determinants of LDC Exporters Performance: A Cross-National Study, *Journal of International Business Studies*, Vol. 24, Issue1, pp. 19-40.

Donthu, N. & Kim, S. H. 1993, Implications of Firm Controllable Factors on Export Growth, *Journal of Global Marketing*, Vol. 7, Issue 1, pp. 47-63.

Down, S. 2010. *Enterprise, Entrepreneurship and Small Business*, Sage Publications Ltd, London.

Economist Intelligence Units, 2008, *the Economist Intelligence Units,* Indonesia, viewed 7 March 2008, <http://www.economist.com/countries/indonesia/profile.cfm?folder=Profile-FactSheet>

Edmund, S. E. & Khoury, S. J. 1986, Exports: A Necessary Ingredient in the Growth of Small Business Firms, *Journal of Small Business Management*, Vol. 24, Issue 4, pp. 54-65.

Edmund, S. & Sarkis, K. 1986, Export: A Necessary Ingredient in the Growth of Small Business Firms, *Journal of Small Business Management*, Vol. 24, Issue 4, pp. 54-65.

Edwards, S. 1998, Openness, Productivity and Growth: What Do We Really Know? *Economic Journal*, Vol. 108, Issue March, pp. 383-398.

Eilon, S. 1990, On Competitiveness, *Omega: International Journal of Management Science*, Vol. 20, pp. i-iv.

Ellis, P. & Pecotich, A. 2002, Macromarketing and International Trade: Comparative Advantage versus Cosmopolitan Considerations, *Journal of Macromarketing,* Vol. 22, Issue 1, pp. 35-56.

Enderwick, P. & Akoorie, M. 1994, Pilot Study Research Note: The Employment of Foreign Language Specialists and Export Success – The Case of New Zealand, *International Marketing Review*, Vol. 11, Issue 4, pp. 4-18.

Erramilli, M. K. & Rao, C. P. 1993, Service Firms' International Entry-Mode Choice: A Modified Transaction-Cost Analysis Approach, *Journal of Marketing*, Vol. 57, Issue 1, pp. 19-38.

Erwidodo 1999, *Effects of Trade Liberalisation on Agriculture in Indonesia: Institutional and Structural Aspects*, Working Paper Series 41, Bogor, United Nations Regional Coordination Centre for Course Grains, Pulses, Roots and Tuber Crops in the Humid Tropics of Asia and the Pacific (CGPRT centre).

Eshgi, A. 1992, Attitude Behavior Inconsistency in Exporting, *International Marketing Review*, Vol. 9, Issue 3, pp. 40-61.

Fillis, I. 2001, Small Firm Internationalisation: An Investigative Survey and Future Research Directions, *Management Decision*, Vol. 39, Issue 9, pp. 767-783.

Fischer, E. & Reuber, R. 2003, Targeting Export Support to SMEs: Owners' International Experience as a Segmentaion Basis, *Small Business Economics*, Vol. 20, Issue 1, pp. 69.82.

Ford, I. D. & Leonidou, L. C. 1991, Research Development in International Marketing, in Paliwoda, S.J. editor, *New Perspectives on International Marketing*, Routledge, London, pp. 3-32.

Fornell, C. & Larcker, D. 1981, Evaluating Structural Equation Models with Unobservable Variable and Measurement Error, *Journal of Marketing Research*, Vol.18, Issue, pp. 39-50.

Frazier, G. Gill, J. & Kale, S. 1989, Dealer Dependent Levels and Reciprocal Actions in a Channel of Distribution in Developing Country, *Journal of Marketing*, Vol. 53, Issue 1, pp. 50-69.

Fryges, H. 2006, *Hidden Champions – How Young and Small Technology-Oriented Firms Can Attain High Export-Sales Ratios*, ZEW Discussion Papers 06-45.

Gankema, G., Snuif, H. & Dijken, V. 1997, The Internationalisation Process of Small and Medium Sized Enterprises: An Evaluation of the Stage Theory, in Donckels, R. & Miettinen, A., editors, *Entrepreneurship and SME Research: On Its Way to the Next Millenium*, Ashgate, Aldershot.

Garnier, G. 1982, Comparative Export Behavior of Small Canadian Firms in the Printing and Electrical Industries, in Czinkota, M. R. & Tesar, G. editors, *Export Management: An International Context*, Praeger Publishers, New York, pp. 113-131.

Gencturk, E. F & Kotabe, M. 2001, The Effect of Export Assitance Programme Usage on Export Performance: A Contingency Explanation, *Journal of International Marketing*, Vol. 9, Issue 2, pp. 51-72.

Gerber, J. 2005, *International Economics*, 3rd edition, Pearson Addison Wesley.

Gomez-Mejia, L. R. 1988, The Role of Human Resources Strategy in Export Perfromance: A Longitudinal Study, *Strategic Management Journal*,Vol. 9, Issue 1, pp. 493-505.

Gorsuch, R. L. 1983, *Factor Analysis* (2nd edition), NJ: Erlbaum, Hillsdale.

Gray, B. J. Profiling Managers to Improve Export Promotion Targeting, *Journal of International Business Studies*, Vol. 28, Issue 2, pp. 387-420.

Green, R. & Larsen, T. 1987, Environmental Shock and Export Opportunity, *International Marketing Review*, Vol. 4, Issue 4, pp. 30-42.

Greenaway, D. & Milner, C. 1986, *The Economics of IIT*, Basil Blackwell, Oxford.

Greenaway, D. & Tharakan, P. K. M. 1986, *Imperfect Competition and International Trade, The Policy Aspects of Intra-Industry Trade*, Wheatsheaf, Sussex.

Grimwade, N. 2000, *International Trade: New Patterns of Trade, Production & Investment*, Routledge, London.

Gripsrud, G. 1990, The Determinants of Export Decisions and Attitudes to a Distant Market: Norwegian Fishery Exports to Japan, *Journal of International Business Studies*, Vol. 21, pp. 469-485.

Gronhaug, K. & Kvitastein, O. 1992, Expansion Strategies in International Markets: An Explanatory Study, in Grunert, K.G. & Fuglene, D, editors, Marketing for Europe – Marketing for the Future, *European Marketing Academy*, Aarhus, pp. 487-504.

Grubel, H. G. & Lloyd, P. J. 1975, *Intra Industry Trade: The Theory and Measurement of Internationally Trade in Differentiated Products,* Wiley, New York

Guilford, J. P. 1954, *Psychometric Methods*, McGraw-Hill, New York.

Gupta, N. 1980, Some Alternative Definitions of Size, *Academy of Management Journal*, Vol. 23, Issue 4, pp. 759-766.

Hadad, M., Lim, J. J., & Saborowski, C. Managing Opennes and Volatility: The Role of Export Diversification, *Economic Premise*, viewed January 2010, <siteresources.worldbank.org/INTPREMNET/Resources/EP6.pdf>.

Hall, C. 2002, Profile of SMEs and SME Issues in APEC 1999-2000, final draft report, viewed 16 December 2009, <http://www.aseansec.org/pdf/sme_policies_1.pdf>

Hair, J. F. Jr., Anderson, R. E., Tatham, R. L. & Black, W. C. 1998, *Multivariate Data Analysis*, Prentice-Hall, Upper Saddle River, New Jersey.

Hanson, D., Hitt, M. A., Ireland, R. D. and Hoskisson, R. E. 2017, *Strategic Management Competitiveness and Globalisation*, 6th edition, Cengage Learning, Australia.

Harveston, P. D., Kedia, B. L. & Davis, P. S. 2000, Internationalisation of Born Global and Gradual Globalizing Firms: The Impact of the Manager, *Advances in Competitiveness Research*, Vol. 8, Issue 1, pp. 92-100.

Hassler, M. 2003, Crisis, Coincidences and Strategic Market Behavior: The Internationalisation of Indonesian Clothing Brand-Owners, *Area*, Vol. 35, Issue 3, pp. 241-250.

Hayashi, M. 2002, The Role of Subcontracting in SME Development in Indonesia: Micro Level Evidence from the Metalworking and Machinery Industry, *Journal of Asian Economics*, Vol. 13, Issue 1, pp. 1-26.

Hayduk, L. A. 1996, *LISREL Issues, Debates and Strategies*, John Hopkins Press, London.

Hayduk, L. A. & Glasser, D. N. 2000, Jiving' the Four-step, Waltzing around Factor Analysis, and Other Serious Fun, *Structural Equation Modeling*, Vol. 7, Issue 1, pp. 1-35.

Hill, H. 1992, Regional Development in a Boom and Bust Petroleum Economy: Indonesia since 1970, *Economic Development and Cultural Change*, Vol. 40, Issue 2, pp. 351-379.

Hill, H. 1995a, The Economic of Recent Changes in the Weaving Industry, *Bulletin of Indonesian Economic Studies*, Vol. 16, Issue 2, pp. 83-103.

Hill, H. 1995b, Indonesia's Great Leap Forward? Technology Development and Policy Issues, *Bulletin of Indonesian Economic Studies*, Vol 31, Issue 2, pp. 83-123.

Hill, H. 1996a, Indonesia's Industrial Policy and Performance: "Orthodoxy" Vindicated, *Economic Development and Cultural Change*, Vol. 45, Issue 1, pp. 147-174.

Hill, H. 1996b, Indonesia: From 'Chronic Dropout' to 'Miracle', *Journal of International Development*, Vol. 7, Issue 5, pp. 775-789.

Hill, H. 2001, Small and Medium Enterprises in Indonesia: Old Policy Challenges for a New Administration, *Asian Survey*, Vol. 41, Issue 2, pp. 248-270.

Hill, C. W. L. 2003, *International Business: Competing in the Global Marketplace*, 4th edition, McGraw-Hil/Irwin, New York, USA.

Hirsch, S. & Lev, B. 1971, Sales Stabilisation Through Export Diversification, *Review of Economics & Statistics*, Vol. 53, Issue 3, pp. 270-277.

Holden, A. 1986, Small Business can Market in Europe: Results from a Survey of U.S. Exporters, *Journal of Small Business Management*, Issue January, pp. 22-29.

Hooper, P. & Kohlhagen, S. W. 1978, The Effect of Exchange Rate Uncertainty on the Prices and Volume of International Trade, *Journal of International Economics*, Vol. 8, Issue 4, pp. 483-511.

Holzmuller, H. H., & Kasper, H. 1990, The Decision-maker and Export Activity: A Cross National Comparison of the Foreign Orientation of Austrian Managers, *Management International Review*, Vol. 3, Issue 3, pp. 217-230.

Holzmuller, H. H. & Kasper, H. 1991, On Theory of Export Performance: Personal and Organisational Determinants of Export Trade Activities Observed in Small and Medium-Sized Firms, *Management International Review*, Vol. 31, Issue March, pp. 45-70.

Hu, L. T. & Bentler, P. M. 1999, Cutoff Criteria for Fit Indexes in Covariance Structure Analysis: Conventional Criteria Versus New Alternatives, *Structural Equation Modeling*, Vol. 6, Issue 1, pp. 1-55.

Hu, L. T. & Bentler, P. M 1998, Fit Indices in Covariance Structure Modeling: Sensitivity to underparamerterized Model Misspecification, *Psychological Methods*, Vol. 3. Issue 1, pp. 424-453.

Humphrey, J. & Schmitz, H. 1996, The Triple C Approachto Local Industrial Policy, *World Development*, Vol. 23, Issue 1, pp. 149-162.

Hutchinson, K., Quinn, B., Alexander N. 2006, SME Retailer Internationalisation: Case Study Evidence from British Retailers, *International Marketing Review*, Vol. 23, Issue 1, pp. 25-53.

Ibeh, K. I. N. & Young, S. 2001, Exporting as an Entrepreneurial Act: An Empirical Study of Nigerian Firms, *European Journal of Marketing*, Vol. 35, Issue5/6, pp. 566-586.

Ibeh, K. I. N., Ibrahim, E. & Ezepue, P. O. 2007, Factors Stimulating Initial Export Activity, *Journal of African Business*, Vol. 8, Issue 2, pp 7-26.

Indonesian Ministry of Cooperative and SMEs 2010, viewed 18 January 2010, <http://www.depkop.go.id/cat_view/35-statistik/37-statistik-ukm/186-statistik-ukm-2007.html>

Isgut, A. 2001, What's Different about Exporters? Evidence from Colombian Manufacturing, *Journal of Development Studies*, Vol. 37, Issue 5, pp. 57-82.

Jaffe, E., Nebenzabl, H. & Pasternak, I. D. 1988, The Export Behavior of Small and Mediumsized Israeli Manufacturers, *Journal of Global Marketing*, Vol. 2, Issue 2, pp. 27-49.

Jain, S. C. 1989, Standardisation of International Marketing Strategy: Some Research Hypotheses, *Journal of Marketing*, Vol. 53, Issue 1, 70-79.

Jannson, H. & Sandberg, S 2008, Internationalisation of Small and Medium-Sized Enterprises in the Baltic Sea Region, *Journal of International Management*, Vol. 14, Issue 1 , pp. 65-77.

Janzen, S. S. & Frost, J. 2000, Alberta Non-Tariff Trade Barriers Study, *Western Centre for Economic Research paper*, Issue 58, November.

Jeannet, J. P. & Hennessey, D. H. 1998, *Global Marketing Strategies*, Houghton Mifflin Company, Boston.

Johanson, J. & Mattson, L. 1988, Internationalisation in Industrial Systems – A Network Approach, in Hood, N. & Vahlne, J.E., editors, *Strategies in Global Competition*, Croom Helm, Kent.

Johanson, J. & Vahlne, J. E. 1977, The Internationalisation Process of the Firm – A Model of Knowledge Development and Increasing Foreign Market Commitments, *Journal of International Business Studies*, Vol. 8, Issue 1, pp. 23-32.

Johanson, J. & Wiedersheim-Paul, F. 1975, The Internationalisation of the Firm – Four Swedish Cases, *Journal of International Management Studies*, Vol. 12, Issue 3, pp. 305-322.

Johnston, W. J. & Czinkota, M. R. 1982, Managerial Motivations as Determinants of Industrial Export Behavior, in Czinkota M. R. & G. Tesar, Editors, Export *Management: An International Context*, Praeger Publishers, New York

Joreskog K. G. & Sorbom, D. 1984, *LISREL VI (Computer Software),* IL: Scientific Software International Inc, Chicago.

Joreskog K. G. & Sorbom, D. 1993, *LISREL VI (Computer Software),* IL: Scientific Software International Inc, Chicago.

Joynt, P. 1982, An Empirical Study of Norwegian Export Behavior, in Czinkota M. R. , & Tesar G. editors, *Export management - An International Context*, editors, Praeger Publishers, New York, pp. 55-69.

Julian, C. & O'Cass, A. 2004, The Impact of Firm and Environment Characteristics on International Joint Venture (IJV) Marketing Performance in Thailand, *International Business Review*, Vol. 46, Issue 4, pp. 359-380.

Kaleka, A. & Katsikeas, C. S. 1995, Exporting Problems: The Relevance of Export Development, Journal of Marketing Management, Vol. 11, Issue 5, pp. 499-515.

Kalwani, M. U. & Narayandas, N. 1995, Long-term Manufacturer-Supplier Relationship: Do They Pay Off for Supplier Firms? *Journal of Marketing*, Vol. 59, Issue1, pp. 1-16.

Katsikeas, C. S. 2003, Advance in International Marketing: Theory and Practice, *International Business Review*, Vol. 12, Issue 1, pp. 135-140.

Katsikeas, C. S. 1994, Perceived Export Problems and Export Involvement: The Case of Greek Exporting Manufacturers, *Journal of Global Marketing*, Vol. 7, Issue 4, pp. 29-57.

Katsikeas C. S. 1994b, Export Competitive Advantages: The Relevance of Firm Characteristics, *International Marketing Review*, Vol 11, Issue 3, pp. 33-53.

Katsikeas, C. S. & Piercy, N. F. 1991, The Relationship between Exporters from a Developing Country and Importers based in Developed Country: Conflict Considerations, *European Journal of Marketing*, Vol. 25, Issue 1, pp. 6-25.

Katsikeas, C S. & Piercy, N. F. 1993, Long-term Export Stimuli and Firm Characteristics in a European LDC, *Journal of International Marketing*, Vol. 1, Issue 3, pp. 23-47.

Katsikeas, C. S. & Morgan, R. E. 1994, Differences in Perceptions of Exporting Problems based on Firm Size and Export Market Experience, *European Journal of Marketing*, Vol. 28, Issue 5, pp. 17-35.

Katsikeas, C. S. 1996, Ongoing Export Motivation: Differences between Regular and Sporadic Exporters, *International Marketing Review*, Vol. 13, Issue 2, pp. 4-19.

Katsikeas, C. S., Leonidou, L. C, & Morgan, N. A. 2000, Firm-level Performance Assessment: Review, Evaluation, and Development, *Journal of the Academy of Marketing Science*, Vol. 28, Issue 4, pp. 493-511.

Katsikeas, E., & Skarmeas, D. 2003, Organisational and Managerial Drivers of Effective Export Sales Organisations, *European Journal of Marketing*, Vol. 37, Issue 11/12, pp. 1723-1745.

Kaynak, E. 1982, Marketing in the Third World, Praeger Publishing, New York, NY.

Kaynak, E. & Kothari, V. 1984, Export Behavior of Small and Medium-Sized Manufacturers: Some Policy Guidelines for International Marketers, *Management International Review*, Vol. 24, Issue 2, pp. 61-69.

Kaynak, E., Ghauri, P. N., Olofsson-Bredenlow, T. 1987, Export Behavior of Swedish Firms, *Journal of Small Business Management*, Vol. 25, Issue 2, pp. 26-32.

Kedia, B. L. & Chhokar, J. 1986, Factors inhibiting export performance of firms: an empirical investigation, *Management International Review*, Vol. 26, Issue 4, pp. 33-43.

Kenen, P. B. & Rodrik, D. 1986, Measuring and Analyzing the Effects of Short-term Volatility in Real Exchange Rates, *The Review of Economics and Statistics*, Vol. 68, Issue 2, pp. 311-315.

Keng, K. A. & Jiuan, T. S. 1989, Differences Between Small and Medium Sized Exporting and Non-Exporting Firms: Nature or Nurture, *International Marketing Review*, Vol. 6, Issue 4, pp. 27-41.

Kessides, C. 1993, *The Contributions of Infrastructure to Economic Development: A Review of Experience and Policy Implications*, World Bank, Washington D.C.

Kindra, G. S. 1984, *Marketing in Developing Countries*, Croom Helm, London.

Kingsbury, D. 2005, *The Politics of Indonesia*, Oxford University Press, South Melbourne.

Kinsey, J. 1987, Marketing and the Small Manufacturing Firm in Scotland, *Journal of Small Business Management*, Vol. 25, Issue 2, pp. 18-25.

Kim, W. C. 1987, Competition and the Management of Host Government Intervention", Sloan Management Review, Vol. 28, Issue 3, pp. 33-39.

Kirpalani V. H. & MacIntosh, N. 1980, Internal Marketing Effectiveness of Technology Oriented Small Firms, *Journal of International Business Studies*, Vol. 11, Issue Winter, pp. 81-90.

Kirpalani, V. H. & Balcome, D. 1987, International Marketing Success: On Conducting More Relevant Research, in Rosson, P.J. & Reid, S.D. editors, *Managing Export Entry and Expansion*, Praeger Publishers, New York, NY, pp. 386-397.

Klein S. & Roth V. J. 1990, Determinants of Export Channel Structure: The Effects of Experience and Psychic Distance, *International Marketing Review*, Vol. 7, Issue 5, pp. 27-38.

Knight, R. V. & Gappert, G. 1989, Cities in Global Society, *Urban Affairs Annual Review*, Vol. 35, Sage Publications, Beverly Hills, California.

Kogut, B. & Singh, H. 1988, The Effect of National Culture on the Choice of Entry Mode, *Journal of International Business Studies*, Vol. 19, Issue 3, pp. 411-432.

Kotabe, M. & Czinkota, M. R. 1992, State Government Promotion of Manufacturing Exports: A Gap Analysis, *Journal of International Business Studies*, Vol. 23, Issue 4, pp. 637-658.

Krugman, P. R. & Obstfeld, M. 2003, *International Economics: Theory and Policy*, 6th edition, Addison-Wesley, Boston, USA.

Kundu, S. & Katz, J. A. 2003, Born-international SMEs: Bi-level Impacts of Resources and Intentions, *Small Business Economics*, Vol. 20, Issue 1, pp. 25-47.

Lages, L. F. & Montgomery, D. B. 2004, Export Performance as an Antecedent of Export Commitment and Marketing Strategy Adaptation: Evidence from Small and

Medium-sized Exporters, *European Journal of Marketing*, Vol. 38, Issue 9/10, pp. 1186-1214.

Lall, S. 1999. *The Technological Response to Import Liberalisation in Sub-Saharan Africa*, Macmillan Press, London.

Lambkin, M & Day, G. S. 1989, Evolutionary Processes in Competitive Markets: Beyond the Product Life Cycle, *Journal of Marketing*, Vol. 53, Issue 3, pp. 4-20.

Lecraw, D. J. 1993, Outward Direct Investment by Indonesian Firms: Motivation and Effects, *Journal of International Business Studies*, 3rd quarter, pp. 589-600.

Lee, W. Y., Brasch, J. J. 1978, The Adoption of Export as an Innovation, *Journal of International Business Studies*, Vol. 9, Issue 1, pp. 85-93.

Leonidou, L.C. 2004, An Analysis of the Barriers Hindering Small Business Export Development, Journal of Small Business Management, Vol. 24, Issue 3, pp. 279-302.

Leonidou, L. C. 1995a, Empirical Research on Export Barriers: Review, Assessment, and Synthesis, Journal of International Marketing, Vol. 3, Issue 1, pp. 29-43.

Leonidou, L. C. 1995b, Export Barriers: Non-Exporters' Perceptions. *International Marketing Review*, Vol. 12, Issue 1, pp. 4-25.

Leonidou, L. C. & Katsikeas, C. S. 1996. The Export Development Process: An Integrative Review of Empirical Models, *Journal of International Business Studies*, Vol. 27, Issue 3, pp. 517-551.

Leonidou, L.C, Katsikeas, C. S. & Samiee, S. 2002, Marketing Strategy Determinants of Export Performance: A Meta Analysis, *Journal of Business Research*, Vol. 55, Issue 1, pp. 51-67.

Leonidou, L. C., Katsikeas, C. S. & Piercy, N. 1998, Identifying Managerial Influences on Exporting: Past Research and Future Directions, *Journal of International Marketing*, Vol. 6, Issue 2, pp. 74-103.

Leontief, Wassily W. 1953. Domestic Production and Foreign Trade: The American Capital Position Re-Examined. Proceedings of the American Philosophical Society, Vol. 97, September, pp. 332-349.

Lesch, W.C., Eshghi, A. & Eshghi, G.S. 1990, A Review of Export Promotion Programmes in the Ten Largest Industrial States, in Cavusgil, S.T. & Czinkota, M.R., editors, International Perspectives on Trade Promotion and Assistance, Quorum, New York, NY, pp. 25-38.

Liargovas, P. G. & Skandalis, K. S. 2008, Export Motivations and Barriers: A Case Study of Greek Firms Exporting to four South-Eastern European Countries, *Global Business and Economics Review*, Vol. 10, Issue 4, pp. 430-448.

Liedholm, C. & Mead D. 1987, Small Scale Industries in Developing Countries: Empirical Evidence and Policy Implications, *International Development Paper* No. 9, Department of Agricultural Economics, Michigan State University, East Lansing, MI. USA.

Lim, J. S., T. W. Sharkey & K. I. Kim 1991, An Empirical Test of an Export Adoption Model, Management International Review, Vol. 31, Issue 1, pp. 51-62.

Lindeman, R. H., Merenda, P. F. & Gold, R. 1980, *Introduction to Bivariate and Multivariate Analysis*, Scott, Foresman, & Co., New York.

Little, I. M., Mazumdar, D., & Page, J. M. 1987, *Small Manufacturing Enterprises: A Comparative Analysis of India and Other Economies*, Oxford University Press, New York.

Long, J. S. 1983, *Confirmatory Factor Analysis*, Sage, Beverly Hills.

Luostarinen, R. & Welch, L. 1990, *International Business Operation*, Kyriiri Oy, Helsinki.

MacCallum, R. C., Browne M. W. & Sugawara, H. M. 1996, Power Analysis and Determination of Sample Size for Covariance Structure Modeling, *Psychological Methods*, Vol. 1, Issue 1, pp. 130-149.

Madsen, T. K. 1989, Sucessful Export Marketing Management: Some Empirical Evidence, *International Marketing Review*, Vol. 6, Issue 4, pp. 41-57.

Malekzadeh, A. R. & Nahavandi, A. 1985, Small Business Exporting: Misconceptions are Abundant, *American Journal of Small Business*, Vol. 9, Issue 4, pp. 7-14.

Manning, C. 2000, Labour Market Adjustment to Indonesia's Economic Crisis: Context, Trends and Implications, *Bulletin of Indonesian Economic Studies* , Vol. 36, Issue 1, pp. 105-136.

Manolova, T. S., Brush, C. G., Edelman, L. F. & Greene, P. G. 2002, Internationalisation of Small Firms, *Internatioonal Small Business Journal*, Vol. 20, Issue 1, pp. 9-31.

Marshall, A, 1920, *Principles of Economics*, Macmillan, London.

Mathieu, J. E. Tannenbaum, S. I & Salas, E. 1992, Influences of Individual and Situational Characteristics on Measures of Training Effectiveness, *Academy of Management Journal*, Vol. 35, Issue 1, pp. 828-847.

McAuley, A. 1993, The Perceived Usefulness of Export Information Sources, *European Journal of Marketing*, Vol. 27, Issue 10, pp. 52-64.

McCawley, P. 1981, The Indonesian Economy Since the Mid Sixties, in Booth, A. & McCawley, P., editors, *The Indonesian Economy During the Suharto Era*, Oxford University Press, Kuala Lumpur.

McGuiness, N. W. & Little, B. 1981, The Influence of Product Characteristics on the Export Performance of New Industrial Product, *Journal of Marketing*, Vol. 45, Issue Spring, pp. 102-122.

Miesenbock, K. J 1988, Small Business and Exporting: A Literature Review, *International Small Business Journal*, Vol. 6, Issue 2, pp. 42-61.

Ministry of Cooperatives and SMEs (MOCSMES), viewed December 2009, http://www.depkop.go.id/depkopgoid2008/index.php/statistik-ukm/cat_view/35-statistik/37-statistik-ukm/186-statistik-ukm-2008.html.

Mintz, I. 1967, Cyclical Fluctuations in the Exports in the United States since 1879 in *A Longitudinal analysis of Total U.S. Exports*, National Bureau of Economic Research, New York.

Mittelstaedt, J. D., Ward, W. A. & Nowlin, E. 2006, Location, Industrial Concentration and the Propensity of Small Firms to Export, *International Marketing Review*, Vol. 23, Issue 5, pp. 486-503.

Moini, A. H. 1997, Barriers Inhibiting Export Performance of Small and Medium-Sized Manufacturing Firms, *Journal of Global Marketing*, Vol. 10, Issue 4, pp. 67-93.

Moon, J. & Lee, H. 1990, On the Internal Correlates of Export Stage Development : An Empirical Invetigation in the Korean Electronics Industry, *International Marketing Review*, Vol. 7, Issue 5, pp. 16-26.

Morgan, R. E. 1997. Export Stimuli and Export Barriers: Evidence from Empirical Research Studies, *European Business Review*, Vol. 97, Issue 2, pp. 68-79.

Morgan, R. E. & Katsikeas, C. S. 1997, Theories of International Trade, Foreign Direct Investment and Firm Internationalisation: A Critique. *Management Decision*, Vol. 35, Issue 1, pp. 68-78.

Mpinganjira, M. 2004, *The Determinants of Export Involvement in Small and Medium Sized Firms: The Case of Malawi*, PhD Dissertation, Newcastle Business School, University of Newcastle, Australia.

Naidu, G. M. & Rao T. R 1993, Public Sector Promotion of Exports: A Need-based Approach, *Journal of Business Research*, Vol. 27,

NAFED 2007, *Indonesian National Agency for Export Development*, Jakarta, viewed 9 March 2007, <http://www.nafed.go.id/exporter.php?ctrl=propinsi>.

OECD 2004, 2nd OECD Conference of Ministers Responsible for Small and Medium-Sized Enterprises (SMEs, *Promoting Entrepreneurship and Innovative SMEs in a Global Economy: Towards a More Responsible and Inclusive Globalisation*, Istanbul, Turkey 3-5 June 2004

Ogbuehi, A. O. & Longfellow, T. A. 1994, Perceptions of U.S. Manufacturing SMEs Concerning Exporting: A Comparison Based on Export Experience, *Journal of Small Business Management*, Vol. 32, Issue4, pp. 37-47.

O'Grady, S. & Lane, H. 1996, The Psychic Distance Paradox, *Journal of International Business Studies*, Vol. 27, Issue 2, pp. 309-333.

Ogram, E. W. Jr. 1982, Exporters and Non-exporters: A Profile of Small Manufacturing Firms in Georgia, in Czinkota, M. R & Tesar G, Eds, *Export Management: An International Context*, Praeger Publishers, New York, pp. 70-84.

Ohlin, B. 1933, *Interregional and International Trade*, Harvard University Press, Cambridge.

Olson, H. C. & Wiedersheim-Paul, F. 1978, Factor Affecting the Pre-export Behavior of Non-exporting Firms, in Leontiades, J., editor, *European Research in International Business*, North Holland, Amsterdam.

Papanek, G. F. 1980, *The Indonesian Economy*, Praeger, New York.

Patterson, P. G. de Ruyter, K. & Wetzels, M. 1999, Modelling Firms' Propensity to Continue Service Exporting: A Cross-Country Analysis, *International Business Review*, Vol. 8, Issue 3, pp. 351-365.

Pavord, W. C & Bogart, R. G. 1975, The Dynamics of the Decision to Export, *Akron Business and Economic Review*, Issue: Spring, pp. 6-11.

Pedersen, T. & Petersen, B. 1998, Explaining Gradually Increasing Resource Commitment to a Foreign Market, *International Business Review*, Vol. 7, Issue 3, pp. 483-501.

Philp, N. & Wickramasekara, R. 1995, The Propensity to Export Among Food Processing Firms in Southern New South Wales and North Eastern Victoria: An Exploratory Study, *Agribusiness Review*, Vol. 3, Paper 8.

Piercy, N. F. & Cravens, D. W. 1995, The Network Paradigm and the Marketing Organisation: Developing a New Management Agenda, *European Journal of Marketing*, Vol. 29, Issue 3, pp. 7-34.

Porter, M. 1990. *The Competitive Advantage of Nations*, Graduate School of Business Administration, Harvard University, Boston, USA.

Powell, W. W. 1987, Hybrid Organisational Arrangements, *California Management Review*, Vol. 30, Issue 1, pp. 67-87.

Propenko, J. 1995, Future Management Strategies, in Propenko, J., editor, *Management for Privatisation*, International Labour Organisation, Geneva.

Pugel, T. A. & Lindert, P. H. 2000, *International Economics*, Irwin/McGraw-Hill, New York.

Rabino, S. 1980, An Examination of Barriers to Exporting Encountered by Small Manufacturing Companies, *Management International Review*, Vol. 1, pp. 67-73.

Ramaswami, S. N. & Yang, Y. 1990, Perceived Barriers to Exporting and Export Assistance Requirements, in Cavusgil, S. T. & M. R. Czinkota, *International Perspectives on Trade Promotion and Assistance*, Greenwood, UK, pp. 187-207.

Rasheed, H. S. 2005, Foreign Entry Mode Strategy and Performance; Moderating Effects of Environmental Factors, *Journal of Small Business Management*, Vol. 43, Issue 1, pp. 41-54.

Raykov, T. 1997, Estimation of Composite Reliability for Congeneric Measures, *Applied Psychological Measurement*, Vol. 18, Issue 1, pp. 63-77.

Raykov, T. 1998, Cronbach's Alpha and Reliability for Congeneric Measures, *Applied Psychological Measurement*, Vol. 21, Issue 1, pp. 173-184.

Reich, R. 1990, But Now We're Global, *Times Literary Supplement*, Issue August, pp. 925-926.

Reid, S. D. 1981, The Decision-maker and Export Entry and Expansion, *Journal of International Business Studies*, Vol. 12, Issue 2, pp. 101-112.

Reid, S. D. 1982, The Impact of Size on Export Behavior in Small Firms, in Czinkota M. R. & Tesar G., editors, *Export Management: An International Context,* Praeger Publishers, New York, pp. 18-38.

Reid, S. D. 1983, Managerial and Firm Influences on Export Behavior, *Journal of the Academy Marketing Science*, Vol. 11, Issue 3, pp. 323-332.

Reid, S. D. 1984, Information Acquisition and Export Entry Decisions in Small Firms, *Journal of Business Research*, Vol. 12, Issue 2, pp. 141-157.

Reuber, A. R. & Fischer, E. 1997, The Influence of the Management Team's International Experience on the Internationalisation Behavior of SMEs, *Journal of International Business Studies*, Vol. 28, Issue 4, pp. 807-825.

Reynolds, P. D. 1997. New and Small Firms in Expanding Markets. *Small Business Economics,* Vol. 9, Issue 1, pp. 79-84.

Rigdon, E. E. 1996, CFI Versus RMSEA: A Comparison of Two Fit Indices for Structural Equation Modeling, *Structural Equation Modeling*, Vol. 3, Issue 4, pp. 369-379.

Roberts, M. J. & Tybout, J. R. 1997, The Decision to export in Colombia: An Empirical Model of Entry with Sunk Costs, *American Economic Review*, Vol. 87, Issue 4, pp. 545-564.

Ronen, S. & Shenkar, O. 1985, Clustering Countries on Attitudinal Dimensions: A Review and Synthesis, *Academy of Management Review*, Vol. 10, Issue 3, pp. 435-454.

Ross, C. A. 1989, Exporters and Non-exporters of Manufactured Products: The Case of Jamaica, *Journal Of Global Marketing*, Vol. 3, Issue 2, pp. 77.103.

Sachs, J. & Warner, A. 1995, *Economic Reform and the Process of Global Integration*, Brookings Papers on Economic Activity.

Sagebien, J. 1990, The Competitive Advantage of Nations by M. E. Porter, *Journal of Macromarketing*, Issue Fall, pp. 94-99.

Sandee H. & Ibrahim B. 2002, *Evaluation of SME Trade and Export Promotion in Indonesia*, ADB Technical Assistance: SME Development, April.

Samiee, S. & Walters, P. G. P. 1990, Influence of Firm Size on Export Planning and Performance, *Journal of Business Research*, Vol. 20, Issue 3, pp. 235-248.

Samiee, S. & Walters, P. G. P. 1991, Segmenting Corporate Exporting Activities: Sporadic Versus Regular Exporters, *Journal of the Academy Marketing Science*, Vol. 19, Issue 2, pp. 93-104.

Samiee, S. & Walters, P. G. P. 1999, Determinants of Structured Export Knowledge Acquisition, *International Business Review*, Vol. 8, Issue 4, pp. 373-397.

Schaper, M. & Volery, T. 2004, *Entrepreneurship and Small Business: A Pacific Rim Perspective*, John Wiley & Sons Australia Ltd.

Schlegelemilch, B. B. & Ross, A. G. 1987, The Influence of Managerial Characteristics on Different Measures of Export Success, *Journal of Marketing Management*, Vol. 3, Issue 2, pp. 145-158.

Schumacker, R. E. & Lomax, R. G. 1996, *The Beginner's Guide to Structural Equation Modeling*, Lawrence Erlbaum Associates, New Jersey.

Seringhaus, F. H. R. 1986, The Impact of Government Export Marketing Assistance, *International Marketing Review*, Vol. 3 Issue 2, pp. 55-66.

Seringhaus, F. H. R. 1987, Export Promotion: The Role and Impact of Government Services, *Irish Marketing Review*, Vol. 2, Issue 1, pp. 106-116.

Seringhaus, F. H. R. & Botschen, G. 1991, Cross-national Comparison of Export Promotion Services: The Views of Canadian and Austrian Companies, *Journal of International Business Studies*, Vol. 22, Issue 1, pp. 115-133.

Seringhaus F. H. R. & Rosson, P. J. 1990, *Government Export Promotion: A Global Perspective*, Routledge, London, UK.

Sethuraman, R., Anderson, J. C. & Narus, J. A. 1988, Partnership Advantage and Its Determinants in Distributor and Manufacturers Working Relationships, *Journal of Business Research*, Vol. 17, Issue 4, pp. 327-347.

Shamsuddoha, A. K. & Ali, M. Y. 2009, Export Assistance in the Garment Industry: An Examination of Awareness, Use and Perceived Benefit, *Journal for Global Business Advancement*, Vol. 2, Issue 4, pp. 381-389.

Shoham, A. & Albaum G. S. 1995, Reducing the Impact of Barriers to Exporting: A Managerial Perspective, *Journal of International Marketing*, Vol. 3, Issue 4, pp. 85.105.

Silverman, M., Castaldi, R. M. & Sengupta, S. 2002, Increasing the Effectiveness of Export Assistance Programmes, The Case of the California Environmental Technology Industry, *Journal of Global Marketing*, Vol. 15, Issue 3/4, pp. 173-192.

Simpson, C.L. & Kujawa, D. Jr. 1974, The Export Decision Process: An Empirical Inquiry, *Journal of International Business Studies*, Issue: Spring, pp. 107-117.

Sjoholm, F., Which Indonesian Firms Export? The Importance of Foreign Networks, *Papers in Regional Science*, Vol. 82, pp. 333.350.

Smith, A. 1776, *An Inquiry into the Nature And Causes of the Wealth of Nations*, United Kingdom, W. Strathan and T. Cadell, Londres.

SMECDA, Pengkajian Produk Unggulan Dalam Meningkatkan Ekspor UKM dan Pengembangan Ekonomi Lokal, viewed January 2010a, < http://www.smecda.com/kajian/files/jurnal/hal_113GB_ok.pdf>

SMECDA, Hambatan Usaha Kecil dan Menengah dalam Kegiatan Ekspor, viewed January 2010, <www.smecda.com/kajian/files/jurnal/hal_99GB_ok.pdf>

Soesastro, H. & Atje, R. 2005, Survey of Recent Developments, *Bulletin of Indonesian Economic Studies*, Vol. 41, Issue 1, pp. 5-34.

Soesastro, H. & Basri, M. C. 2005, *The Political Economy of Trade Policy in Indonesia*, Economics Working Paper Series, viewed June 2008, http://www.csis.or.id/papers/wpe092.

Souchon, A. L. & Damantopoulos, A. 1996, A Conceptual Framework of Export Marketing Information Use: Key Issues and Research Propositions, *Journal of International Marketing*, Vol. 4, Issue 3, pp. 49-71.

Stanley, J., Ingram, D. & Chittick, C. 1989, *The Relationship between International Trade and Linguistic Competence: Report to the Australian Advisory Council on Languages and Multicultural Education*, Australian Government Publishing Service, Canberra.

Stottinger, B. & Schlegelmilch, B. B. Explaining Export Development through Psychic Distance: Enlightening or Elusive? *International Marketing Review*, Vol. 15, Issue 5, pp. 357-372.

Strange, R. & Katrak, H. 2002, *Small-scale Enterprises in Developing and Transitional Economies*, Palgrave, Basingstoke.

Suarez-Ortega, S. M. 2003, Export Barriers: Insights from Small And Medium-Sized Firms, *International Small Business Journal*, Vol. 21, Issue 4, pp. 403-420

Suarez-Ortega, S. M. & Alamo-Vera, F. R. 2005, SMEs Internationalisation: Firms and Managerial Factors, *International journal of Entrepreneurial Behavior and Research*, Vol. 11, Issue 4, pp. 258-279.

Sullivan, D. & Bauerschmidt, A. 1988, Common Factors Underlying Incentive to Export: Studies in the European Forest Products Industry, *European Journal of Marketing*, Vol. 22, Issue 10, pp. 41-55.

Sullivan, D. & Bauerschmidt, A. 1990, Common Factors Underlying Incentive to Export: Studies in the European Forest Products Industry, *European Journal of Marketing*, Vol. 22, Issue 10, pp. 41-55.

Tambunan, T. T. H. 2000, *Development of Small-Scale Industries During the New Order Government in Indonesia*, Aldershot, Ashgate.

Terpstra V. & Sarathy R. 2000, *International Marketing*, Dryden Press, Forth Worth, London.

Tharakan, P. K. M. 1983, *Intra-industry Trade: Empirical and Methodological Aspects*, Elsevier Science, Amsterdam.

Tesar, G. & Tarleton, J. 1982. Comparison of Wisconsin and Virginia small and medium-sized exporters: aggressive and passive exporters in M. Czinkota & G. *Tesar. Export Management-An International Context*, Editors, pp. 39-54, New York, Praeger.

Tesform G. & Lutz, C. 2006, A Classification of Export Marketing Problems of Small and Medium Sized Manufacturing Firms in Developing Countries, *International Journal of Emerging Markets*, Vol. 1, Issue 3, pp. 262-281.

Thomas, M. J. & Araujo, L. 1985, Theories of Export Behavior: A Critical Analysis, *European Journal of Marketing*, Vol. 19, Issue 2, pp. 42-52.

Trimeche, M. 2004, The Changing Business Environment in Tunisia: Implications for Multinationals, Journal of African Business, Vol. 5, Issue 2, pp. 71-92.

Tsai, W. M., MacMillan, I. C. & Low, M. B. 1991, Effects of Strategy and Environment on Corporate Venture Success in Industrial Markets, *Journal of Business Venturing*, Vol. 6, Issue 1, pp. 9-28.

Tseng, J. & Yu, C. M. J. 1991, Export of Industrial Goods to Europe: The Case of Large Taiwanese Firms, *European Journal of Marketing*, Vol. 25, Issue 9, pp. 51-63.

Tybout, J. R. 2000, Manufacturing Firms in Developing Countries: How Well Do They Do and Why? *Journal of Economic Literature*, Vol. 38, Issue March, pp. 11-44.

UNCTAD 2010, *United Nations Commodity Trade Statistics Database*, viewed 10 March 2010, <http:// http://comtrade.un.org/pb/FileFetch.aspx?type=volumes&docID=3406

UNESCAP 2009, *Globalisation of Production and the Competitiveness of Small and Medium-sized Enterprises in Asia and the Pacific: Trends and Prospects*. Viewed 4 January 2010, <http://www.unescap.org/tid/publication/tipub2540 chap1.pdf>

Urata, S. 2000, *Policy Recommendations for SME Promotion in the Republic of Indonesia, Report of JICA Senior Advisor to the Coordinating Minister of the Economy*, Finance and Industry, JICA, Tokyo, 26 July, pp. 16-32.

Ursic, M. L. & Czinkota, M. R. 1989, The Relationship Between Managerial Characteristics and Exporting Behavior, *Developments in Marketing Science*, Vol. 12, pp. 208-210.

Van Diermen, P. 1998, Sistem Kewirausahaan: Industri Garmen dan Furniture Kayu di Indonesia, PT Pustaka CIDESINDO Jakarta and Massey University, New Zealand.

Velicer, W. F., Peacock A. C., & Jakcson, D. N. 1982, A Comparison of Component and Factor Patterns: A Monte Carlo Approach, Multivariate *Behavioural Research*, Vol. 17, Issue 1, pp. 371-388.

Vernon, R.. 1966, International Investment and International Trade in the Product Life Cycle, *Quarterly Journal of Economics*, Vol.80, Issue 2, pp. 190-207.

Vona, S. 1991, On the Measurement of Intra-industry Trade: Some Further Thoughts, *Review of World Economics*, Vol. 127, Issue 4, pp. 678-700.

Wade, R. H. 2003, What Strategies are Viable for Developing Countries today? The World Trade Organisation and the Shrinking of 'Development Space' *Review of International Political Economy*, Vol. 10, Issue 4, pp. 621-644.

Wakelin, K. 1998, Innovation and Export Behaviour at the Firm Level, *Research Policy*, Vol. 26, Issue 1, pp. 829-841.

Walters, P. G. P. 1983, Export Information Sources – A Study of Their Usage and Utility, *International Marketing Review*, Issue Winter, pp. 34-43.

Watson, K. & Hogarth-Scott, S. 2003, *Understanding the Influence of Constraints to International Entrepreneurship in Small and Medium-Sized Export Companies, Frontiers of Entrepreneurship Research*, Research Working Papers.

Weaver, K. M. & Pak, J. 1990, Export Behavior and Attitudes of Small and Medium-Sized Korean Manufacturing Firms, *International Small Business Journal*, Vol. 8, Issue 4, pp. 59-70.

Weaver, K. M., Berkowitz, D. & Davies, L. 1998, Increasing the Efficiency of National Export Promotion Programmes: The Case of Norwegian Exporters, *Journal of Small Business Management*, Vol. 36, Issue 4, pp. 1-12.

Welch, L. & Wiedersheim-Paul, F. 1980), Initial Exports – A Marketing Failure?, *The Journal of Management Studies*, Vol. 17, Issue 3, pp. 333-344.

Wengel, J. & Rodriguez, E. 2006, SME Export Performance in Indonesia After the Crisis, *Small Business Economics*, Vol. 26, Issue 1, pp. 25-37.

Westhead, P. 1995, Exporting Non-exporting Small Firms in Great Britain, *International Journal of Entrepreneurial Behavioral and Research*, Vol. 1, Issue 2, pp. 6-36.

Westhead, P., Binks, M. Ucbasaran, D., and Wright, M. 2002, Internationalisation of SMEs: A Research Note, *Journal of Small Business Enterprise Development*, Vol. 9, Issue 1, pp. 38-48.

Wie, T. K. 2000, The Impact of the Economic Crisis on Indonesia's Manufacturing Sector, *The Developing Economies*, Vol. 38, Issue 4, pp. 420-453.

Wie, T. K. 2006, Policies for Private Sectors Developments in Indonesia, ADB *Institute Discussion Paper* No. 46.

Wiedersheim-Paul, F., Olson, H. & Welch, L. S. 1978, Pre-export Activity: The First Step in Internationalisation, *Journal of International Business Studies*, Issue Spring/Summer, pp. 47-58.

Wignaraja, G. 2003, *Competitiveness Strategy in Developing Countries: A Manual for Policy Analysis*, Routledge, London.

Wignaraja, P. A. et al. 1991, *Participatory Development*, Oxford University Press, Karachi.

Wijaya, T. 2008, Kajian Model Empiris Perilaku Berwirausaha UKM DIY dan Jawa Tengah, *Journal of Management and Entrepreneurship*, Vol. 10, Issue 2, pp. 93-104.

Wilkinson, T. & Brouthers, L. E. 2006, Trade Promotion and SME Export Performance, *International Business Review*, Vol. 15, Issue 1, pp. 233-252.

Williams, D. A. 2008, Export Stimulation of Micro and Small Locally Owned Firms from Emerging Environments: New Evidence, *Journal of International Entrepreneurship*, Vol. 6, Issue 3, pp. 101-122.

Wolff, J. & Pett, T. L. 2000, Internationalisation of Small Firms: An Examination of Export-Strategy Approach, Firm Size, and Export Performance, *Journal of Small Business Management*, Vol. 38, Issue 2, pp. 34-47.

World Bank 1998, *Oil Windfalls: Blessing or Curse?* Oxford University Press, New York.

World Bank 1993, The *East Asian Miracle: Economic Growth and Public Policy*, Oxford University Press, New York.

World Bank 1991, *World Development Report*, Oxford University Press, New York.

World Development Indicator, viewed 4 January 2010, < http://0-ddp-ext.worldbank.org.library.newcastle.edu.au/ext/DDPQQ/report.do?method=showReport>.

WTO, World Trade Organisation statististics[1], viewed February 2010a, <http://www.wto.org/english/news_e/pres10_e/pr598_e.htm>.

Wood, A. & Jordan, K. 2000, Why Does Zimbabwe Export Manufactures and Uganda Not? Econometrics Meets History, *The Journal of Development Studies*, Vol. 37, Issue 2, pp. 91-116.

World Trade Organisation statistics[2], viewed February 2010,b <http://www.wto.org/english/news_e/sprr_e/china_e.htm>

World Trade Organisation, *Participation of developing countries in World Trade: Overview of major trends and underlying factors*, viewed June 2009, <http://www.wto.org/english/tratop_e/devel_e/w15.htm>.

Wortzel, L. H. & Wortzel, H. V. 1981, Export Marketing Strategies for NIC and LDC based Firms, *Columbia Journal of World Business*, Vol. pp. 51-59.

Yang, Y. S., Leone, R. P. & Alden, D. L. 1992, A Market Expansion Ability Approach to Identify Potential Exporters, Journal of Marketing, Vol. 56, Issue January, pp. 84-96.

Yaprak, A. 1985, An Empirical Study of the Differences Between Small Exporting and Non-Exporting US Firms, *International Marketing Review*, Vol. 2, Issue Summer, pp. 72-83.

Yeoh, P. L. 1994, Entrepreneurship and Export Performance: A Proposed Conceptual Model, in Axinn, C.N., editor, *Advances in International Marketing*, Vol. 6, JAI Press, Greenwich, CT, pp. 43-68.

Young, S. 1995, Export Marketing: Conceptual and Empirical Developments, *European Journal of Marketing*, Vol. 29, Issue 8, pp. 7-16.

Zhao, H. & Zou, S. 2002, The Impact of Industry Concentration and Firm Location on Export Propensity and Intensity: An Empirical Analysis of Chinese Manufacturing Firms, *Journal of International Marketing*, Vol. 10, Issue 1, pp. 52-71.

Zou, S. & Stan, S. 1998, The Determinants of Export Performance: A Review of the Empirical Literature between 1987 and 1997, *International Marketing Review*, Vol. 15, Issue 15, pp. 333-356.

Appendices

Appendix 2.1: Programmes to Promote SME Development in Indonesia

Technology	1969	MIDC (Metal Industry Development Centre) established.
	1974	BIPIK (Small Industry Development) Programme formulated as technical support programme for SMEs.
	1979	Under BIPIK programme, LIK and PIK (Small Industries Estate) provided technical assistance extended to SMEs in or near LIK/PIK mainly through UPT (Technical Service Unit) Staffed by TPL (Extension Field Officers).
	1994	BIPIK programme finished and PIKM (Small-scale Enterprises Development Project) launched.
Marketing	1979	Reservation Scheme introduced to protect markets for SMEs.
	1999	Anti-Monopoly Law enacted.
	2007	Review on marketing promotion models for SMEs was conducted by the Deputy VII of Ministry of Cooperatives and SMEs (MOCSME) Review on market infrastructure utilisation was conducted by the Deputy VII of MOCSME
Financing	1971	PT ASKRINDO established as a state-owned credit insurance company.
	1973	KIK (Credit for Small Investment) and KMKP (Credit for Working Capital) introduced as government-subsidised credit programmes for SMEs
	1973	PT BAHANA founded as a state-owned venture capital company.
	1974	KK (Small Credit), administered by BRI (Indonesia's People's Bank) launched and later (1984) changed to KUPEDES scheme (General Rural Savings programme) aimed at promoting small business.
	1989	SME Loans from state owned enterprises (1 to 5% benefits) introduced.
	1990	Government-subsidised credit programmes for SMEs (KIK/KMKP) abolished and unsubsidised KUK (Credit for Small Business) scheme introduced.
	1998	The Liquidity Credit Scheme restarted.
	1999	The responsibility of directed credit programmes transferred from Bank Indonesia (the central bank) to PT PNM (State-owned Corporation for SMEs) and Bank Export Indonesia.
	2000	Major government credit programme for SMEs, including KUK, abolished
	2002	Financial and non-financial supports were granted through business development centres.

	2008	Review on SMEs credit effectiveness was conducted in all development centres
General	1973	Ministry of Light Industry and Ministry of Heavy Industry merged into Ministry of Industry.
	1976	Deletion (Localisation) Programmes for commercial cars introduced (motorcycles in 1977 and some other products such as diesel engines and tractors later on)
	1978	Directorate General for Small-scale Industry established (in Ministry of Industry).
	1984	Foster Father (Bapak Angkat) Programme introduced to support SMEs
	1991	Foster Father-Business Partner Linkage extended to a national movement.
	1991	SENTRAs (Groups of Small-scale Industry) in industrial clusters organized as KOPINKRA (Small-scale Handicraft Cooperatives).
	1993	Deletion Programmes for commercial cars finished and Incentives Systems adopted.
	1993	Ministry of Cooperatives started handling small business development.
	1995	Basic Law for Promoting Small-scale Enterprises enacted.
	1997	Foster Father (Bapak Angkat) Programme changed to Partnership Programme (Kemitraan).
	1998	Ministry of Cooperatives and Small Business added medium business development to its responsibilities.
	1998	SME promotion emphasised in People's Economy as a national slogan.
	1999	New Automobile Policy announced, and Incentive Systems finished.
	2002	Business Development Centres for SMEs were established in 11 provinces around Sumatera, Java, Nusa Tenggara, Kalimantan and Sulawesi islands.
	2005	MOCSME introduced competency-based support and promotion system.
	2008	MOCSME conducted supply chain management system training to empower SMEs in the agricultural sector.

Source: Wie (2006: 101-112), internal documents prepared by the Indonesian Ministry of Industry and Trade, and the study on the Indonesian Ministry of Cooperatives and SMEs policies.

Appendix 5.1: Path Diagram of the Construct of Internal Barriers

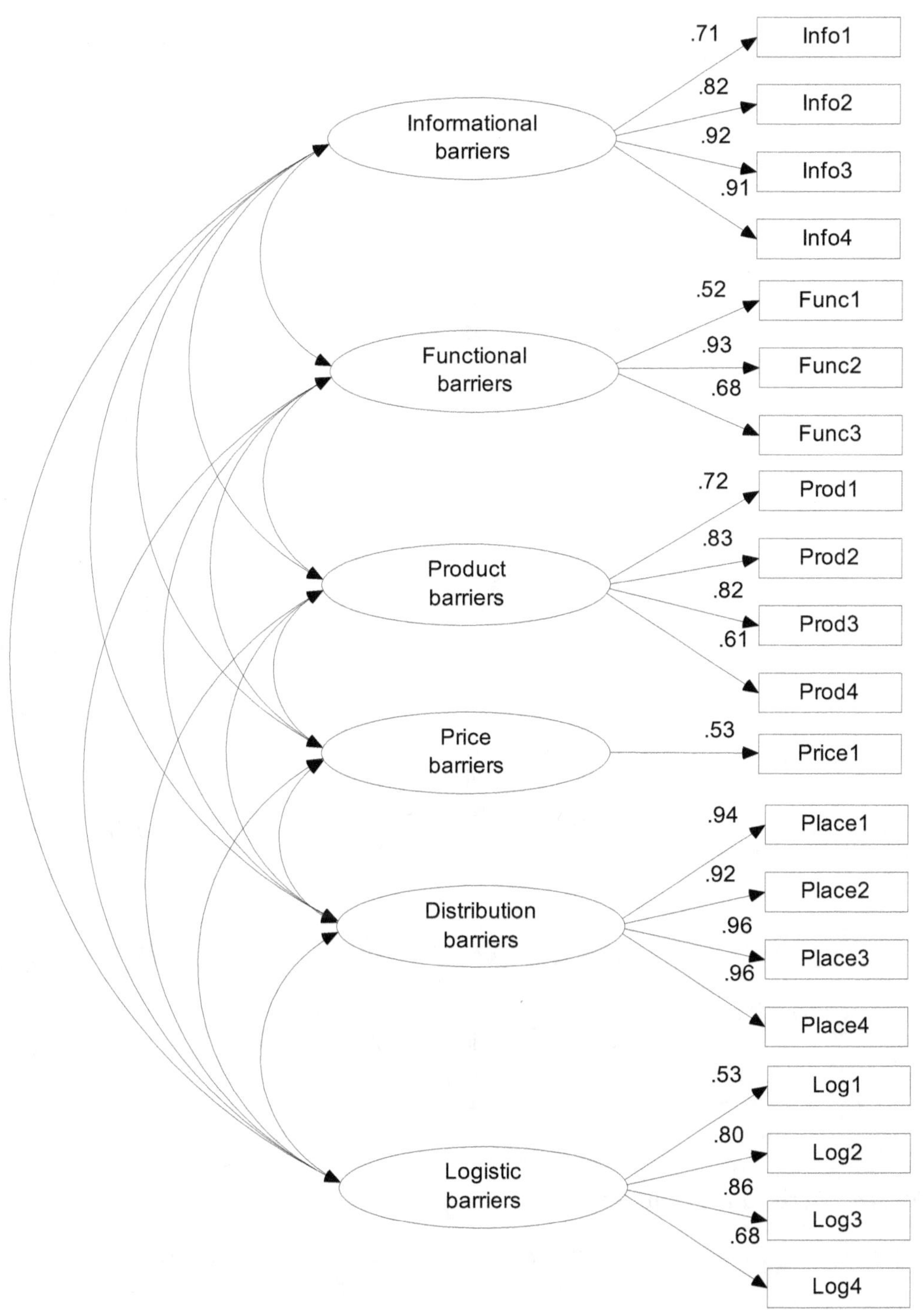

Source: Derived from survey data.

Appendix 5.2: Path Diagram of the Construct of External Barriers

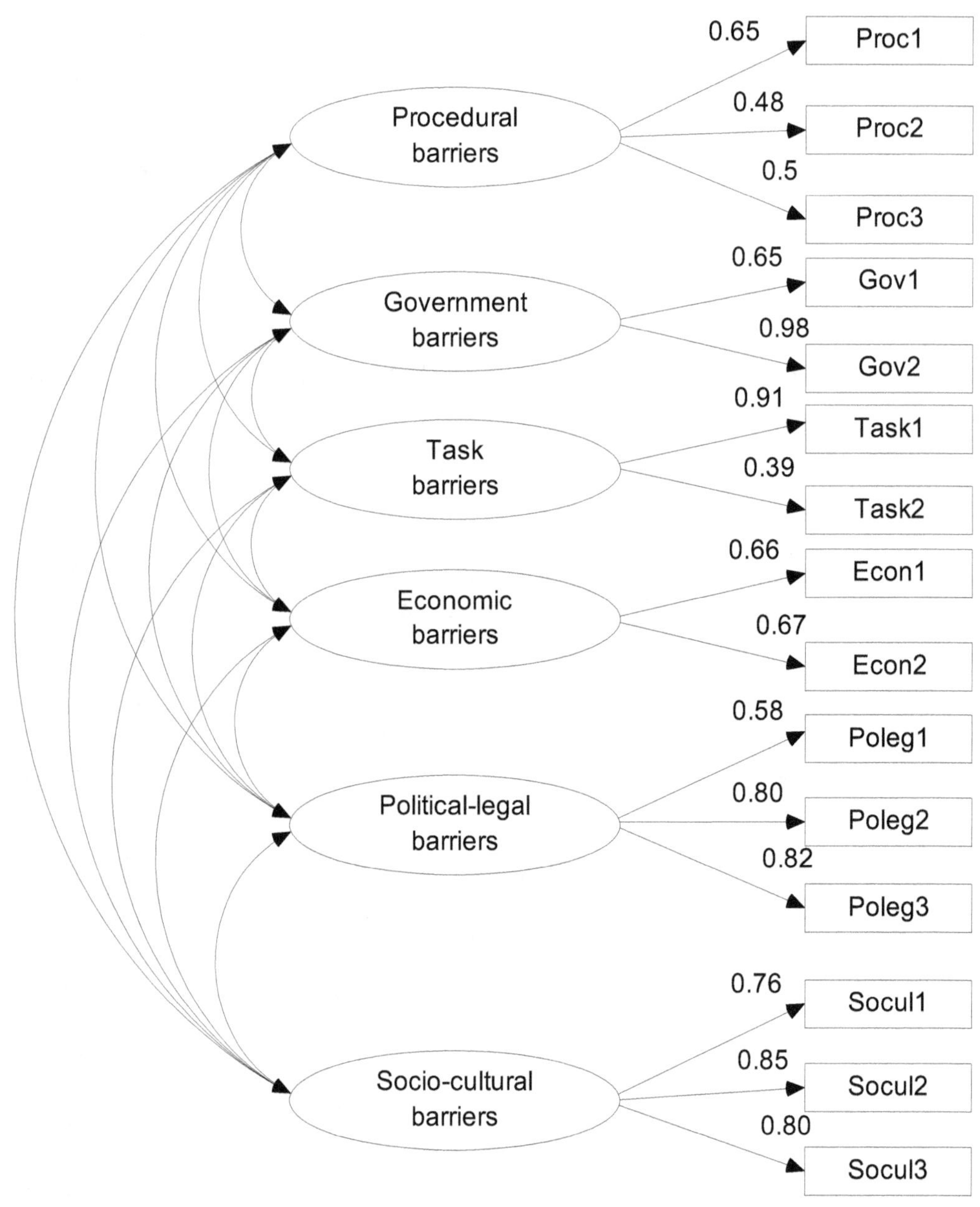

Source: Derived from survey data.

Appendix 5.3: Path Diagram of the Construct of Internal and External Barriers

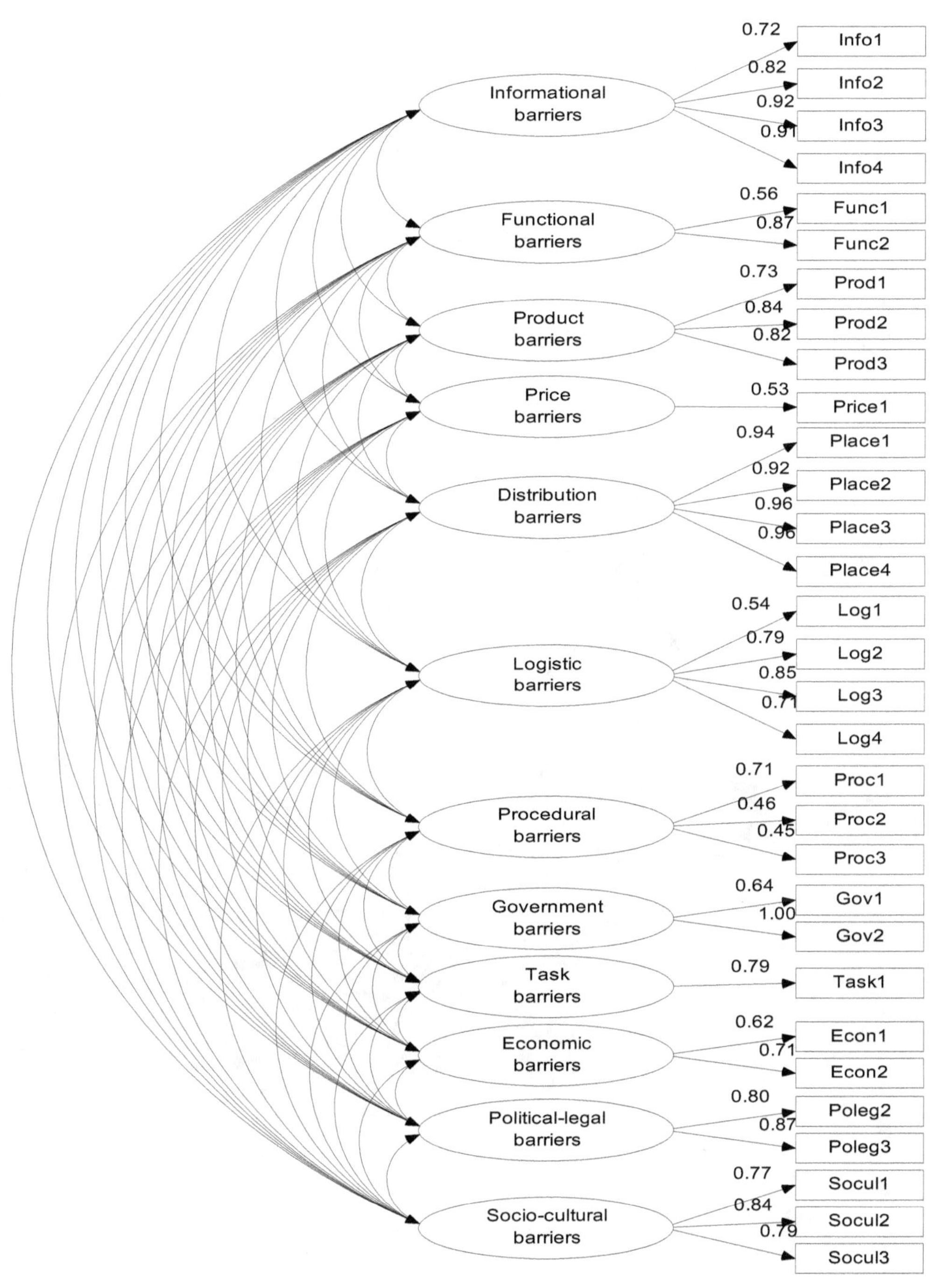

Source: Derived from survey data.

Appendix 6.1: Path Diagram of Perceptions of Export Barriers Affecting Export Development, Export Propensity, and Export Intensity – Saturated Model

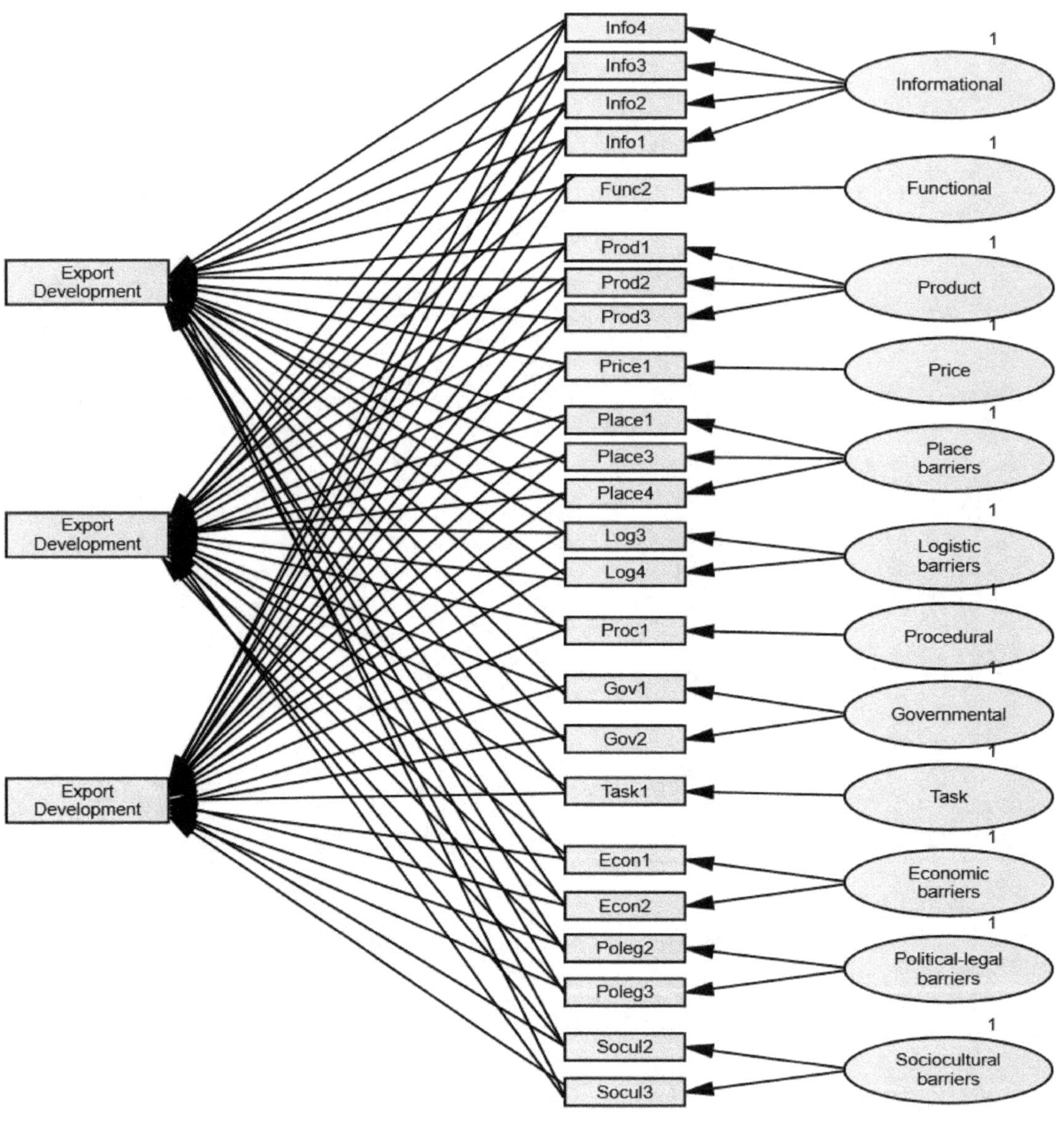

Source: Derived from survey data.

Appendix 6.2: Perceptions of Export Barriers Affecting Export Propensity

	r	Unstandardized Coefficients		Standardized Coefficients	t	Sig.
		B	S.E.	βeta		
Export prop ‹— Informational1	-0.134	0.041	0.061	0.047	0.670	NS
Export prop ‹— Informational2	-0.092	0.063	0.072	0.074	0.876	NS
Export prop ‹— Informational3	-0.192	0.014	0.092	0.016	0.151	NS
Export prop ‹— Informational4	-0.222	-0.135	0.086	-0.159	-1.568	NS
Export prop ‹— Functional2	-0.096	0.008	0.057	0.009	0.137	NS
Export prop ‹— Product1	0.009	-0.006	0.059	-0.007	-0.103	NS
Export prop ‹— Product2	-0.110	-0.020	0.065	-0.024	-0.307	NS
Export prop ‹— Product3	-0.070	0.055	0.062	0.068	0.889	NS
Export prop ‹— Price1	0.044	0.049	0.051	0.058	0.947	NS
Export prop ‹— Distributional1	-0.135	0.183	0.098	0.239	1.868	*
Export prop ‹— Distributional3	-0.177	-0.169	0.116	-0.223	-1.454	NS
Export prop ‹— Distributional4	-0.166	0.040	0.112	0.053	0.352	NS
Export prop ‹— Logistic3	-0.110	0.057	0.057	0.069	0.988	NS
Export prop ‹— Logistic4	-0.072	0.137	0.061	0.161	2.242	**
Export prop ‹— Procedural1	-0.227	-0.084	0.058	-0.104	-1.434	NS
Export prop ‹— Governmental2	-0.023	0.051	0.046	0.067	1.117	NS
Export prop ‹— Task1	-0.094	0.083	0.063	0.093	1.318	NS
Export prop ‹— Economic1	-0.070	-0.060	0.051	-0.070	-1.174	NS
Export prop ‹— Economic2	-0.087	-0.069	0.052	-0.086	-1.340	NS
Export prop ‹— Political-legal2	-0.177	-0.017	0.059	-0.02	-0.278	NS
Export prop ‹— Political-legal3	-0.209	-0.019	0.061	-0.025	-0.314	NS
Export prop ‹— Socio-cultural2	-0.303	-0.180	0.071	-0.205	-2.538	**
Export prop ‹— Socio-cultural3	-0.230	0.002	0.068	0.002	0.033	NS

Source: Derived from survey data.

Appendix 6.3: Perceptions of Export Barriers Affecting Export Intensity

		Unstandardized Coefficients		Standardized Coefficients		
	R	B	S.E.	Beta	T	Sig.
Export inty ‹— Informational1	-0.147	0.019	0.027	0.030	0.688	NS
Export inty ‹— Informational2	-0.156	-0.004	0.032	-0.006	-0.122	NS
Export inty ‹— Informational3	-0.244	0.003	0.041	0.005	0.079	NS
Export inty ‹— Informational4	-0.220	-0.017	0.038	-0.027	-0.441	NS
Export inty ‹— Functional2	-0.203	0.042	0.025	0.067	1.674	*
Export inty ‹— Product1	-0.011	-0.009	0.026	-0.014	-0.329	NS
Export inty ‹— Product2	-0.103	0.032	0.029	0.053	0.554	NS
Export inty ‹— Product3	-0.054	0.015	0.027	0.026	0.554	NS
Export inty ‹— Price1	0.092	0.020	0.023	0.033	0.884	NS
Export inty ‹— Distributional1	-0.379	0.015	0.044	0.027	0.350	NS
Export inty ‹— Distributional3	-0.362	0.013	0.051	0.024	0.257	NS
Export inty ‹— Distributional4	-0.411	-0.007	0.050	-0.012	-0.136	NS
Export inty ‹— Logistic3	-0.334	-0.021	0.025	-0.035	-0.818	NS
Export inty ‹— Logistic4	-0.319	0.023	0.027	0.038	0.855	NS
Export inty ‹— Procedural1	-0.388	-0.061	0.026	-0.105	-2.359	**
Export inty ‹— Governmental2	-0.072	0.022	0.020	0.039	1.076	NS
Export inty ‹— Task1	-0.154	0.015	0.028	0.024	0.546	NS
Export inty ‹— Economic1	0.046	0.017	0.023	0.027	0.753	NS
Export inty ‹— Economic2	0.040	0.025	0.023	0.044	1.112	NS
Export inty ‹— Political-legal2	-0.233	0.020	0.026	0.034	0.751	NS
Export inty ‹— Political-legal3	-0.374	-0.089	0.027	-0.158	-3.302	****
Export inty ‹— Socio-cultural2	-0.311	-0.033	0.032	-0.052	-1.045	NS
Export inty ‹— Socio-cultural3	-0.312	0.020	0.030	0.030	0.652	NS

Source: Derived from survey data.

www.ingramcontent.com/pod-product-compliance
Lightning Source LLC
LaVergne TN
LVHW081352060426
835510LV00013B/1789
* 9 7 8 1 9 3 9 1 2 3 9 9 2 *